360-DEGREE
PREACHING

360-Degree Preaching

Hearing, Speaking, and Living the Word

Michael J. Quicke

Baker Academic

A Division of Baker Book House Co
Grand Rapids, Michigan 49516

PATERNOSTER PRESS

© 2003 by Michael J. Quicke

Published by Baker Academic
a division of Baker Book House Company
P.O. Box 6287, Grand Rapids, MI 49516-6287
www.bakeracademic.com

and

Paternoster Press
an imprint of Authentic Media
P.O. Box 300
Carlisle, Cumbria CA3 0QS, UK
www.paternoster-publishing.com

Printed in the United States of America

Library of Congress Cataloging-in-Publication Data
Quicke, Michael J., 1945–
    360-degree preaching : hearing, speaking, and living the Word / Michael J. Quicke.
        p.   cm.
    Includes bibliographical references and index.
    ISBN 0-8010-2640-7
    1. Preaching. I. Title: Three hundred sixty-degree preaching. II. Title.
BV4211.3.Q53 2003
251—dc21   2003048495

British Library Cataloguing in Publication Data
A catalogue record for this book is available from the British Library
ISBN 1-84227-247-0

Scripture quotations are from the New Revised Standard Version of the Bible, copyright 1989 by the Division of Christian Education of the National Council of the Churches of Christ in the USA. Used by permission.

The diagrams on pages 173–74 are from Paul S. Wilson, *The Practice of Preaching* (Nashville: Abingdon, 1995), 180–81. Used by permission.

For more information about Michael J. Quicke's ministry, see www.michaelquicke.com.

To
my wife, Carol—best friend,
resilient listener, candid critic,
and unwavering believer
that God could use my preaching
(and just possibly this book)

Contents

Acknowledgments

I owe more than I know to others, and it is impossible to give an adequate list of those who have influenced me during my thirty-five-year preaching journey. I am particularly indebted to my church congregations in Blackburn, Cambridge, and Wheaton, Illinois, for helping me believe in 360-degree preaching. And deep thanks go to my students at Spurgeon's College in London and Northern Seminary in Lombard for fanning my enthusiasm as they responded to early prototypes of this book.

I am grateful to Spurgeon's College for granting me sabbatical leave in 1998 (while I was a busy principal) and to colleagues John Colwell, Peter Stevenson, and Stephen Wright for their early encouragement. Parts of this book first emerged in lectures: E. Y. Mullins (United States), Lester Randall (Canada), College of Preachers (Britain), Olwyn Abbott (Australia), J. C. Barry (United States), and Hiller (United States). These occasions, supplemented by countless ministers' conferences, have nourished a lively band of pilgrims, fellow believers in preaching, who have taught me much along the way.

Parts of this book were read and critiqued by gracious friends and gifted scholars: Gerry Borchert, Ian Chapman, Steve Holmes, Dan Lee, Barry Morrison, Greg Sharf, Jim Stamoolis, and Noel Vose. I owe much to their honesty and insights. Of course, they bear no responsibility for my many opinions and prejudices. Tony Campolo kindly agreed that a sermon of his could be a case study. Jon Lederhouse, swimming coach at Wheaton College, gave invaluable insights into my "preaching swim" metaphor. I also owe much to Baker Book House—the encouragement of Robert N. Hosack and the editing skills of Melinda Van Engen.

My daughter-in-law, Lori Quicke, gave useful advice, and the rest of my family, especially my wife, Carol, coped stoically with my worrying

9

absences in body and mind while writing. I wrote this book out of the conviction that our Triune God—Father, Son, and Spirit—who empowers preaching, could also help me write about preaching. My hope is that somewhere in its pages there might be an insight or two that, by God's power, will inspire preachers along the way.

Introduction

It is one of the best kept secrets of homiletics that our lives are full of holy places and experiences.

Henry H. Mitchell, *Celebration and Experience in Preaching*

Most books, even textbooks, make more sense as you catch glimpses of the author. Forgive me for being personal, but I don't think you will understand this book's passion and emphases without a little insight into who I am.

I belong to the British Baptist family, in which commonly those who sense a call to ministry are heard in their local churches so that they can be commended for seminary training. And so in 1969, I was invited to preach in West Norwood Baptist Church in southeast London. It was a preaching center, near its peak in terms of size and influence. Gratefully, I was given a midsummer date when the pastor and many others were away on vacation, reducing the number of critics. My few previous attempts at preaching had been, frankly, lamentable. In spite of diligent preparation, scriptural orthodoxy, and a sincere desire to succeed, my sermons had always disappointed.

On Sunday morning, August 3, 1969, I preached to a fairly full church on Ephesians 3:14–21. It was a tidy, worthy effort, and I appeared to please people with my brevity. I had survived the first test. The evening service was better attended, with over five hundred people crowding into the main body of the church and its gallery. I preached on the divided reactions to Jesus in John 10:19–20. Some were saying, "He has a demon and is out of his mind. Why listen to him?" while others were saying, "These are not the words of one who has a demon. Can a demon open the eyes of the blind?" I had lived with this passage for weeks and had visualized its life and felt some of its power. Untidily and inexpertly, its challenge about responding to the person of Christ tumbled out of me.

In the middle of this sermon, I had my one and only experience (so far) of God unmistakably speaking to me. I realize that such language may alienate some readers who may draw negative conclusions about my naivete, conceit, and even sanity. But the more I reflect on what happened, the more I realize that there is no other way to express it. Suddenly, with intensity and stillness, even while I was speaking, I heard another voice clearly say, "Michael, I call you to preach." Unlike any faith experience up to that point, including my conversion and baptism as a believer, it was the very last thing I was expecting. A few hearers commented later that they knew something significant had happened to me. Afterward, though there were several visible responses to the challenge of the sermon, life quickly returned to normal. I kept my experience private for many years.

Nothing remotely like this has happened to me since. Of course, psychologists could explain how the pressures of that situation might have created an unusual disturbance in my psyche, therefore hyping up my imagination. But as the years have passed, I have become more and more convinced that this experience was truly of God. He gave inadequate me a vivid, lifelong commitment to preach, "whether the time was favorable or unfavorable" (2 Tim. 4:2). I can honestly say that this call has never felt glamorous and has never pandered to conceit; it has demanded hard work and humility. Yet inch by inch, transformation has taken place through years of service in local churches in which ordinary people have come to faith, been nurtured, and made a difference through their changed lives.

Actually, that Sunday evening I felt as though I were being called to plunge into something that would always be uncomfortably too deep. I think that feeling has much to do with my choice of swimming as a metaphor for preaching, which I develop in this book. Do I think all preachers need to go through a similar experience? Of course not. God calls in a wide variety of ways. But I am convinced that he called *me*, and that call has transformed my life.

After three years in seminary and seven years as a local pastor in Blackburn, Lancashire, I moved to a Baptist church in the center of Cambridge, England. There I witnessed firsthand the power of consistent preaching in a local church. When I arrived in 1980, there were roughly seventy elderly members in the congregation, which was lost in a fine building that could seat one thousand people. The church's history was redolent with great preachers, including C. H. Spurgeon, who had been a member as a teenager on his way to becoming the "prince of preachers." However, its condition had deteriorated until several wondered out loud whether the church would survive. Yet during the next thirteen years, events occurred that I had only read about in books with titles such as *How My Church Took Off!* The congregation doubled, tripled, quadrupled, and beyond with conversions and a fast-expanding mission program. The church committed itself to build and staff a seven-day-a-week mission center for the city. Eventually, there were fourteen full-time staff members, and over four thousand people visited the center every week to use its restaurant, job clubs, and counselors. Homeless people were sheltered each winter, and young people had their own rooms for church youth programs. And when you asked the members how this had all come about, they spoke about God's grace, prayer, and preaching.

Behind this story is another profound personal experience. In the summer of 1987, I became ill with a neurological disease called dystonia. Damaged muscles in my neck so twisted my head downward with painful spasms that I could no longer walk or stand properly. I could not cut my own food or dress myself easily. Driving was forbidden as my entire body became misshapen. A specialist warned my wife that I would never be able to minister publicly again. The story of how the entire church held a prayer vigil for me and of the medical breakthroughs that put me in the first British clinical trials for botulinum toxin injections would delay us unnecessarily. Suffice it to say, doctors cautioned that I would need to continue injections for the rest of my life and that stress-induced adrenaline would likely increase the spasms. The act of preaching, therefore, could disable me. But the injections proved effective. On Easter day 1988, after seven months of being unable to preach, I went back. People still mention how, at the very moment I stood up to preach, they saw my body visibly straighten and free up. I knew a surge of joy as God gave me back a preaching ministry, and I sensed a greater urgency than ever.

In 2000, I was invited to the United States to fill the C. W. Koller Chair of Preaching and Communication at Northern Seminary in Chicago. Koller was a homiletics giant whose book *Expository Preaching without Notes* is still used.[1] After thirty years of preaching, I now have time to read, reflect, teach, and write about my lifelong passion for biblical preaching. The older I become, the more impatient I am with dull preaching that anesthetizes the faithful and pretty preaching that tickles listeners' taste buds and the more convinced I am that when preaching is honestly and humbly offered to God, he can do things through it as with nothing else. I believe in preaching.

Now, please hear me. I do not offer this book as a preaching expert but as a local preacher who keeps making more mistakes than I care to think about. I struggle weekly to preach, and sometimes, I confess, it seems more difficult than ever. Preaching never ceases to humble. Throughout the entire time I was writing this book, I was the interim preacher at First Baptist Church in Wheaton, Illinois. Preaching twice every Sunday morning kept my feet to the fire. Weekly cycles of panic and tiredness were punctuated by unique preaching opportunities, especially in the aftermath of the terrorist tragedy of September 11, 2001.

I was speaking at a ministers' conference recently. Over a meal before the final session on Saturday, I mentioned to ministers at my table how much pressure I was feeling about preaching the next day. Rather dramatically I said, "Preaching every week—it's a killer!" Immediately, one of the ministers said to me, "That's the most helpful thing you've said throughout this conference. You understand how I feel." Yes, I do.

So this book's convictions, definitions, metaphors, models, and style of teaching are birthed in large doses of realism. Its pages chart much of my own preaching odyssey as I have struggled to make sense of a theology of preaching as well as understand a world that is changing around me. It will become evident where my vision for the future outruns my practical experience. And much of my analysis is untried in wider courts of opinion and needs to be exposed to better minds and greater experience.

My story is different from yours, and any book on preaching should recognize the uniqueness of preachers and the complexities of their tasks. Like others, I have been attracted to the comment attributed to Oliver Wendell Holmes: "I don't give a fig for the simplicity this side of complexity but I would die for the simplicity on the other side of complexity."[2] A necessary complexity engages our best thought and action as we approach the subject of preaching. We must resist bandying generalizations about such as "The TV age has finished off preaching"; "Technology ruins community"; "Nobody can sit still for twenty minutes"; "The longer you preach the more worthy is its quality"; "Never use notes"; "The old ways are the best"; and "The only way forward is the new."

Anyone attempting to summarize the principles and practice of preaching will be in danger of simplism offering a panacea of simple solutions, slogans, and stereotypes. I confess at the outset, as I negotiate a way through issues raised by complex theology and changing culture, that this book's charts and diagrams will necessarily oversimplify many issues.

Part 1 offers some vital principles for biblical preaching. Chapter 1 looks at preaching's scriptural roots, proposes a definition, and refers to preaching's importance in church history. Sadly, in too many places, twenty-first-century preaching is not working well; chapter 2 provides a brief analysis of the current situation. I believe the way forward lies in a recommitment to preaching's trinitarian dynamic—what I call 360-degree preaching in chapter 3. Preaching has no future unless it recovers its dynamics. But there must also be courageous and thoughtful engagement with culture, which forms the focus of chapter 4. The person of the preacher is critical for preaching's effectiveness, and chapter 5 looks at the preacher's spirituality and offers four models. Some of the implications of preaching to changing times are summarized in chapter 6.

Who would dare to give an overview of modernity, postmodernity, and shifts in orality (how spoken words work) in just a few pages? My 360-degree model for preaching, however, seeks to offer a more complex and therefore satisfying outcome and hopefully enables readers to recognize fresh possibilities for their own preaching journey.

Part 2 focuses on preaching practice and invites preachers to join in the "preaching swim." This is my model for the rigorous, practical journey all preachers must make each time they preach. Its five stages relate to issues raised in the earlier parts of this book and have emerged out of my own preaching and teaching experiences. Chapter 7 proposes the model and considers some general, practical issues. Chapters 8 to 12 trace the different stages from source to destination as a preacher prepares, delivers, and experiences the outcomes of preaching. Appendix A contains an outline of these stages, and Appendix B includes a sermon that emerged as I took doses of my own advice. Appendix C offers an example of a sermon evaluation form created by one of my classes.

Since coming to the United States in the summer of 2000, I have been introduced to the word *doable*. A persistent complaint I have often heard from busy preachers at conferences and seminars is that some homiletics professors or celebrity preachers offer what is just not "doable" in their pressured lives. And students sometimes complain that their teachers have forgotten what it is like for those with tentative, nervous beginnings. I intend for the principles explained in this book to refresh body, mind, and spirit for the tasks ahead and to be doable. I am convinced that God continues in the business of calling and creating preachers in the twenty-first century. He's not finished with preaching yet.

Part 1

Preaching Realities

1

Preaching Roots

God decided, through the foolishness of our proclamation, to save those who believe.

1 Corinthians 1:21

We should never become desensitized to the fact that, within a dazzling range of divinely imaginative options, God invented and decided to use *preaching* to impact his world. This plan goes deeply into both Old and New Testaments, where the key attributes of biblical preaching are rooted and nourished. Four of preaching's qualities are particularly significant: It is prophetic, transformational, incarnational, and diverse. Only after considering each of these will I be able to offer a definition of preaching and to highlight preaching's role in church renewal.

Prophetic Preaching

When Jesus Christ emerged into public ministry, his first recorded action was the following: "Jesus came to Galilee, proclaiming the good news of God" (Mark 1:14). Thomas Goodwin the Puritan remarked that "God had only one Son and he made him a preacher." George Buttrick simply entitled his preaching classic *Jesus Came Preaching.* He says:

> It is a fair presumption that Jesus could have written books. Instead, "Jesus came preaching." He trusted his most precious sayings to the blemished

reputation and the precarious memory of his friends. . . . Of a truth it is a printed New Testament that remains, but its vital power is drawn from a word and a Person. . . . The gospel was and is a living impact.[1]

Yngve Brilioth claims that Jesus' synagogue sermon (Luke 4:16–21) not only roots Christian preaching in Jewish proclamation but also provides the key to understanding the history of Christian preaching ever since.[2] His analysis of this event in Luke 4 identifies three primary elements that can be used to study all subsequent Christian sermons: The liturgical element emphasizes the worship context; the exegetical element underlines the significance of interpreting the text; the prophetic element stresses that when Jesus declares, "*Today* this scripture has been fulfilled in your hearing" (v. 21), he "gives to every text its interpretation and its address for every time and place; he is the one who gives to every text its eternal content."[3] This prophetic element is closely connected with the power of the Spirit: Jesus returned "filled with the power of the spirit" (v. 14), and "the Spirit of the Lord is upon me" (v. 18). Brilioth acknowledges that there are other kinds of sermons, such as missionary sermons that occur outside the usual liturgical context, and sermons that focus on ethical admonition or the care of souls. But most preaching can be assessed by these three elements, particularly by the prophetic, when preachers are "grasped by divine reality,"[4] when they have an awareness that God's Spirit is empowering their words and actions.

Sometimes the term "prophetic preaching" is used loosely and extravagantly, as when a preacher appears to have particular intensity or deals with justice issues.[5] Someone said to me that its two characteristics seem to be sweat and noise. But prophetic preaching is about the "today-ness" of divine reality when Christian preachers respond to Scripture as Old Testament prophets did when they heard the word of the Lord. When prophets declared, "Listen to the word of the Lord," they had a conviction that God had spoken and was now present, expressing himself through the prophet's words.

Clearly, there are dangers associated with likening preachers to Old Testament prophets, whose messages were derived directly from God. They were in fact mouthpieces of God: "If you utter what is precious, and not what is worthless, you shall serve as my mouth" (Jer. 15:19). John Stott warns about making comparisons because Christian preachers do not have direct access to original, personal revelation; rather, they are responsible for declaring the revelation given in Christ and in Scripture.[6] However, there are some striking parallels.

Sidney Greidanus identifies three characteristics common to both Old Testament prophets and New Testament apostles.[7] First, both represented God. Second, both spoke God's Word. Third, both understood

God's Word to be God's deed. Both prophets and apostles were "sent-persons" who testified to what they witnessed firsthand. The apostle Paul claimed to speak on behalf of God and could describe his message as "the word of God": "We also constantly give thanks to God for this, that when you received the word of God that you heard from us, you accepted it not as a human word but as what it really is, God's word, which is also at work in you believers" (1 Thess. 2:13). Greidanus claims that preachers share the last two characteristics with prophets and apostles. Because the authority of preachers is rooted in Scripture and enlivened by the Holy Spirit, preachers can claim both to speak God's Word and to understand God's Word to be God's deed. The refrain "the word of the LORD came to me" expressed both the source of and the energy for a prophet's task (see, for example, the frequent recurrence of this phrase in Ezekiel 6:1; 7:1; 12:1; 13:1; 14:2; and so on). Once a word came from the Lord, it moved unstoppably on its way. "The Lord GOD has spoken; who can but prophesy?" (Amos 3:8). Jeremiah described a similar compulsion: "If I say, 'I will not mention him, or speak any more in his name,' then within me there is something like a burning fire shut up in my bones; I am weary with holding it in, and I cannot" (Jer. 20:9). Similarly, preachers are effective because God's Word is heard through them and is sharper than a two-edged sword (Heb. 4:12). The Holy Spirit who first inspired its words when they were spoken and written down goes on inspiring each generation of preachers as it hears and speaks again.

Preachers are also God's sent-persons whose sense of "call" involves a total commitment to preach. God calls, gifts, and employs preachers so that through them his truths might impact and change lives. Paul's apostleship was tested and authenticated through the changed lives of his hearers (2 Cor. 3:1–3).

When Timothy is charged to preach the word (2 Tim. 4:2), he stands in the new order of Christian preaching, in continuity with the apostolic commission. Klaas Runia and others argue that Paul's words in 2 Corinthians 5:18–20 embrace all Christian preachers.[8] "So *we* are ambassadors for Christ, since God is making his appeal through *us*" (v. 20). From this point on there is an immediacy of revelation because of the continuing work of Christ and the Holy Spirit through God-breathed Scripture. The stunning claim rings out that "whoever speaks must do so as one speaking the very words of God" (1 Peter 4:11). "For the Spirit who spoke through the prophets is still speaking today through preaching which passes on the messages of God's prophets and apostles."[9]

No other kind of public speaking is therefore in the same league with prophetic preaching. They operate at different levels. Of course, preaching shares certain characteristics with public speaking such as the need to focus on a topic, design a message, and deliver it skillfully with voice and body. But while people can be trained to become more effective public speakers, effectual preaching first requires God's call upon a preacher. No amount of natural skills can ever compensate for a lack of divine reality, a sense that God is empowering a spiritual event.

The Holy Spirit is intimately involved in the process of identifying a preacher's call. We need to rehabilitate the language of "anointing" by the Holy Spirit—which James Forbes describes as a "process by which one comes to a fundamental awareness of God's appointment, empowerment, and guidance for the vocation to which we are called as the body of Christ."[10] This process can be lengthy and complex and includes several features such as nurture in a family and faith community, vocational readiness, obedience to the Spirit, power from beyond oneself, and courage to bear witness.

Preachers therefore should never select themselves. Indeed, many have gone to great lengths to avoid selection. Reluctance rather than enthusiasm marked the call of Moses, Jeremiah, and Jonah. Overeagerness smacks of immaturity. Preachers should ask whether they could do anything else. Colin Morris admonishes, "Preach—if you must."[11] Martin Luther wrote, "Preaching is not the work of men. . . . For to this day I, an old and experienced preacher, am still afraid of preaching."[12] Preachers need to test their call by sensitively asking and listening: Is there any evidence of anointing? Intertwined with a speaker's talents are there signs of submission of tongue and life to God? Is there resonance of the holy?

A preacher's call belongs within God's wider call to the body of Christ to ministry. Those set apart as preachers are involved in equipping all the saints for their vocations (Eph. 4:12), and these saints need to discern necessary qualities in their preachers. These include:

- a gift for preaching: They should communicate authentically.
- humility: They should be aware of the need to listen to God in his Word and to people in their need.
- spiritual sensitivity: They should have a sense of rightness about God's call on their lives.
- good relationships: They should have integrity in their dealings with others.
- divine reality: They should have an experience of holy encounter with God through their words and lives.

Different denominational groups have developed ways by which an individual's call can be tested within the wider church's mission.

Transformational Preaching

Jesus Christ seemed to leave no room for neutrality or boredom whenever he preached. From explosive beginnings in Nazareth, he created impact every time. At first there was a positive response as "all [*pantes*] spoke well of him and were amazed at the gracious words that came from his mouth" (Luke 4:22). Yet at the conclusion, "all [*pantes*] in the synagogue were filled with rage. They got up, drove him out of the town, and led him to the brow of the hill . . . so that they might hurl him off the cliff" (Luke 4:28–29). The emphatic restatement of *pantes* serves to illustrate the power of Jesus' proclamation both to amaze and to antagonize. Amazement and antagonism remain the predominant outcomes throughout the Gospels. People are continually "astounded" (as in Matt. 7:28; 13:54; 22:33; Mark 1:22; 11:18; Luke 4:32).

Amazement and antagonism mark the apostles' preaching too. At the birth of the church, it is by Peter's preaching that the gospel is heard and responses are made (Acts 2:14–41). It is a sermon presenting Christ crucified and risen that brings hearers to crisis, repentance, and faith; they are "cut to the heart," and "about three thousand persons were added" (Acts 2:37, 41). Though it all begins in the unrepeatable "sound like the rush of a violent wind" and "tongues as of fire," it is by repeatable words of frail preachers that God chooses to birth his church. At key breakthroughs in mission, preaching is essential, as in Samaria (Acts 9:20–31) or with Cornelius (Acts 10:34–47). Paul's missionary preaching makes a dramatic impact wherever he goes, with the unfortunate exception of Eutychus, who fell asleep (Acts 20:9). The actual word used in Acts 20:9 is *dialegomai*, "to discourse and argue." Its occurrence throughout the latter part of Acts is associated with a common pattern of astonishing people with good news as well as antagonizing religious leaders (see Acts 17:2; 19:8; 20:7).

Preaching also has long-term effects in the nurturing of new churches. The reference in 1 Corinthians 14:3 to "those who prophesy" relates strongly to intelligible speech (v. 9) and therefore to preaching. Its three outcomes are listed as "building up" (*oikodomē*), "encouragement" (*paraklēsis*), and "consolation" (*paramythia*). Peter Adam stresses the "building up" aspect of preaching with reference to Ephesians 4:12 and defines preaching as "the explanation and application of the Word to the congregation of Christ in order to produce corporate preparation for serving, unity of faith, maturity, growth, and up building."[13] The themes of encouragement and comfort emphasize the way in which persuasive preaching can both excite and calm listeners. In 2 Timothy 4:2, further outcomes are mentioned: Preaching should convict (*elenchō*) and rebuke (*epitimaō*).

Astonishment, antagonism, conviction, conversion, strengthening, encouraging, and consolation result from preaching. In the New Testament, some preaching bears immediate fruit, while other preaching brings long-term results in the formation of congregational life. Always, however, something happens. Preaching changes people. "God decided, through the foolishness of our proclamation, to save those who believe" (1 Cor. 1:21). Preaching is not *telling* about good news; it *is* good news. It is not a pointer to *potential* divine promise somewhere else; it is God's promise that is effective *now*. Preaching rooted in Scripture and inspired by the Spirit possesses prophetic reality to transform. Leander Keck describes how "the preacher who has wrestled with the text can . . . become a prophetic spokesman on behalf of the text."[14] Karl Barth defined preaching in the following way: "Preaching is the Word of God which he himself has spoken; but God makes use, according to his good pleasure, of the ministry of a man who speaks to his fellow men, in God's name by means of a passage of Scripture."[15] No wonder early on the priority of preaching needed to be safeguarded as pastoral pressures built in the new church in Jerusalem. The apostles recognized that they could not fail in their key task: "It is not right that we should neglect the word of God in order to wait on tables" (Acts 6:2). They appointed others, while they devoted themselves "to prayer and to serving the word" (Acts 6:4).

Incarnational Preaching

Christian theology places faith within culture. The incarnation of Jesus Christ as the "Word made flesh" (John 1:14) roots the gospel inextricably in culture. Born in Bethlehem, at the time of the Augustinian census (Luke 2:1–2), Jesus was immersed historically in the world, identifying with humankind at a particular time and place. The repercussions of his life, death, and resurrection are eternal, but they happened in time and in culture. Scripture's story similarly tells of God's dealings with his people at particular times and places before, during, and after the incarnation of Christ.

Yet the good news (gospel) of Jesus Christ is Jesus proclaiming himself and living out his own story. He *is* the story as the Word becomes flesh. As Marshall McLuhan put it in a conversation with Pierre Babin, "That is the only case in which the medium and the message are perfectly identical." Babin continues, "And in explaining the term *message*, he insisted that it was not the *words* spoken by Christ but *Christ himself* and all the ministries that extend from him that produce an effect on us. The message is conversion."[16] Because the gospel's truth and experience reside in the person of Jesus, his big story or "grand narrative" remains constant even though human cultures continually shift and the story is heard in different ways. Telling God's timeless story in our time remains the critical task for all preachers everywhere. The other main timeless truth is that humankind needs salvation.[17]

As we will see, the fact that Jesus never wrote a book but lived a story and taught through stories is an exhilarating foundation for all subsequent preaching. Humankind needs salvation, and the same story has to be told to each generation. Its source is in Jesus the Word made flesh, yet it has to be told through the words, experiences, and flesh of preachers. Preachers must therefore stand *under* Scripture and the lordship of Christ and also *in* the contemporary world to embody God's Word in their words and persons. This has huge implications for understanding the times, as we will see.

Diverse Preaching

For convenience, I have so far referred to New Testament preaching as though it were one phenomenon. However, nearly thirty Greek words may be translated using the single word *preaching*. Each struggles to represent the new phenomenon of the in-breaking kingdom of God and to describe a unique event that had never happened before.

One of these, *kēryssō*, means "I herald" and is suggestive of a town crier in a market square. But it "does not mean the delivery of a learned and edifying or hortatory discourse in well chosen words and a pleasant voice. It is the declaration of an event."[18] Repent! Other expressive terms surprise us with their range. For example, in Acts we find words such as these: *euangelizomai* (Acts 14:7), meaning "I bring good news, I preach good tidings, I instruct concerning the things that pertain to Christian salvation,"[19] from which we derive the word *evangelist; didaskō* (Acts 4:2; 5:25), meaning "I teach, hold discourse with others in order to instruct them, deliver didactic discourses";[20] *apophthengomai* (Acts 2:4, 14), which means "I pronounce (not belonging to everyday speech but to dignified and elevated discourse)";[21] and *dialegomai* (Acts 17:17; 18:4; 19:8; 20:9; 24:25), meaning "I converse, discourse with one, argue, discuss,"[22] from which the word *dialogue* comes. Some have constructed theories about how some of these words have technical significance. C. H. Dodd contrasted *kēryssō* (which he saw as proclamation outside the church) with *didaskō* (teaching inside the church).[23] But this oversimplified the evidence, for if significant differences were meant to be understood this way, they would be much clearer in the text.

This sample of New Testament words underlines the rich variety of preaching practice and sounds out a warning about making simple generalizations. There is little evidence that early preaching resembled what has become the norm for many of us in our worship services. True, Jesus preached in the synagogue (Luke 4:16–21), an event that provides some significant criteria for subsequent Christian preaching. But his incarnation makes his preaching unique and unrepeatable. He *is* the story.

Preachers can learn much from studying Jesus' and the apostles' teaching ministries, but they will not find examples of sermons that closely resemble their own. For example, the sermon of Acts 2:14–39 seems to summarize only the highlights of a missionary sermon. So we must be cautious about assuming that we know what the word *preaching* means. No one can be dogmatic about what a sermon should look like or can generalize from his or her own experience how all preaching should be. There are no uniform packages or pigeonholes in the New Testament. What Craig Loscalzo says about evangelistic preaching holds true for other kinds as well: "One problem with evangelistic sermons is that they look and sound like evangelistic sermons."[24] No one can say for certain what a sermon should look like. In the twenty-first century, no one can authoritatively declare that one size fits all or that there is only one biblical pattern. There has never been one ordained pattern, and in our age of turbulent change, we should expect just as much diversity as we find in the New Testament.

A Definition of Preaching

Preaching's diversity in the New Testament, and ever since, makes it difficult to construct a single workable definition. Indeed, *preaching* is such a slippery word that almost anyone can construct a definition based on his or her personal experience and preference that can then be read back into favorite New Testament references.

Phillips Brooks's well-known definition of preaching, "truth mediated through personality," was developed by George Sweazey into "truth through personality, *in the midst of personalities*."[25] Bernard Manning states, "Preaching is a manifestation of the Incarnate Word from the Written Word by the spoken word."[26] Harry Fosdick regards preaching "as drenching the congregation in one's life's blood."[27] Some are more explicit in detail. Haddon Robinson states, "Expository Preaching is the communication of a biblical concept, derived from and transmitted through a historical, grammatical, and literary study of a passage in its context, which the Holy Spirit first applies to the personality and experience of the preacher, then through the preacher applies to the hearers."[28]

Because preaching is prophetic, transformational, and incarnational, I am drawn to a definition that focuses on its dynamic impact. My conviction is that preaching is nothing less than sharing the in-breaking of God's good news to create new people in new community. Christian preaching, at its best, is a biblical speaking/listening/seeing/doing event that God empowers to form Christ-shaped people and communities. "At its best" expresses a realism that much preaching sadly falls short, yet it also dares to raise expectations about what preaching can and should be. "Biblical speaking/listening/seeing/doing" conveys a dynamic eventfulness that has implications for all the senses, all the person, and all the community. The word *seeing* refers not only to multisensory words and the person of the preacher but also to the possibilities of new technology. But most importantly, this definition contains the theological conviction that God empowers preaching events to form Christ-shaped people and communities. Preaching is about God communicating his will and purpose with power and immediacy to effect change—an emphasis that will resonate throughout this book. Preaching, at its best, is a God happening, empowered by Father, Son, and Holy Spirit.

To borrow from Walter Brueggemann, it is "the evoking of an alternative community that knows it is about different things in different ways."[29] When Jesus Christ came proclaiming (Mark 1:14), his primary concern was not to impart new information but to announce a new way of living in his kingdom. "Repent and believe in the good news." This is not a tinkering with life as we know it but an invitation to a new way of being never imagined. It is not a dabbling with surface issues of passing significance but a dealing at depth with our reasons for existence in his kingdom—issues of eternal consequence.

When the charge rings out from God's throne room, "Proclaim the message; be persistent whether the time is favorable or unfavorable" (2 Tim. 4:2), it is not a charge for a domestic activity for religiously inclined people but God's urgent word to create an alternative reality. In a context of "itching ears" that want palatable affirmations, preaching confronts with sound doctrines that convince, rebuke, and encourage for the finishing of the one good fight, the one race that matters, which comes with "the crown of righteousness, which the Lord, the righteous judge, will give me on that day" (v. 8). Preaching puts people, communities, nations, and the world on a new course, with new possibilities and new outcomes. Preaching offers another way of living that is not a gloss on the status quo but a change to abundant life.

Peter Berger the sociologist wrote of "signals of transcendence"[30] that discerning people see in the world as evidence of God's presence. Preachers are called to the task of announcing signals of transcendence. Jesus Christ has broken into the busy self-preoccupied world with transforming power for kingdom living today. God is involved in dynamic change. John Ruskin described preaching memorably: "Thirty minutes to raise the dead in."[31] The Helvetic Confession (1566) majestically stated, "The preaching of the Word of God is the Word of God."[32] James Stewart challenged preachers, "Every Sunday morning when it comes ought to find you awed and thrilled by the reflection—'God is to be in action today, through me, for these people.'"[33]

These claims about evoking an alternative community thrust preaching into a strategic role in God's purposes. Brueggemann calls for prophetic ministry "to nurture, nourish, and evoke a consciousness and perception alternative to the consciousness and perception of the dominant culture around us."[34] Dominant cultures are characterized as being numb to the possibilities of newness. The prophetic task goes against the numbness of a self-seeking, self-perpetuating, dominant culture. For Brueggemann, all acts of ministry should lead to this evoking and confronting. "Prophetic ministry seeks to penetrate despair so that new futures can be believed in and embraced."[35]

Preaching is unlike any other activity, for its distinctive language creates new community. It has a subversive quality that undermines conventional wisdom with perceptions of deeper verities. William Willimon captures this well in *Peculiar Speech: Preaching to the Baptized*, when he pleads with passion for peculiar speech that evokes a new people out of nothing. Preachers need to understand, as he puts it, that they "talk funny." Elsewhere he writes of the "weirdness of the gospel." "While preaching struggles for connections, associations, between my life and the word of the gospel, it also expects disassociation, gaps and tension between my story and the gospel."[36]

Some may find this broad, dynamic definition of preaching unsatisfying. Why does it not mention, for example, a key word for many evangelicals—*expository*? For many, this word seems to guarantee legitimacy through a particular style of verse-by-verse preaching that is claimed to reflect Scripture most accurately. However, Robinson correctly states that expository preaching "at its core is more a philosophy than a method."[37] As he comments, whether a person is an expositor or not depends on how he or she answers the question, "Do you, as a preacher, endeavor to bend your thought to the Scriptures, or do you use the Scriptures to support your thought?"[38] Exposition is primarily a matter of being "exposed" to the message of Scripture and "exposing" hearers to its power. Rather than being tied to a particular format, it depends on the quality of relationship, of humble interaction, between preacher and Scripture. There are no ready-made, prepackaged preaching styles that guarantee this relationship, as though preachers can be spiritually cloned. Each has a unique responsibility, by God's calling and under the authority of his Word in Christ and in Scripture, to find his or her own voice for his or her own hearers in his or her own times.

The Church and Preaching throughout History

Every spiritual surge in the church's story since the first century has owed its life to God's presence and action—"not by might, nor by power, but by my spirit says the LORD of hosts" (Zech. 4:6). Yet one continuous sound has been heard throughout—the words of preachers. It has been estimated that over three billion sermons have been preached since the day of Pentecost.[39] No other formal group activity can come close to this impressive statistic.

Incontrovertibly, the church's story cannot be told without reference to its preaching. Preaching is a part of the DNA of church; it is not just a part of its high profile moments but its daily life. "Renewal comes, not through isolated, heroic thinkers, but rather in the church through the everyday activity of people. . . . We believe that renewal comes through an appreciation of the continuing empowerment by word and sacrament, which in each age creates a church worthy to hear the Word and to receive the body and blood of Christ."[40] Believing comes through hearing the Word from preachers who are in the right places at the right times. That is what makes their feet beautiful (Rom. 10:15).

Consistently and stubbornly, preaching echoes through the millennia, sometimes fortissimo, often pianissimo, but always vital for the church's life. At the heart of this book lies the conviction that preaching at its best has always accompanied church life at its best. Whenever God has breathed fresh life into his people, it has led to a vibrant missional church with vibrant missional preaching. Lively preaching and lively church mission share mutual energy and creativity within the empowering of God's Spirit. Leander Keck claims, "Every renewal of Christianity has been accompanied by a renewal of preaching. Each renewal of preaching, in turn, has rediscovered biblical preaching."[41] Church historian Edwin Dargan comments, "Decline of spiritual life and activity in the churches is commonly accompanied by a lifeless, formal, unfruitful preaching, and this partly as cause, partly as effect. On the other hand, the great revivals of Christian history can most usually be traced to the work of the pulpit, and in their progress they have developed and rendered possible a high order of preaching."[42] Peter Forsyth adds, "With its preaching Christianity stands or falls. Preaching is the most distinctive institution within Christianity."[43] Nothing conveys God's saving truth as effectively as preaching does, and nothing may contribute to church renewal more.

Originating in the synagogue traditions of Jewish Christianity, preaching was influenced by such things as the Greek homily and Latin rhetoric. The church's greatest thinkers and leaders did their thinking and their leading through preaching. Often without realizing it, preachers today build on earlier work of preaching giants such as Origen, Augustine, and Luther.

Origen (c. 185–c. 254) was trained in Alexandria, an important intellectual center, and studied the work of the philosopher Philo, who developed a method of bringing together Jewish thought and Greek philosophy.

Origen employed three senses by which to understand Scripture: a *literal* sense, a *moral* sense that applied to the listener's situation, and a *mystical* sense that brought a person into a relationship with Christ and the church. For moral and mystical understandings, he made strong use of the allegory, a tool that is prone to abuse but that, when used with caution, can make positive connections between texts and contemporary meanings—"this text means this." Paul Wilson pleads today for an appropriate use of allegory and the reemployment of "four senses," as they ultimately became known in the early church: the literal sense—the literal historical event; the allegorical sense—a text's theological doctrine; the moral sense—a text's call for changes in hearers' lives; the prophetic sense—a text's implications about the next life.[44] Through Origen, "exegesis and preaching were so firmly united that . . . long afterwards they remained intertwined."[45]

Preachers who stress the twin tasks of understanding a Scripture passage correctly in order to preach it persuasively probably owe more than they realize to Augustine (354–430), who was trained in rhetoric and taught it as a professor in Milan. Augustine forged a link between a solid understanding of a text (he wrote some of the first commentaries on Scripture) and the need to design persuasive preaching. Toward the end of his life he wrote the first preaching textbook, *De Doctrina Christiana*, book 4, in which he applied rules of classical rhetoric to preaching. He quoted the definition of a speaker's task given by the Latin rhetorician Cicero: *Docere* ("to teach"), *delectare* ("to delight"), *flectare* ("to influence").[46] These tasks appeal to intellect, feeling, and will and model three types (genus) of speech: *submissum* ("restrained"), *temperatum* ("moderate"), and *grande* ("grand"). Augustine was concerned that listeners respond to all three *intelligenter* ("intelligently"), *libenter* ("willingly"), and *obedienter* ("obediently").

According to Brilioth, because of Augustine's preaching, which combined a deep commitment to Scripture with passionate, fiery sentences and sermons (many less than ten minutes), there was no worthier representative of prophetic preaching before the Reformation. "Above all else . . . Augustine conceived of himself as a steward of the mysteries of God."[47] The marriage between preaching and rhetoric remains a critical union for all preaching.

The Reformation is supremely associated with the preaching of the Word, especially with regard to Martin Luther. Brilioth claims, "No person, before or since, has so exalted the word, not only the written word but the living word: 'The New Testament office is not written on dead tablets of stone, instead it is entrusted to the sounds of living speech.'"[48] In each sermon, Luther concentrated on one Scripture passage, with a passion for simplicity. "Christ has spoken in the most simple way and yet he was eloquence personified—therefore the highest eloquence is to speak simply."[49] Luther had a deep consciousness of being entrusted with in-breaking good news, which had to be told as urgently and simply as possible.

Many branches of the church family honor different breakthrough eras when fresh preaching reinvigorated their lives and missions. Protestants treasure the golden era of the Reformation, with the preaching of Luther and Calvin, and the late-eighteenth-century revivals in the Western church, associated with the preaching of George Whitefield and John Wesley, as high points in powerful preaching. Yet "Lutherans, Calvinists and Anglicans were not the only ones to restore the word of God to its place of honor. In the Roman Catholic church, the Council of Trent insisted that all priests should preach on Sundays and teach the faithful."[50]

But not just preachers had a critical influence within the history of preaching. A chief example is Johannes Gutenberg, who, between 1440 and 1456, invented movable type, which spurred extraordinary developments in preaching. Pierre Babin describes what happened as nothing less than "an inspired act on the part of the church to seize on this new medium. . . . They created a different way of communicating faith, which was based on the potential of the new print medium. . . . The most important factor in the religious revival of the sixteenth century, both Catholic and Protestant, was the effort to ensure that the ordinary people learned the theological foundations of Christianity,"[51] which happened through uniformly precise printed leaflets. The Protestant Reformation, therefore, was spread through the fusion of two mediums—preaching and printing. "Protestantism was born with printing and has been the religion in which printing—the printed Bible, the catechism, newspaper and journal—has played a vital part."[52] Printing changed the ways in which people were able to think and preachers could communicate. Words could be mass produced, and people could learn the catechism. The task of preaching became more about explaining what people had already learned through print.

The story of preaching should not be told without reference to the impact of shifts in communication. Preaching has its own speaking/listening/seeing/doing dynamics, but they operate within cultural contexts that change. Past pulpit giants are giants partly because they grasped opportunities to proclaim timeless truths in changing times. Just as preachers once saw new opportunities in printing, so contemporary preachers are confronted by opportunities in the electronics revolution. Is there evidence of "an inspired act on the part of the church to seize on this new phenomenon"? This important question will command some attention later.

As I reflect on preaching's high role in God's past mission break-throughs, I plead for contemporary preaching, in God's name and by his power, to take primary responsibility for church renewal today. Nothing is more significant to human existence than announcing the in-breaking of God's good news to create new people in new community. Effective churches resonate with God's alternative reality, called the kingdom of God, live out his grace of forgiveness within their memberships, and have a passion for mission and service that reaches far beyond their boundaries. Authentic preaching has always opened up new ways of living and being in Christ. It never has merely conveyed safe information to shore up the status quo but has helped to form a new people for the sake of a lost world. It offers not cushions but life jackets, not comfortable platitudes but rescue and restoration. It seeks not approval of the already committed but urgent responses of those still seeking.

Transformational, individual-saving, community-forming preaching creates churches at their best. That is why mission and leadership flow from healthy preaching. Common descriptions of preaching, whether positive (energetic, lively) or negative (dull, boring), can entirely miss the point. Preaching's awesome task is about evoking an alternative community that lives for a different agenda—for God, for the wider community, and for the world. Preaching needs to be experienced as prophetic, transformational, incarnational, and diverse. Catalytic, life-changing preaching accomplishes deep outcomes in God's purposes.

If it were possible to run a spiritual seismometer over Christian history to record its major tremors, every quake would correspond to a renewed sense of God's presence in preaching. This claim for preaching in the past, however, seems to ring hollow in the present. Whatever preaching may have done in the past, honesty compels us to admit that the present does not seem to be a time of life and renewal. To this sorry state of affairs we must now turn.

2

Current Realities

Preaching is in trouble everywhere.

J. Sittler, *The Anguish of Preaching*

Recently, I asked the students in one of my preaching classes whether they look forward to the preaching they hear in their churches. Of twenty-three students, only eight raised their hands. "Does that mean the rest of you do *not* look forward to the preaching you hear?" I asked. One commented, "Yes, it's so often dull, boring, and long-winded," and others nodded in agreement. The music in worship can be inspiring and the fellowship genuine, but the preaching nearly always disappoints.

I know I should not draw conclusions from one such experience, and many readers may protest at such negativity. Obviously, there are some bright exceptions. But many times I have asked other groups the same question and have encountered disturbingly similar results. During the last ten years, for every preacher I have heard described as interesting, thoughtful, powerful, and anointed, I have heard of another two who are uninteresting, predictable, lacking in courage, and long-winded. It is not that churchgoers say they believe any less in the significance of preaching or that preachers appear to be less committed to the task. Surveys continue to show that churchgoers have high expectations of preaching. When it comes to preaching, hope springs eternal. But the plain fact is that in too many places preaching does not seem to be working well. There is a plague of dullness. As with a story repeatedly told by a garrulous, elderly relative, we have heard it all before. Though the

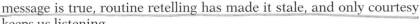

message is true, routine retelling has made it stale, and only courtesy keeps us listening.

The few brilliant pockets of preaching creativity must not mislead, for often they shine brightly because of the surrounding dark tracts of dead and dying churches. Too many churches are pathetically grateful that their doors are still open and that attendances at morning services are holding up, while mass society tragically bypasses churches in its own "spiritual" search. Too much preaching appears to have lost its power to change anything. Frankly, the words *prophetic* and *transformational* seem inappropriate in regard to preaching.

Ineffectual preaching has dire consequences for God's church and mission in the twenty-first century. A crisis in preaching means a crisis in the health and life of the local church. Of course, local churches live and die for many reasons. Strong churches with authentic worship and a vital mission owe much to factors such as gifted leadership, spiritual vitality, prayer, vision, and above all the grace of God. But preaching has primary responsibility, and when it is weak and sick, the local church and its mission are weak and sick.

A Serious Malaise

Much analysis of current church life makes for miserable reading on both sides of the Atlantic. Thomas Bandy claims that "most Christendom congregations have been on the longest losing streak in denominational history: decreasing worship attendance, smaller Sunday schools, aging participants, less outreach, closure. The laity are demoralized, the clergy are unhappy and the fans are beyond critical; they have given up."[1] Thomas Reeves paints a depressing picture of seven denominations within North American Protestantism that have lost between one-fifth and one-third of their members since the 1960s and have a marked inability to retain children. In 1995, a researcher found that the United States Methodist Church had lost one thousand members every week for the previous thirty years. Newell Williams is quoted: "Many people now see no reason to be Christian. The mainline churches are just plain boring."[2]

Cardinal Murphy-O'Connor made British newspaper headlines in September 2001 by claiming that Christianity had almost been vanquished in Britain. "Christ was being replaced by music, New Age beliefs, the environmental movement, the occult and the free-market economy," he said, and the extent to which Christianity informed modern culture and intellectual life in Britain had been hugely diminished. "You see quite a demoralized society, one where the only good is what I want, the only rights are my own, and the only life with any meaning or value is the life I want for myself."[3] In many parts of Western Europe, Christian faith has been marginalized. It no longer has a public role for all but is a private hobby for a few.

Callum Brown's *The Death of Christian Britain* goes further. It offers a cultural analysis that so-called "discursive Christianity," as summed up in those factors that make up personal Christian identity—behavior, dress, speech—held wide social significance until it suddenly "died" in the 1960s. "British people re-imagined themselves in ways no longer Christian—a 'moral turn' which abruptly undermined virtually all of the protocols of moral identity."[4] This controversial assessment is based on widespread interviews with people who spoke about their "identity."

In most places, the gospel is met by massive indifference. Christian distinctives are becoming less and less evident as a declining Christian community acculturates to twenty-first-century mores. George Barna has amassed statistics that show a similarity in behavior between "born-again Christians" and those "outside the church." In terms of divorce, the figures are 34 percent compared with 27 percent; giving money to a homeless person, 17 percent compared with 24 percent.[5]

It would be unnecessarily dispiriting to pursue further evidence of decline. We have already seen enough to raise sharp questions about preaching's role. While other causes contribute to this malaise, preaching bears much culpability. Says Reeves, "In mainline churches all over America, sermons are too often hastily prepared and deadly dull. . . . An amazing number of pastors are 'rhetorically challenged.' I have sat through hundreds of sermons based largely if not exclusively on the repetition of religious cliches."[6] Some complain that sermons have lost their declamatory voice. "Deplorable is the state of the sermon. . . . The surest evidence that Protestantism has abandoned its glorious heritage . . . is the demise of kerygmatic preaching, preaching that consists in retelling the story of God's gift of salvation in Jesus Christ. Sermons are didactic more than kerygmatic, more centered on moral concerns than on the gospel."[7] William O'Malley gives a salutary commandment for preachers: "Presume disinterest. While you are poring over the Scriptures for next Sunday's homily, presume a cold audience. Presume that they would rather feed their children to crocodiles than listen to you."[8]

A. W. Tozer once quipped, "Give me a new Christian before he has met too many other Christians and heard too many sermons," and Reginald White, in a passing mood of facetious cynicism, defined preaching as "a monstrous monologue given by a moron to mutes."[9] Self-deprecating humor has always been a preacher's defense mechanism, but nothing can disguise the low regard in which much preaching is held. When I was appointed to my chair in 2000, I titled my installation address "The

Wheel Is Turning, but the Hamster Is Dead."[10] Since then, several listeners have told me how my message resonated with their experiences of repetitive church routines and preachers feebly caught in the cyclical pattern of committees and church life.

In too many places, preaching has been reduced to an anemic, religious non-event. Faint is its power to proclaim an alternative reality, the kingdom of God, and faded is its conviction about transforming communities. Gone are its prophetic voice and its mission thrust. Missing is its gloriously subversive way of challenging the status quo to create communities of light and service. Preaching has become a shadow of its richly diverse New Testament forbears. Often it merely peddles texts and stories to affirm or, even worse, amuse a cautious remnant.

Preachers have also lost the art of leadership through the proclaimed Word. There is too little courage and too much safe predictability, too little confrontation of evil by Christ's power and too much soothing of the already convinced. Fewer people can imagine that revival and renewal could ever come from preaching. Preaching has been customized, relativized, banalized, and sidelined by what appears to hold more promising developments for the church, such as worship renewal. We seem to be reliving the tragedy of 1 Samuel 3:1: "The word of the LORD was rare in those days; visions were not widespread."

Does anyone care about this decline apart from self-interested preachers? When was the last time a non-preacher wrote a book pleading for biblical preaching? Rather than slide into depression, preachers need to confront criticisms and negative factors, assess their validity, and respond honestly. To these factors we now turn.

Objections to Preaching

David Norrington's book *To Preach or Not to Preach?*[11] raises some fundamental questions about the validity of sermons. He finds no evidence in Scripture to support the contemporary practice of preaching sermons but rather locates its origin in Greek and Roman rhetoric. He argues that following these pagan sources has had dangerous consequences, beguiling preachers into acting like egotistical primadonnas who inevitably induce listeners to become dependent on them. Far from doing good, sermons can seriously damage a congregation's health, functioning as "deskilling agents" that stunt the growth of listeners.

Norrington criticizes preaching's elitist expectation that for one period each week someone who is more gifted than the rest will speak and everyone else will attend in silence. Because congregations contain members who have a wide range of knowledge and rates of spiritual growth, to say nothing of contrasting concentration spans, he claims that monologue sermons without participation fail to develop listeners' thinking and analytical skills. One-way communication reinforces passivity, fortifies domination by clergy, and fosters immaturity among believers.

There are glaring weaknesses in Norrington's argument. He seems to define preaching narrowly as speech and pays little attention to the significance of Jesus' preaching in Luke 4 as the origin of Christian preaching. While the Greek homily and Latin rhetoric certainly had a later influence on preaching, as noted in Origen's and Augustine's contributions, Christian preaching has deeper roots than Norrington allows. He omits any discussion about preaching's theology and its relationship with Scripture and the Holy Spirit—all of which we will consider later. He makes little room for anointed preaching, for which the first apostles were set aside (Acts 6:4, 7). Indeed, he seems to take the positive aspects of the Holy Spirit's work in developing Christian maturity and place them uncritically within the model of small groups.

Yet painfully, preachers must hear his charge of mediocrity against much contemporary preaching and admit to an all-too-common failure to create active, mature congregations. Jeremy Thomson raises similar issues: "For all the effort of preparing, delivering and listening to sermons, most church members are not as mature as we might expect as a result."[12] He complains that the rich variety of New Testament preaching has become a monologue and argues for dialogical preaching that encourages more congregational interaction.

Some challenges to preaching are subtler. They are found in what writers do *not* say. Much current literature that calls for the church to change reveals only embarrassing silence about preaching's future role. For example, Bandy advocates a new role for Christian leaders that he calls "coaching."[13] His term for traditional ministers is "professionals," whom he describes as those trained in seminaries, who act like CEOs, are at home with programs, and relate as preacher to congregation. Instead of "professionals," he claims that the future church needs "coaches" who are grown and mentored within congregations, act as motivators of teams, are at home in chaos, and relate as friend to friend. Preaching is excluded from the animation, synergy, and passion of his team-building model for the future. His glowing picture of the future church, transformed by teams and technology, has no room for preaching.

Christian Schwarz, in his worldwide survey and analysis of the factors that make for healthy, growing churches, highlights eight characteristics of "natural church growth."[14] You would expect one of them, "inspiring worship," to promote preaching, but instead there is minimal reference. Another popular leadership book, *Leading Congregational Change*, outlines a process for congregational transformation but again makes little explicit reference to preaching. Its thesis is, "If you keep doing what you've been doing, you'll keep getting what you've been getting. Can you live with that?"[15]

The suspicion is that preaching inevitably maintains the status quo and specializes in survival and playing it safe. Many church observers presume that preachers function in maintenance mode and are more concerned with devotional thoughts for the committed than with living on the cutting edge with the uncommitted. According to many experts, the future church does not need preachers.

Negative Factors Affecting Preaching

Along with some disquiet about preaching's value, certain negative factors have also affected preaching at the beginning of the twenty-first century. These are a loss of holistic engagement with Scripture, a poverty of Holy Spirit power, increased pressure on preachers, fewer good models to follow, and changing times. The first four issues relate to dynamics *within* preaching and anticipate chapter 3, while the last issue deals with dynamics *outside* preaching. Understanding culture in a changing world occupies chapter 4.

A Loss of Holistic Engagement with Scripture

Holistic engagement with Scripture means responding to Scripture with all the senses so that it captures head and heart, intellect and imagination, emotions and will. The command to love God "with all your heart, and with all your soul, and with all your strength, and with all your mind" (Luke 10:27) also applies to engagement with his Word. Such engagement involves not just knowing about Scripture, having a grasp of its contents, but being immersed in its life, grasped by its power, involved in its story, and convicted by its word. A preacher's relationship with Scripture is interactive and needs a vocabulary with words such as immerse, listen, question, visualize, enter, taste, experience, love, and obey.

But in too many places, such interactive commitment is missing. Much preaching suffers from one-dimensional engagement. Scripture has been limited to the head or to the heart. "The two edged sword becomes a plastic butter knife."[16] Many preachers, trained in the discipline of exegesis to ask questions about historical context and literary content, aided and abetted by Bible commentaries, have a tendency to engage Scripture only with their minds. Their preaching can become cerebral. In contrast, preachers who fail to do exegesis and engage only with their hearts, focusing on feelings and reducing everything to tidy applications, are in danger of becoming vacuously emotional. Both heads and hearts have to be involved. God's Word needs to become visceral, embodied, thought out, experienced, and lived out. As G. Robert Jacks challenges, "Don't think of yourself as being 'responsible for' the Word. God is, not you. Let it come to life in you! Better yet: Let it bring you to life!"[17]

Such holistic engagement with Scripture requires more than a sound doctrinal commitment to the orthodoxy of Scripture. Of course, an interactive relationship with Scripture requires a belief in Scripture's inspiration and authority. Second Timothy 3:16 is preaching's touchstone. But what a preacher actually allows Scripture to do in practice is most significant. Donald McKim's survey of doctrinal beliefs about Scripture, for example, outlines a range of possible beliefs, yet he emphasizes that the practical use of Scripture matters most. He invites preachers to place themselves in one or more of fourteen theological movements ranging from classical Roman Catholic and Protestant teaching to liberation, black, Asian, and feminist theologies. He gives each a slogan, such as liberal theology's "Scripture as experience," fundamentalism's "Scripture as proposition," scholastic theology's "Scripture as doctrine," and neo-orthodoxy's "Scripture as witness." However, he concludes, "The Church needs always to remember that the use of Holy Scripture is more important than debates about its authority."[18]

Bluntly put, much contemporary preaching lacks energy. Thomas Long warns that "when the voltage drops in the Bible, preachers desperately plug the sermon into any outlet that promises a jolt of energy: psychotherapy, narrative, image, communication theory, personal disclosure—the list goes on."[19] This plunge in scriptural voltage has disabled much contemporary preaching. Too many preachers have become disengaged from Scripture. Unless they are alive in Scripture, they will never be alive to listeners.

Leander Keck parodies much contemporary preaching by likening it to the bound figure of Lazarus (John 11). Several negative influences, such as lost confidence in preaching's significance, society's revolt against authority, and a failure to relate "biblical criticism" to what he calls "conservative piety," are like cloths wrapped around the face. Keck calls preachers to understand the historical nature of Scripture and to master critical methods yet at the same time to "establish an intimate first hand religious relationship with the text."[20] Scholarship should go hand in hand with a personal, experiential encounter with the text. Preachers have to stop preaching on easy passages, avoiding texts that ask difficult questions, and start living according to the alternative reality that Scripture presents. Preachers must discern how the biblical story interprets the world rather than interpret Scripture through contemporary lenses.

A Poverty of Holy Spirit Power

Another critical factor is an absence of spiritual authenticity in much preaching. To misquote 1 Thessalonians 1:5, there is preaching simply with words and *not* in power, in the Holy Spirit, or with full conviction. James Forbes claimed in his Lyman Beecher Lectures in 1986, "If a greatly improved quality of preaching is to be experienced in our time, it will stem from the renewing power and presence of the Holy Spirit."[21] Talk about Holy Spirit power seems awkward for preachers who appear to be allergic to the pneumatic. In addition to theological concerns about the supernatural, they may have temperamental distaste for and perhaps even fear of experimentation with the Spirit. Many preachers, skilled at controlling words, have been trained to close out spiritual vitality. Though they may claim to worship the God of the impossible, they fervently hope that he will not do anything impossible where they are.

Many are also suspicious of Holy Spirit power because of the excesses seen on the fringes, where music and testimony in worship are used at the expense of the Word and tend to push out doctrine and truth. While unhelpful charismatic manifestations do exist, they must not blind preachers to the empowering role of the Holy Spirit and the need to have a working theology of his involvement. "Warned of false fire by fireless men, we have settled for no fire at all."[22]

This book stresses the trinitarian dynamics of preaching, with an understanding that Father, Son, and Holy Spirit are active at every point of effective preaching. (This idea will be developed as 360-degree preaching.) Of the Persons of the Trinity, the Holy Spirit is particularly identified with the anointing of preachers and the convicting of listeners. Yet sadly, the Holy Spirit often seems so absent that much contemporary preaching has become binitarian. Much recent practice has been so preoccupied with techniques that it has logic chopped homiletics, microscopically dissected texts, and imaginatively constructed sermons with minimal reference to the Holy Spirit. Twenty-first-century preaching needs less function and more unction, an older word that needs rehabilitation. "Unction" speaks of the seal of God, the "not in word only but also in power" reality of authentic divine-human encounter—the spiritual vitality that is often missing.

Forbes claims that "the preacher makes a statement about the Holy Spirit just by entering the pulpit. . . . The preaching event itself . . . is a living, breathing, flesh-and-blood expression of the theology of the Holy Spirit."[23] Tragically, much preaching seems to contradict this high hope. Controlling and closed rather than liberating and open, shallow and predictable rather than deep and restoring, sermons are often dull, cerebral non-events or frothy ephemera.

People commonly say that the missing quality in contemporary preaching is passion. "Call it passion, life, authenticity, naturalness, conviction, sincerity or being animated."[24] Only by holistic engagement with Scripture energized by Holy Spirit power can there be genuine passion. Remember the old adage: "All Word and no Spirit—we dry up; all Spirit and no Word—we blow up; both Spirit and Word—we grow up."

Increased Pressure on Preachers

Another significant, though more prosaic, reason preaching is in trouble relates to increasing pressures on preachers as pastors. Changing priorities of church leadership in the last four decades have brought fresh waves of pressure. During the 1970s there was a greater emphasis on counseling ministry, followed by an emphasis on church growth and leadership skills through the 1980s and into the 1990s. Pastor preachers were expected to develop teams, evaluate strategies, and empower church members. As charismatic renewal made an impact, there was a shift toward congregational participation and a greater informality in communication and worship styles. Models of seeker-sensitivity, purpose drivenness, and natural church growth have called for fresh requirements of energy and commitment.

Many pastors testify to increasing workloads. In addition to perhaps two sermons a week that need to be prepared, there are hurting people to be supported, strategies to be implemented, worship priorities to be harmonized, gifts among members to be mobilized, new converts to be integrated, mission to be stimulated, and a neighborhood community to be served.

A survey of pastors' workloads found that within an average work week of fifty-five hours, almost half of that time is spent on administration. The figures were: administration, twenty-five hours; preparation for preaching/teaching, thirteen hours; pastoral care, counseling, conflict mediation, nine hours; and personal spiritual development, six hours.[25] As administrative tasks gobble up increasing amounts of time, other duties suffer, especially sermon preparation. Preaching that involves holistic engagement with Scripture inevitably takes time and intellectual, spiritual, and emotional effort. It can only flow out of a spiritual lifestyle that integrates every part of a preacher's weekly life.

Remember Harry Fosdick's definition of preaching as "drenching the congregation in one's life's blood"? John Killinger also emphasizes the cost of love: "The preacher's first calling, therefore, is to love. . . . We must love people and love God's vision of the community. Then we can preach."[26] Authentic preaching cannot bypass personal cost, yet many preachers find themselves stretched by pastoral busyness.

A preacher's career commonly begins with the highest expectations and the best efforts—at least thirteen hours preparation for preaching/teaching. But as pastoral and family pressures increase and perhaps the hard-won sermons seem to garner meager responses, certain nagging questions arise: Is preaching really worth all the effort? All these hours, week after week, and for what? So passing years see sights lowered. Few in the congregation appear to notice the preacher's diminished commitment—in fact, sadly, listeners almost seem to expect less and less. Spiritual discipline drops a notch or two, and preachers settle for second or third best.

Some churches can unwittingly trap preachers in a cruel contradiction. On the one hand, they claim that preaching is all-important. Consumer trends in church attendance often focus on whether there is good preaching or not. Yet on the other hand, the need for "church success" can drive a minister to focus on areas other than preaching. I recall someone saying, "Anyone can preach, but only a few can lead, and our church needs leaders." Many preachers are deeply frustrated by the tension between high expectations for preaching and practical demands on their time.

Fewer Good Models to Follow

There is yet another reason preaching is in trouble. Fewer good models mean less contagious preaching. The bland follow the bland. Men and women who sense a call to Christian service often seem more drawn to tasks other than preaching.

"Celebrity preachers" do not always help the cause of the pastor either. Their reputations for effective preaching, often developed through television exposure, raise congregational expectations while at the same time leave local preachers dazzled, envious, and dismayed at their own lack of skills and charisma. Some of the newer forms of preaching have also been criticized because they do not promote workable methodologies. Richard Eslinger, for example, is critical of Charles Rice's "preaching as story" because it "fails to draw attention to the sermonic methods appropriate to preaching the story."[27] Whenever I read a volume of highly rated sermons or look at the way an author has treated one noteworthy sermon as a detailed case study, I always want to ask, What did they preach the next week? It is within the realities of weekly church life, both its restraints and its opportunities, that a new generation of preachers needs to be motivated afresh to mentor enthusiasm in others.

 Changing Times

Already I have made passing references to changes in culture and their effects on preaching. Many in fact criticize preaching for its cultural irrelevancy. Who wants to listen to a talking head in church? Indeed, advocates of biblical preaching have long warned about the impact of the communications revolution. In 1971, D. Martyn Lloyd-Jones identified the growing influence of radio and television on the church and preaching,[28] and in 1982, John Stott highlighted the influence of the cybernetics revolution as television and computers brought new learning processes.[29] Both men wished to safeguard traditional preaching in the midst of change.

But others have no such desire to preserve traditional preaching. Meic Pearse and Chris Matthews, agreeing with David Norrington's arguments (presented earlier), strongly object to the centrality of sermons:

> We inhabit a culture in which learning from spoken words is very difficult. Countless studies demonstrate that most people remember only a tiny fraction of what they have heard; most of us are increasingly visually oriented. TV is the dominant medium of our society. . . . The centrality of preaching in an increasingly post-literate, visually oriented society helps to make "church" an impenetrable subculture for the unchurched.[30]

Many argue that in an age in which attention spans have supposedly shrunk to three minutes, television has mastered the message in a minute (or less), and the visual now complements and sometimes overwhelms the spoken word, monologue preaching is obsolete.

Important though such criticisms are regarding the medium of preaching, the issue of changing times is further reaching. It takes us far beyond TV, video, and talking heads. Profoundly disturbing culture shifts are in the process of sweeping in a sea change that affects the Western world's way of thinking and living. Such changes are so important that chapter 4 concentrates on some of their implications. Unless we invest time and effort to understand and respond to the cultural changes around us, preaching will become increasingly irrelevant and "a chasing after wind" (Eccles. 2:26).

However, the first priority is to address issues *within* preaching: a loss of holistic engagement with Scripture, a poverty of Holy Spirit power, increased pressure on preachers, and a lack of good models. These issues betray a weak preaching dynamic. They challenge us to consider the way in which preaching works and to commit to a more adequate model.

3

Toward a More Adequate Model

Preaching is meant to be an occasion when, so to speak, God *happens;* when that strange and yet familiar moment comes upon us, and we know we have been addressed, healed, confronted and kindled by the one who made us and loves us.

N. T. Wright, introduction to Donald Coggan,
A New Day for Preaching

We can drive a car without knowing how an internal combustion engine works. I can testify to this fact. We defend ourselves by saying, "What does it matter how an engine works as long as turning the key ignites its power?" Preaching, however, cannot be thoughtlessly ignited. If preachers pay too little attention to how it works, they can miss the core elements that are foundational for communicating within all cultures and changing times. From its New Testament beginnings, preaching has had certain key factors that combine to make preaching powerful, and we must make an effort to understand them.

All preaching models involve connecting various pieces. Thomas Long identifies these pieces as congregation, preacher, sermon, and presence of Christ, all of which belong together in what he calls a kind of "solar system." He suggests that they work together because they share "an inner dynamic; its [preaching's] parts are arranged into an active system. . . . We have to stand somewhere in this solar system of preaching in order to be able to see the positions of the other planets."[1]

The key to identifying this "inner dynamic" lies in asking, What makes preaching eventful? How does God empower effective preaching? Most listeners quickly discern whether a sermon "works" or not. Is it "good" and "real," or is it "bogus"? T. Keir describes the difference as that "between reading an article about life in the army and being handed your call-up papers; between discussing a dogma and meeting the living God."[2]

Put simply, a sermon "works" when God empowers it. But how best can we picture God working in the preaching event? Is there a model that holds together the complex dynamics that make biblical preaching eventful and empowered?

A simple span model has been offered to explain what happens in preaching. John Stott, for example, is associated with the metaphor of "bridge building," with an arc between Scripture and hearers through the preacher.[3] On one side is the biblical text. On the other side is today's context for contemporary listeners. The preacher links these two worlds as an interpreter and communicator, making Scripture relevant (see fig. 1). As Stott says, "Our task is to enable God's revealed truth to flow out of the Scriptures into the lives of men and women today."[4]

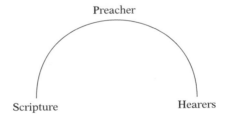

Fig. 1. The Preaching Bridge: 180-Degree Model

This bridge model has many merits, not least that it appears solid and straightforward with two fixed points that need to be connected through vital communication. Stott warns about those who fail to make the connection: the theological conservative, who lives on the Bible side of the gulf and whose trajectory goes straight up into the air and does not land on the other side; and the theological liberal, who lives on the contemporary side and has the opposite problem. Stott commends an incarnational model of communication as the way to enter and connect Scripture and people's worlds of thought and feeling. Such communication is "authoritative in expounding biblical principles, but tentative in applying them to the complex issues of the day."[5] Others have used imagery similar to bridge building. For example, Jean-Jacques von Allmen envisages "two poles in preaching, the Word of God and those to whom it is addressed, the first of these determines the second."[6] I call bridge building the 180-degree model.

How Does God Work in a Preaching Event?

In spite of the depressing class survey mentioned earlier, I have also found that the great majority of my students have witnessed at least one memorable preaching event that they would describe as "effective preaching." Hopefully that's true for you as well. Pause and ask yourself why the preaching was effective on that particular occasion. The more you reflect and the deeper your analysis probes, the more complex the factors are likely to be. When I have asked groups this question, responses have included words such as authenticity, humor, personal testimony, interactive, visual, incarnational, multisensory, transcendence, passion, authority, and "afterglow."

I remember an occasion in April 1999 when I attended a large annual event in Britain called Spring Harvest. This particular evening Tony Campolo was the speaker. I had not heard him before, but aware of his reputation, I confess I bore a measure of prejudice against him. So-called "star preachers" with their dazzlingly polished "celebrity sermons" often seem to be more about virtuoso performance than spiritual encounter.

Yet I can still recall vividly what happened. Campolo began by reading Luke 4:16–19, emphasizing the final words that repeat Isaiah 61:2: "to proclaim the year of Jubilee." In a loud passionate voice, he explained how Jesus proclaimed his kingdom at every point of his life and how Jubilee is a part of celebrating kingdom life. He referred to Leviticus 25 and the opportunity for poor people to make a new start in the Jubilee year, when land was given back and debts were settled. He painted a picture of Luke 4 that made us feel as though we were in the crowd listening to Jesus as he confronted them with the reality that he is the promised Messiah: "In case you didn't get it, folks, I'm it." As Campolo sounded out the words *kingdom* and *Jubilee* and engaged us in the story of Luke 4, I heard another powerful voice—that of Scripture itself.

I also recognized in Campolo's sermon a great skill in the way he presented Scripture. His words were active and interesting. "The synagogue is full. Mary undoubtedly has rounded up the crowd. You know how mothers are. 'My son is going to be down at the central synagogue. He's really a spellbinder. You won't want to miss it.' The place is packed." He used multisensory language to help us visualize and experience the scene.

Some of his teaching was demanding. He drew attention to the fact that Jubilee was never actually observed, and he explained what it means to say that Christ views the poor sacramentally. His humor surfaced often, yet this contrasted well with moments of somberness. Throughout, in an ebb and flow between Scripture and the present, Campolo used language that was lively and appropriate, keeping the congregation involved and responsive. He personified authentic sharing. He seemed to believe what he was saying. I found myself being drawn into a genuine encounter with God.

At one point Campolo described the atonement in the language of Einstein's general theory of relativity, that time is relative to motion. The faster you travel, the more time is compressed. He explained that if we were able to travel at the speed of 186,000 miles per second, the speed of light, everything would be compressed into an eternal "now." He asked us to marvel at the fact that Jesus is God incarnate and can experience time as though it were at the speed of light. On the cross there was a simultaneous identification as he became sin for us. "When Jesus was hanging on the cross two thousand years ago, he was and he is simultaneous with you sitting here. Hear me. Jesus from Calvary is looking straight at you." There was a quiet intensity as he gave an appeal to come to the cross.

The way Campolo had preached on God's new revolution of the Jubilee had already opened up several powerful possibilities for living differently and daringly for Jesus. His final appeal for people to volunteer to serve the poor in Latin America brought a surging response as people streamed to the front to make a commitment. Here was evidence that the message had not just engaged minds but had moved people to a serious, new commitment.

As I reflect on that preaching experience and its impact, I recognize that several factors combined to make it effective for me. First, the message was rooted in *Scripture.* Campolo used language about kingdom and Jubilee and included a lively presentation of Luke 4 so that we could enter its experience. The message had authority and dynamism because of his careful use of the Bible.

His choice and use of *words* were also effective. They engaged with both humor and pathos. I sensed that *God the Father* was addressing me through him. In the stillness of his extended analysis of Jesus' crucifixion, there was a pervading sense of the presence of *Jesus Christ* in our midst. At the conclusion, it was possible to sense the *Holy Spirit* challenging us. I had an experience of being spoken to directly and relevantly. Something spiritual occurred in that sermon through which God was real to me.

Other factors also contributed to the effectiveness of this preaching event. The *preacher* called for respect and trust. Not just his high level of competence but also his "transparency" and "presence"[7] were somehow conveyed to us. As the preaching continued, I became convinced that Campolo was not just an experienced speaker in celebrity mode but someone who deeply and passionately cared about his message and his audience. I would not have been surprised to learn that he had prayed long and hard before preaching his message because he showed a dimension of spiritual integrity. I have since heard him respond to an interview question about the source of power in his preaching by saying, "It's prayer. Every morning when I wake up I just load up!"[8] But there was also a down-to-earth matter-of-factness in his preaching.

Though I was positively affected, and the entire congregation seemed similarly influenced, there were probably some people who responded negatively. Perhaps they were irritated by Campolo's personality and humor. Maybe they had heard some of his preaching stories before or were unhappy about his high profile. For others, however, their negative reactions probably owed less to the speaker and more to an argument they had had with their spouse before coming to the service, or to the cold draft they had sat in, or to the misbehaving child in front of them. Two additional factors, therefore, influence a sermon's effectiveness: the *listener* and the *worship context.*

Based on this event and others like it, I have concluded that preaching is most effective when several factors positively combine: Scripture, words (combined with images), God (the Father, Son, and Holy Spirit), the person of the preacher, the listener, and the worship context. All these aspects belong and work together as the trinitarian God empowers the preacher's words and the hearers' responses.

The bridge model of 180 degrees seems woefully inadequate to describe what actually happens in effective preaching. In fact, it may even do a disservice by misleading preachers into thinking that *they* bear all the responsibility to connect the two poles—Scripture and hearers. This model is also static and partial, for it fails to do justice to the activity of our Triune God, who initiates the preaching event in his revealed Word and empowers many factors, integrating them to achieve his purpose. Therefore, we must move toward a more adequate model, that of 360-degree preaching.

360-Degree Preaching

Preaching is much more than a communication arc of 180 degrees with the Bible and listeners at its two ends and a preacher making a con-

nection. Many sources of power combine to make preaching eff
A model of preaching, therefore, needs to be more open and untidy to accommodate the various factors that help to empower the preaching event within the grace of the Triune God.

Peter Forsyth commented provocatively that the sermon "is the Word of the Gospel returning in confession to the God who gave it. It is addressed to men indeed, but in truth it is offered to God. Addressed to man but offered to God—that is the true genius of preaching."[9] Preaching occurs within a returning dynamic as the Lord gives his Word, which must necessarily return to him. Strikingly, Isaiah 55:10–11 compares God's Word to the cycle of rain and snow falling from heaven and returning after they have watered the earth and caused seed to grow. "So shall my word be that goes out from my mouth; it shall not return to me empty, but it shall accomplish that which I purpose, and succeed in the thing for which I sent it" (v. 11).

Preaching flows from God the Father, who addresses us in Scripture and in Christ, through the responses of the preacher and the people, and then back to God in the form of worship, witness, and service. It involves movement through 360 degrees of eventfulness as God—Father, Son, and Holy Spirit—speaks through his Word *and* empowers the preacher *and* convicts the listeners *and* transforms the lives of the preacher and the listeners. Christ stands with those who gather in his name (Matt. 18:20) and prays for all believers (John 17:20–26), and the Holy Spirit helps them in their weaknesses (Rom. 8:26), actively creating spiritual apprehension (1 Thess. 1:5). The preaching event involves revealing, preaching, listening, and responsive living. Its dynamic, found in God and driven by God, returns to God as individuals and communities are transformed—all within the grace of the Triune God. Preaching is a God happening.

Martin Luther boldly claimed that "there is in the divine Trinity a *pulpit:* as God the Father is an eternal speaker, so the Son is spoken in eternity, and the Holy Spirit is an eternal listener. God's triune being is an eternal conversation, and since the Holy Spirit tells us what he hears we are taken into this conversation."[10] Christoph Schwobel sees hearers as "conversation-partners who are drawn into the conversation of the divine life."[11]

James Torrance, in *Worship, Community, and the Triune God of Grace*, contrasts two views of worship—unitarian and trinitarian.[12] Sadly, many people are practical unitarians who have a view of worship that

has no doctrine of the mediator or sole priesthood of Christ, is human-centered, has no proper doctrine of the Holy Spirit. . . . We sit in the pew watching the minister "doing his thing," exhorting us "to do our thing," until we go home thinking we have done our duty for another week.[13]

A trinitarian view of worship sees worship as "the gift of participating through the Spirit in the incarnate Son's communion with the Father."[14] An incarnational, trinitarian model that supports this view focuses not on human faith but on the relationship between Jesus and the Father. "By his Spirit he draws men and women to participate both in his life of worship and communion with the Father and in his mission from the Father to the world."[15]

Torrance describes the double movement as:

(a) a God-humanward movement, from *(ek)* the Father, through *(dia)* the Son, in *(en)* the Spirit and (b) a human-Godward movement to the Father through the Son in the Spirit.[16]

He develops these two movements by referring to the intercessions of Christ and the Spirit: "In Jesus Christ, the Word made flesh, and in the Spirit we are led to the Father."[17]

It must be shamefully confessed that too often preachers are practical unitarians who appear to "do their own thing" without conscious commitment to the dynamics of trinitarian worship. No genuine encounter with God in preaching can occur except through gracious revelation of the Father, Christ's interceding presence, and the empowering of the Holy Spirit, who enabled Scripture to be inspired and now enables it to be interpreted, shared, and lived out in faith. Preaching is a Father event, a Christ event, and a Spirit event, or else it is merely resounding gongs or clanging cymbals.

Ever since the incarnation, we have had to live with the paradox that God—Father, Son, and Spirit—chose to express his Word in flesh. God's love and purpose were revealed through the flesh and blood ministry of Jesus Christ, and it fell to some fishermen and their successors to carry on the task of preaching the gospel—"Word in flesh" and subsequent "words in flesh." Christian preachers have to live with the awesome responsibility of proclaiming God's Word and appropriating his promise of empowering their preaching.

The kind of model that does justice to preaching God's Word is a 360-degree model (fig. 2). Whereas a 180-degree model is appealingly manageable, this model is not. It is untidy, multidimensional, and risks confusion. It contains many arrows flowing in many directions and shows how preaching happens within a trinitarian framework through a symbiosis of human and divine actions. It illustrates the role of preaching in moving the community of God from worship to service and witness to the world.

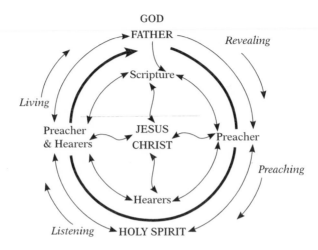

Fig. 2. Dynamics of a 360-Degree Preaching Event

Notice how the Triune God begins and finishes the process and is involved at every point in between. God the Father has revealed his truth in Scripture, through Christ, and by the Holy Spirit and is intimately involved in nourishing connections between preacher and hearers as the entire community is challenged. Here is something on the move. Each arrow describes additional points of impact that contribute to the joint outcome. This model of preaching is summarized by the following: "We declare to you what we have seen and heard so that you also may have fellowship with us; and truly our fellowship is with the Father and with his Son Jesus Christ" (1 John 1:3).

Since preaching moves in returning response to God, whose Word will not come back empty, we should expect things to happen. Sometimes Scripture reveals explicit evidence of outcomes in hearers' lives. We noted earlier (in the section on transformational preaching) how amazement and antagonism are often the result of hearing God's Word. At times there is visible astonishment—*ekplēssomai* ("to be greatly struck")—as in Matthew 7:28; 13:54; 22:33; Mark 1:22; 6:2; 11:18; Luke 4:32; Acts 13:12. Other outcomes include upbuilding or edifying *(oikodomiē)*, encouragement *(paraklēsis)*, and consolation *(paramythia)* (1 Cor. 14:3); convincing *(elenchō)* and rebuking *(epitimaō)* (2 Tim. 4:2). God makes things happen through preaching.

While it is often difficult to analyze a paradox, let alone the paradox of God empowering humans for the task of preaching, it deserves our close attention. Too often preaching's spiritual empowerment has been treated as an unknowable "given." In effect, many preachers have trusted in its mystery, putting a premium on ignorance by assuming that somehow it would work for them. But such an attitude can do serious harm as preachers fail to see their responsibility within the 360-degree preaching dynamic.

The rest of this chapter unpacks some of the implications of 360-degree preaching using elements identified earlier in Campolo's preaching.

The Power of Scripture

Earlier we noted the devastating effect that a loss of holistic engagement with Scripture has had on much contemporary preaching. Only when preachers interact with Scripture, engaging in its life with heads and hearts, can there be powerful preaching.

This raises a fundamental question. Does a preacher's imagination, creativity, or energy make Scripture come alive for hearers, or does Scripture have its own power to energize the preaching event? Put bluntly, does Scripture's energy depend on what preachers bring to it?

In practice, some preachers treat Scripture as a unique resource book that comes alive through their skills and spirituality. In other words, Scripture inspires preachers to be inspired so as to make Scripture inspiring. Preachers do need to be called and gifted, but dynamic preaching requires an expectation and commitment to Scripture's own inimitable power: "All scripture is inspired by God and is useful for teaching, for reproof, for correction, and for training in righteousness" (2 Tim. 3:16).

The description of Scripture as inspired, "God-breathed" (NIV), evokes powerful images of blowing wind and moving Spirit. A "wind from God swept over the face of the waters" in creation (Gen. 1:2), gusted into dry bones so that they become a vast army (Ezek. 37:1–14), enables the act of being "born from above" (John 3:3, 7), and continues to breathe divine energy in and through Scripture's text. Dual authorship intimately cocreates at every turn. As Sidney Greidanus puts it:

> The mystery of divine inspiration is that the Bible is 100% divine while it is 100% human. . . . Hermeneutically, the mystery of inspiration means that interpreters of the Bible acknowledge that *God* speaks his word through these writings of human authors and redactors; the mystery of inspiration

calls for a holistic biblical interpretation which probes beyond historical reconstruction and verbal meanings for the message of *God*.[18]

Within this dual authorship, God has the life-transforming initiative to reveal who he is. How could we know anything about God unless God chose to reveal himself? I like Robin Gill's analogy: "I guess an ant might find it quite difficult to talk meaningfully to another ant about the human mind. Even while crawling over a human skull—on the way to being swiped by a human hand—there may not be too much that an ant knows about what goes on inside that skull."[19] Instead of hoping in the silence, antlike, that God is not cold, distant, and inarticulate, we gasp with wonder that he has shown us that he is loving, close, and articulate. His words in Scripture have broken the silence.

The God-breathedness of Scripture also empowers relationships. Its words not only address our minds but also embrace everything we are and do. As Donald Coggan sums it up, "If we ask: 'Why is the Christian's God a God who speaks?' the answer must be: 'He speaks *because he loves.*'"[20] Scripture records the way in which God has spoken in history in the greatest story ever told. Its sixty-six books are a cumulative revelation of God's dealings with his people, expressed in proposition and narrative, dealings that are crowned by God's revelation in the incarnation of the Word become flesh. Our relationship with Scripture should never be cerebral only, as though God is primarily sharing information. He is sharing himself—"O taste and see that the LORD is good" (Ps. 34:8). Scripture empowers holistically—whole persons in the whole church for the whole of life.

Preachers must realize that Scripture not only *says* things but also *does* things—it is "useful for teaching, for reproof, for correction, and for training in righteousness" (2 Tim. 3:16). Scripture's words have four functions. However they are unpacked, their purpose is to influence whole persons (and entire communities) to live differently. "Teaching" leads to right understanding of truth, "reproof" sheds light on a person's wrong thinking and lifestyle, "correction" holds out the possibility of a new life, and "training in righteousness" emphasizes the ongoing disciplines of living in relationship with God and others. Scripture has its own practical agenda to create long-lasting change. "While current theological debate about Scripture concentrates on its authority, inspiration, infallibility, and inerrancy, the New Testament has a different agenda. Its most important claim about Scripture (in this case the Old Testament) is that it is effective."[21]

Scripture should be heard firsthand. Elizabeth Achtemeier contrasts preaching phrases such as "the Bible says our sins are forgiven" with the directness that results when they are spoken in the present tense. "How different is that indirect use of the Bible from a direct employment of it, in which its words are spoken immediately to the congregation—'Your sins are forgiven.' . . . 'Come unto me'—all set in the gracious story of the man from Nazareth."[22] Scripture's God-breathed directness gives power to biblical preaching, providing its prophetic voice—its today-ness in the present tense. Biblical preachers live and speak in Scripture's power, not contriving to make Scripture come alive but coming alive through God, who reveals and relates in Scripture and in Christ by the power of the Holy Spirit.

G. Robert Jacks emphasizes Scripture's primary role in shaping a preacher.[23] It reverses normal speaking priorities—me, my audience, my message—and instead puts God and his message first.[24] He warns, "There is a God—and you're not it!" Preachers always know who speaks first in 360-degree preaching.

The Power of Words

Few things reveal a personality more than the way in which a person uses words, and few things reveal the level of personal engagement with Scripture more than the way in which a preacher uses words. When a preacher clearly lives in a Scripture text, its images, sounds, tastes, and challenges spill out through multisensory words. But when a preacher plods through a text, using the head only, flat, dull, and passive language is likely to result. Yet another preacher can craft words cleverly and speak passionately but leave hearers feeling manipulated. The way in which a preacher uses words affects preaching. This is no surprise. Words can be used positively (Isa. 55:11) but also negatively—"How great a forest is set ablaze by a small fire! And the tongue is a fire" (James 3:5–6).

Words derive their power from the foundational truth that God reveals and creates through words (Gen. 1:3). Communicators have always been fascinated by words' innate power, when words are used both individually and together. The ancient discipline of rhetoric, developed in Greek and Roman culture, concerned the art of persuasion through the skilled use of words. From Augustine's integration of rhetoric into preaching to Martin Luther King Jr.'s "I have a dream" speech, people have been stirred by carefully crafted speech.

Preaching has always lived in uneasy alliance with rhetoric: "My speech and my proclamation were not with plausible words of wisdom, but with a demonstration of the Spirit and of power, so that your faith might rest not on human wisdom but on the power of God" (1 Cor. 2:4–5). Several big names in preaching history, such as Martin Luther and John Calvin, vehemently criticized rhetoric as dangerously manipulative. Yet they were extremely persuasive with words themselves. The truth is that words always have a capacity to persuade. What matters is whether it is ethical or unethical persuasion.

Andre Resner, in *Preacher and Cross,* analyzes *ēthos* (the rhetorical power of the orator's person) in three sources: classical rhetoric, homiletical theory, and Paul's Corinthian letters. He helpfully contrasts the "efficacy" of preaching, understood theologically (*kata stauron,* "according to the cross"), and its "persuasiveness," understood rhetorically (*kata sarka,* "according to the flesh"). "*Kata sarka* uses of ethos selfishly serve the preacher; *kata stauron* uses of ethos serve Christ and God's continuing mysterious and redemptive activity in the world."[25] Preachers must resist a chronic temptation to abuse rhetoric's power of "persuasiveness," *kata sarka.* Remember David Norrington's criticism of preachers who are more concerned about their oratory than their congregations' spiritual growth? The way in which preachers use words requires urgent care and attention today.

The Power of God the Father

Though it is important to emphasize the power of Scripture and the power of words, it must be made explicit that their energy owes everything to the originating power of God the Father. Effective preaching begins with God the Father and returns to him because his Word will not return empty (Isa. 55:11).

As noted, Genesis 1:3 is the foundational truth that God reveals and creates through words: "Then God said, 'Let there be light; and there was light.'" Until Genesis 1:3 the earth was formless, empty, and dark—an absence of speech meant an absence of life outside God. Yet God awesomely and repetitively broke the silence by his litany of creation: "And God said . . . and it was so" (Gen. 1:6–7, 9, 14–15, 20, 24, 26). God's language reached a crescendo in verse 26: "Then God said, 'Let us make humankind in our image, according to our likeness.'" In his own speaking image, God created human beings who speak. Human beings are constituted by God's words to live by God's words and to communicate by words.

God's words are never mere sounds to communicate; they are also deeds to perform. They are charged with power to get things done. The Hebrew word *dabar* can be translated as either "word" or "deed." *Dabar* is a "word event" or "event word." "By the word of the Lord the heavens were made. . . . For he spoke, and it came to be" (Ps. 33:6, 9).

Peter Adam suspects that some contemporary theologians are unhappy about the claim of a "speaking God" because of "a desire to preserve the transcendence of God and a belief that words are too feeble a vehicle adequately to convey more than a poor reflection of divine truth. . . . Is God too transcendent to speak?"[26] He rejects this as a false view of transcendence:

> For transcendence is not at the cost of God's involvement and interaction with the universe he created; that would be a deistic transcendence. Theistic, biblical transcendence means that the sovereign God is totally free to be involved in the intimate detail of his creation without compromising his transcendence. . . . The sovereign transcendence of God means he can be immanent within his universe, act within it, and communicate within it, without losing his transcendent power. . . . The biblical assumption is not only that God may use human words to reveal himself, but that he has done so."[27]

God has designed the universe so that words are vehicles for creative power. Nothing expresses this more powerfully than the way the crowning revelation of Jesus Christ is described as the "Word made flesh."

The Power of Christ

A great promise is that given by Jesus: "Where two or three are gathered in my name, I am there among them" (Matt. 18:20). For preachers, nothing equals Christ's promised presence. He remains the unique word-event who says what he does and does what he says—the medium and the message. He presides over the preaching event.

Steve Holmes believes that the way to understand any ministry in the church, such as preaching, is by realizing that "the Church participates through the Spirit in the ministry of Christ which was given him by the Father."[28] The 360-degree model reflects something of this participation in Jesus Christ's ministry. It places him central to empower relationships in several directions simultaneously. The Lord of all authority (Matt. 28:18) cannot be excluded from any part of preaching.

Karl Barth memorably expressed a threefold dynamic for the Word of God: the Word *revealed*, who is Jesus Christ; the Word *written* in Scripture; and the Word *proclaimed* in preaching.[29] All three belong symbiotically together. They are not three different "words"; rather, they are mutually bound together. Barth gave central place to Jesus Christ, who is the incarnate Word of God and who meets us in this threefold way. Through God's grace, and only by grace, Jesus Christ is the unique word-event in history given in flesh and words. Yet by his continuing presence, he empowers. "It is from a relationship with Jesus Christ that all other important aspects of the sermon flow, however we might name them: the contributions of the congregation and preacher; biblical and contemporary interpretation; teaching; judgment; correction; conversion; prophecy; pastoral care; witness; grace; justice; and various kinds of mission activities."[30]

Barth stressed that each of the threefold ways in which God's Word is expressed has a human and a divine aspect. On the one hand, there is the human aspect: the Word made flesh, the Scriptures written by people, and the all-too-human words and personality of the preacher. Yet on the other hand, each has a divine aspect: the eternal Word, the God-breathed Scriptures, and God speaking today though his preachers. This combination of human and divine enables the highest possible claims to be made for preaching. "Preaching is human talk about God . . . in and through which God speaks about himself and to which God commits himself absolutely 'in such a way that like the existence of Jesus Christ himself *it is God's own proclamation.*'"[31] Probably the highest claim ever made for preaching is found in the words of Heinrich Bullinger in the Second Helvetic Confession: "The preaching of the Word of God is the Word of God."

Everything in preaching depends on Christ the word-event. It is not his past preaching in Galilee or his first commissioning of disciples to preach or even the heart of the gospel message in its proclamation of Christ crucified that is most critical for preaching. Rather, it is the present, supreme reality that he is eternally the Word of God. Preachers are sent as ambassadors to "proclaim Christ crucified" (1 Cor. 1:23), yet the once crucified and now risen Christ is always present in the preaching task. "Preaching does not cause Christ to be present. It is possible only because Christ is already present and to speak in Christ's name is to claim Christ's own promise, 'The one who hears you, hears me' (Luke 10:16)."[32]

Christ's continuing presence in preaching propels us toward an understanding of preaching that borders on the sacramental, sacrament defined as "the means by which God brings home to us the reality of his redeeming love."[33] Several authors use this language. Fred Craddock states, "Preaching lies very near the sacrament and is to be understood as opening mind and heart in faith to receive the sacrament."[34] David Schlafer says, "We need preaching that *is* sacramental, rather than preaching that *just talks* about the sacramental quality of God's self-revelation in history."[35] Paul Wilson adds, "Our task is not to bring Christ to the church, but to find Christ there and to bring our people before God's throne of judgment and grace."[36] Christian preaching cannot occur without Christ working in its midst.

The Power of the Holy Spirit

Though we risk theological clumsiness in an attempt to separate the responsibilities of the Persons of the Trinity, certain aspects of divine activity may be identified with each. Early church theologians grappled with relationships within the Trinity. For example, the Cappodocian theologian and preacher Basil the Great (c. 330–79) defined relationships within the Trinity in this way: The Father is the origin (first cause) of every divine work, the Son (the efficient cause) carries it out, and the Spirit (the perfecting cause) brings it to completion.[37] Developing a sophisticated trinitarian theology for preaching is beyond the scope of this book, but it is possible to relate preaching to the Trinity: The Father speaks forth his Word in creation and revelation, the Son is the eternally spoken Word, and the Spirit causes the Word to be heard and preached.

The doctrine of the interpenetration of Father, Son, and Spirit is known as *perichōrēsis*, which holds that the Persons of the Trinity cannot be separated as though they are distinct from one another. However, each Person of the Trinity also has what the early church fathers called "appropriations" or *proprium*. "The *proprium* of a person of the Trinity is not one-third of the triune God, as if God could be separated into three parts."[38] As God the Father acts in the Son, who is witnessed to in Scripture, the Son works by the Holy Spirit in the church's life. "Preaching, as an important part of the life of the Church can therefore be called a *proprium* of the Holy Spirit. . . . It is God himself who acts through the Holy Spirit in Christ, who wants to make Himself known by the preaching of the sermon."[39] Of all the Persons of the Trinity, the Holy Spirit seems specifically associated with preaching power.

Though words have innate energy, their spiritual efficacy to transform lives resides in the Spirit's power. "Our message of the gospel came to you not in word only, but also in power and in the Holy Spirit and with full conviction" (1 Thess. 1:5). This threefold qualification of "in power," "in the Holy Spirit," and "with full conviction" goes to the heart of preaching. Words can stir minds and hearts, inform and even inspire action, but power, the Holy Spirit, and full conviction belong to God alone. Older books on preaching sometimes spoke of the "plus of the Spirit" as a sermon's moving power. Discussions about "unction" and a preacher's "anointing" similarly focus on the Holy Spirit's work, though sometimes his action seems falsely limited to the act of delivery itself.

One writer set the scene in this way:

The deskwork has been done. The prayers have gone up. The gestation period is over. The hour of delivery has arrived. A company sits waiting, expectant, watching God's man in the pulpit. . . . We need that strange condition which used to be called *unction*—a word so little used today. . . . It is a quality that pervades the man and his teaching—the anointing of the Holy One.[40]

This sounds alarmingly like a patient in an emergency room urgently needing resuscitation. Unless, at the last minute, the Holy Spirit revives the heart, the preacher and the people are doomed to dead preaching! Let's be clear. The Holy Spirit is vital for *all* aspects of preaching, not just sermon delivery. As expressed in the 360-degree model, the Holy Spirit is everywhere—in the revealing, preaching, listening, and living. Minds, hearts, mouths, ears, individual lives, and communities are all within his influence.

Mysteriously, when it comes to revealing himself, God is both the object of our knowing and also the subject. Trevor Hart describes this paradox:

> He is the one who initiates and brings to completion the act of knowing by, on the one hand, positing himself objectively to be known, and on the other, entering into us as the Holy Spirit and creating the faith which responds appropriately to this self-manifestation. . . . Thus the term revelation refers *not to the objective self-manifestation alone, but equally to the act of faith in which it is heard and received and obeyed.*[41]

God is involved at every point, revealing who he is and by his Spirit enabling us to hear and respond. "When true preaching takes place, the main actor is not the preacher, nor the congregation, but the Holy Spirit. . . . The most active part . . . is taken by the third person of the blessed Trinity. Without him and his creative and re-creative activity there can be words, there can be essays . . . but there can be no preaching."[42] Nothing happens without the Spirit's blessing.

As noted in chapter 2, the Spirit's blessing is especially associated with anointing. Jesus applied the anointing of Isaiah 61 to himself (Luke 4:18–21), and James Forbes sees this emphasis retained in apostolic tradition by Peter's words: "how God anointed Jesus of Nazareth with the Holy Spirit and with power" (Acts 10:38). Anointed preaching "expects that the God of creation will be present to transform spoken words into deeds of liberation and massive reorientation of life for the sake of the kingdom. Jesus' life was the Amen."[43]

Another significant theme for preachers is found in Jesus Christ's teaching on the Paraclete in John 14–16, where the description of the Holy Spirit as one "called" *(klētos)* "alongside" *(para)* particularly applies to his role as empowering collaborator. The relationship between Christ and the Paraclete is extraordinarily close. Christ comes to us in the Paraclete (John 14:16), yet the Paraclete is not identical with Christ and comes only after Jesus has departed (John 16:7). His characteristics parallel those of Jesus: They are both truth, both are given by the Father, both have tasks to glorify the Father, and neither speaks on his own authority as he teaches, bears witness, and convinces the world (16:8–11). The Paraclete, therefore, comes to disciples to dwell within them (14:16), to teach them (14:26), to guide them (16:13), and to remind them of all that Jesus said (16:26). With regard to the world, the Paraclete puts it on trial (16:8) with a strong sense of advocacy. In the church's ministry, the Paraclete is the driving force continuing Christ's ministry and is particularly "called alongside" preachers.

The Holy Spirit's role reinforces the "sacramental" nature of preaching. "The prime actor in the Sacrament of the Word is the Holy Spirit."[44] Coggan suggests that Paraclete is better translated as "Stimulator-Spirit" or "Awakener," and he boldly compares the act of preaching with baptism and communion. On the one hand, sacraments of baptism and communion are God's *verba visibilia*, visible words that appeal to the eye. On the other hand, there are the words of the preacher—God's *verba audibilia*—audible words for the ear. Preaching's startling reality is that God is at work through it, encountering men and women at exactly their points of need.

"Charismatic renewal" in the latter part of the twentieth century was said to have "rediscovered" the Third Person of the Trinity in many congregations. Ironically, while this renewal led to a much greater participation in worship, it did not seem to have a positive effect on preaching. The Spirit's gifting and working in preaching often went unmentioned.

The Power of the Hearer

The hearer's role in preaching seems obvious. Active listening makes preaching authentic, while unheard preaching is a waste of breath. No wonder that Jesus calls out, "Let anyone with ears to hear listen" (Matt. 11:15; 13:9; Mark 4:9, 23; 7:16; Luke 8:8). C. E. B. Cranfield likens the command "listen" to the way Israel's daily recited creed, the *Shema*, opens: "Hear, O Israel" (Deut. 6:4). "It is both an appeal to hear aright and at the same time a solemn warning of the possibility of a wrong hearing."[45] By the command "hearers are summoned to hear at a deeper level than mere sense perception . . . to apply it to themselves and thus ultimately to hear the word of God that can save them."[46] Hearers need to hear with ears, minds, and hearts, to put words into practice rather than be like a foolish person who builds a house upon the sand (Matt. 7:26).

So strategic is a hearer's responsibility that George Sweazey claims, "The skills of the hearers are more important than the skills of the preacher."[47] He pleads for hearers to be instructed in preaching, comparing them to concert goers who benefit so much more when they know "something about how music is put together and performed. Church goers need to know what the various sorts of sermons are getting at and why they are important."[48]

The danger of this analogy is that it runs the risk of reinforcing the idea of preaching as "performance." Winston Fletcher parodied "sermon tasting" by imagining the way in which thirty-seven British cathedrals might be improved:

> Sermons should be drafted centrally and distributed by fax. And they should be interactive. Each member of the congregation should have a remote control console with a red button to press when bored. More than 50% press their buttons and a red light shines in the pulpit warning the preacher to get on with it. Three reds and he's out. Soon every pew would have its own mini TV, networked so that cathedral-goers can choose which of the 37 services on offer look the most heavenly. Soon costs would be veritably slashed with only the best two or three services serving all 37 cathedrals.[49]

Hearers of sermons are not consumers in church to score a sermon's "edutainment" level on a scale of one to ten. They are a congregation drawn together by God to participate in worship. They are a community of the baptized, "a holy priesthood, to offer spiritual sacrifices acceptable to God through Jesus Christ" (1 Peter 2:5). "The church comes into being because God's Word is spoken."[50] Everything in 360-degree preaching concerns the people of God. The grace of our Triune God holds together preacher *and* hearers so that God's Word does not return empty. James Forbes emphasizes this dynamic. "It is the Spirit who opens our hearts and minds to receive anew God's self-disclosure as the living word. . . . It seems to follow that the quality of the preaching is affected most significantly by the level of awareness of the movement of the Spirit shared by those in the pulpit and the pew."[51]

Hearers, therefore, have responsibilities before, during, and after a sermon. Just as they need to love God with all their hearts, and with all their souls, and with all their strength, and with all their minds (Mark 12:30), they need to listen and respond to preaching with all they are.

The Power of the Worship Context

Because hearers are not individual consumers but members of a congregation drawn together to worship, there is also power in the corporate worship context itself. Worship is our response to God's grace. Yet as we participate together, God makes new qualities of relationship possible. Indeed, James Torrance claims that this participation in worship "means that perhaps we are never more truly human than at the Lord's Table when Christ draws us into his life of communion."[52]

Ever since Luke 4, most Christian preaching has occurred within a worship context as part of a corporate event. In the ebb and flow of word and response, worshipers are drawn into an experience of worshiping in spirit and truth (John 4:23). God addresses his people through the call to worship, the reading of Scripture, the sermon, and communion. People respond with songs, prayers, giving, and above all commitment of their lives. Lives deepen in corporate worship.

Preachers readily recognize the contrast between preaching within a worshipful congregation that is united in prayer and expectancy and one that is not. Within one there is a palpable quality of openness and responsiveness. Preachers partner with congregations within the rhythm of listening and responding as God's Word returns to him. Together they experience the humbling reality of Christ's new way of living. "Come to him . . . like living stones, let yourselves be built into a spiritual house" (1 Peter 2:4–5). "But you are a chosen race, a royal priesthood, a holy nation, God's own people, in order that you may proclaim the mighty acts of him who called you out of darkness into his marvelous light" (1 Peter 2:9). But when a congregation is unresponsive, there is instead dullness and flatness.

The Power of the Preacher

Among the factors contributing to 360-degree preaching, one more needs examination: the person of the preacher. By definition, incarnational preaching occurs only through "words in flesh." Because preaching is primarily about a personal encounter, great weight rests on *who* the preacher is. "In preaching Person comes to persons through person."[53] Incarnational preaching requires that preachers stand *under* Scripture and the lordship of Christ and also *in* the contemporary world to embody God's Word in their words and persons.

Clyde Fant calls preachers to have a "partial participation in culture,"[54] which means that they are not overimpressed or underimpressed by culture. They must understand the times but not sacrifice or accommodate God's truth to them. For Fant, preaching combines both the subjectivity of a preacher's existence with the objectivity of God's Word so that the timeless Word (which is objective) can be heard in contemporary language and experience (which are subjective). God's Word has to be fleshed out in changing times.

I will delay considering the person of the preacher until chapter 5. Because incarnational preaching is rooted in the contemporary world, it is vital that we turn next to the nature of changing times so that we can better understand what it means for a twenty-first-century preacher to refuse to be overimpressed or underimpressed by culture.

4

Understanding
the Times

One cannot help feeling that the catastrophic drop in church attendance
since the 1960s has been largely self-induced by a fatal misreading of
culture by the churches and the theologians who supposedly service their
needs.

Kieran Flanagan, *The Enchantment of Sociology*

I was on a flight to Columbus, Ohio. Next to me was a businessman in
his forties. Hearing my English accent, he struck up a conversation. He
told me he was a business consultant who advised firms on logistics of
stock control and delivery. "And what about you?" he asked. "I work at
a seminary. I teach preaching and communication." "Oh." Long pause.
"What kind are you?" "I'm a Baptist." Another long pause. I thought that
admission had killed the conversation. Then leaning forward earnestly,
he said, "I'm Lutheran. Can you answer something for me? Can you tell
me why preachers are just not willing to realize that a twenty- to thirty-
minute sermon isn't working anymore? My teenagers are totally turned
off. When there are so many technological possibilities, sermons could
be so different. My kids learn and live in a different world. I don't like
MTV, but my kids do. But when I talk to our two pastors, they just don't
want to know. They just want to do what they have always done."

As a pastor born in the 1940s, I sympathized with this man's pastors
and felt defensive. How dare he decree that sermons just aren't working?
But I also felt the shock of recognition that this man was speaking for a

generation that regards traditional preaching as irrelevant. His concern about changing times and preachers who have been left behind is one of the toughest issues facing twenty-first-century preachers.

First Chronicles 12 lists warriors who dared to join the outlaw David in Hebron. Some were large, well-armed groups: "the people of Judah bearing shield and spear numbered six thousand eight hundred armed troops" (v. 24). However, a much smaller group made a distinctive, strategic contribution. "Of Issachar, those who had understanding of the times, to know what Israel ought to do, two hundred chiefs, and all their kindred under their command" (v. 32). They probably possessed some conventional weaponry, but their most important attribute was their spiritual discernment of their times. Others might be nostalgic, naive, or confused, but not them.

Wise understanding has always been an important theme for the people of God. People are commanded to obey the laws of life, for this shows wisdom and understanding to the nations (Deut. 4:6). Timothy is commanded to "think over what I say, for the Lord will give you understanding in all things" (2 Tim. 2:7).

Preachers should be latter-day members of the tribe of Issachar. Our turbulent times of change call for wise understanding so that the people of God know what they should do. We need to engage in what John Stott calls "double listening." "We listen to the Word with humble reverence, anxious to understand it, and resolved to believe and obey what we come to understand. We listen to the world with critical alertness, anxious to understand it too, and resolved not necessarily to believe and obey it, but to sympathize with it and to seek grace to discover how the gospel relates to it."[1]

Traditionally, dictionaries of preaching have included entries such as "history of preaching," "rhetoric and preaching," and "biblical studies and preaching." Each of these subjects needs continual updating. "Biblical studies," for example, have shifted dramatically "from historical criticism to literary criticism, from history to genres."[2] However, within the limits of this book, I wish to add six words to the vocabulary of twenty-first-century preaching: *culture, paradigm shifts, modernity, postmodernity, orality shifts,* and *hermeneutics.* Some of these have become almost faddish words, splattered about without much clarity, but preachers need to give each careful attention if they are to understand the times.

Culture

It is not surprising that many recent preaching textbooks make reference to culture and the need to understand and relate the gospel to it, though often their analyses prove to be relatively slight.[3]

Frequently, the word *culture* is used in a limited sense. When a church contains people from different ethnic and social backgrounds, it is called "multicultural." We talk about "youth culture" and "popular culture" and even "subcultures," like the church described by Meic Pearse and Chris Matthews at the end of chapter 2. Because preaching occurs in local contexts with their own cultural mixes, preachers need to understand the "cultures" of their listeners. Several books stress the importance of evaluating congregations. These include Rick Ezell's *Hitting a Moving Target*[4] and Mark Greene's *Three-Eared Preacher.*[5] Some focus on communicating with particular generational groups such as Jimmy Long's *Generating Hope: A Strategy for Reaching the Postmodern Generation.*[6]

Today's preachers need to understand popular culture. Unfortunately, preachers in general are perceived as clueless about popular taste in TV, film, video, music, news, and web sites. Bill Hybels, of Willow Creek fame, claims that most non-churchgoers think pastors are woefully out of touch with reality, as sermon illustrations and applications all too often painfully demonstrate. One of his tongue-in-cheek goals in ministry is "to complete however many years God gives me without ever using a Spurgeon's illustration."[7] He asks, Who wants to hear about a dead Englishman? Occasionally referring to our spiritual history is valid, but only when it is embedded in contemporary relevance.

Popular culture contains many surprises. For example, in a 2001 survey of American college and high school students, the name most associated with the word *Christian*, other than Jesus, was not Billy Graham or the pope but a guy named Ned Flanders in the *Simpsons* TV cartoon sitcom. According to some, he is "television's most effective exponent of a Christian life well-lived."[8] Preachers cannot discount the *Simpsons'* huge popularity or its many messages about Christianity. "*Simpsons* fans treat Sunday as a day of worship. Not early mornings at church; 8 pm in front of the holiest of holies, the TV tuned into the Fox network."[9] Being heard in terms relevant to audiences has never been more critical than in this media-saturated, generational-sensitive, entertainment-oriented popular culture. (We will deal with this challenge later.) When a preacher interprets Scripture, however, he or she must not be overimpressed or underimpressed by culture.

However important these limited uses of the word *culture* are, the word needs to be widened in two ways—first, by seeing its bigger picture, and second, by emphasizing the significant connection between communication and culture.

First, *culture* needs a definition that includes the characteristics of an entire group of people at a given period of time. Culture is the total context in which we live, work, play, and preach. Generational differences, ethnic and social contrasts, and popular tastes are subsets within the sweep of an underlying culture. In his seminal work, *Christ and Culture,* H. Richard Niebuhr argued that culture should be as inclusive as the concept of civilization. "It comprises language, habits, ideas, beliefs, customs, social organization, inherited artifacts, technical processes and values."[10] Preachers in the Western world need to discern the times for "Western culture" and its deep tides of change in this wide context.

Second, preachers need to see communication's role within culture. The most common communication theory is called the "transmission model." It contains several elements that form an elliptical loop: a *source*, which transmits a *message* through a *medium* to an *audience* with *feedback* to the source. It recognizes the possibility of *interference* between source and audience and the influence of a wider *context*. Many theorists have expressed dissatisfaction with this model because its loop encourages an oversimplistic understanding that is crudely mechanical. Everyone recognizes that communication embraces both verbal and nonverbal language and operates within nuances of complex relationships. No one can guarantee the impact of a message independent of an audience's subjective responses.

For Christians, the primary objections to the transmission model stem from its exclusion of God and its lack of biblical understanding that words were God's idea. God broke the silence in the beginning—"Then God said" (Gen. 1:3)—and ever since, words have had God-given power to cause things to happen, including creating culture. Quentin Schultze claims, "God gives us the gift of communication so that we can actively cocreate our *culture*, our whole way of life. When we communicate, we expand God's original creation by making and sharing our ways of life."[11] He describes human culture as a symphony. When people communicate well, in tune with God's "score," they make great music, but poor communication only adds to dissonance and despair. Schultze introduces a challenging concept of the "stewardship" of words, encouraging us to use them responsibly so as to develop communities of justice and peace—shalom.

This "cultural model" of communication makes God's grace central to the big picture. It opens up vistas to encourage and humble. On the one hand, preachers have a key role as responsible cocreators of culture for the sake of God's shalom. They are not powerless in the face of changing Western culture. But on the other hand, the sheer scale of change keeps preachers modest. High claims can be made for preaching, but there can be no pretentious triumphalism.

Tragically, in the Western church, changes in culture have often overwhelmed preaching, drowning out its good news. Some preachers have ignored the changes and shipwrecked dwindling congregations. Others have accommodated too easily. Schultze warns that biblical preachers "must discern the spirit of contemporary culture or they will become false prophets." He quotes Eugene Peterson, who says that most lies are "90 percent the truth. So you swallow the lie, and subtly, the edge of the gospel is blunted; you think you're preaching the gospel, and you're not. You don't even know it."[12]

Preachers must recognize the tumultuous impact of changing culture and the dangers of neglect or compromise if they are to proclaim God's in-breaking good news and reclaim and reorder culture according to God's shalom.

Paradigm Shifts

The language of "paradigm shifts" has been widely and freely adopted to describe almost any kind of change. The word *paradigm* is associated with Thomas Kuhn, a physicist and historian of science. It is defined as "the relationship of ideas to one another in philosophy of science, a generally accepted model of how ideas relate to one another forming a conceptual framework."[13] Kuhn's particular insights as to how scientific knowledge develops have been summarized by missiologist David Bosch:

> It does not really grow cumulatively (as if more and more knowledge and research brings us ever closer to final solutions) but rather by way of "revolutions." A few individuals begin to perceive reality in ways *qualitatively* different from their predecessors.[14]

Paradigms can be thought of as lenses through which the world is viewed. New discoveries and inventions revolutionize worldviews and the way we see ourselves, which in turn change our preconceptions about reality. Obvious paradigm shifts occurred when Christopher Columbus discovered the new world of the Americas, shifting flat-earth thinking to round-earth thinking, and when Copernicus discovered that the earth orbits the sun and is not the center of the universe. But less obviously, Christian history can be viewed through a series of paradigms, lenses, by which succeeding generations have understood and expressed Christian faith. In our present time of cultural change, several Christian thinkers have articulated their views of the new paradigm, the "revolution in Christian worldview," for today. Robert Webber argues that the value of such paradigm thinking lies in its ability to help us understand the past contextually, appreciate the variety and diversity of the great models of the past, and deal with times of transition in an intelligent way. We need to identify the "core elements which do not change in order to carry forward what has been true of the church from its past."[15]

Webber focuses on five eras in Western church history and the means used to interpret the Christian faith in each.

Ancient	Medieval	Reformation	Modern	Postmodern
Mystery	Institutional	Word	Reason	Mystery
Community			Systematic and Analytical	Community
Symbol				Symbol
			Verbal	
			Individualistic	

Table 1. Paradigms of Church History. Taken from Robert E. Webber, *Ancient-Future Faith: Rethinking Evangelicalism for a Postmodern World* (Grand Rapids: Baker, 1999), 34. Used by permission.

Notice that the characteristics of the most recent culture shift, postmodernism, actually parallel those of the early church. Webber challenges evangelicals to rethink an "ancient-future faith" for the postmodern world. He claims that the early church's context, which was pagan, pre-Constantinian, and marked by spiritual hunger, is similar to the contemporary situation, which is neo-pagan, post-Constantinian, and also manifests spiritual hunger. He pleads for a rediscovery of core elements—mystery, community, and symbol—in order for the missional church to be effective today.

Changes "under our noses" are always more difficult to assess than those blessed by hindsight. Short-term waves can disguise profound sea changes, and certain features in culture can overimpress, eventually turning out to be minor. Yet Christians, especially preachers, need to watch for paradigm shifts and treat them with utmost seriousness. One such paradigm shift, as shown in table 1, is that from modernity to postmodernity.

Modernity

Many observers agree that Western culture is in transition from modernity to postmodernity. Modernity held sway over the last 250 years and is so ingrained in our thinking, inside our skins, that most of us find it difficult to conceive that our familiar, modern culture is shifting to something else. Being called "modern" was a compliment. It meant we were contemporary and on the cutting edge. But there is mounting evidence that the cutting edge has moved.

Modernity was birthed in the Renaissance, as human reason reigned supreme, and was crowned in Enlightenment culture. Modern Western culture was sustained by a sublime confidence in the human mind's abilities to question ideologies and explain all of life. Human progress was seen as the inevitable outcome of asking the right questions and finding the right answers. The patron of modernity, René Descartes, turned a phrase of Augustine's into a creed: "I think therefore I am." This Enlightenment thinking had a reassuring, overarching sense of rational coherence. Webber, in table 1, describes it using the following words: reason, systematic and analytical, verbal, and individualistic.

In modernity, people looked for a set of absolute and good principles by which to understand the world, and they found them. Modernity involved not only the philosophical world of ideas but also economics, technology, and social factors. With optimism, such people saw science and technology as instruments of reason and progress. Andrew Walker identifies some of modernity's sociological characteristics: "functional rationality," dominated by the clock and by money; "structural pluralism," which moved the Christian faith out of the public arena and into the private sphere; and "cultural pluralism," by which Christian distinctives were lost.[16]

George Hunter summarizes Enlightenment thinking by stating its five convictions.[17] First, the universe functions like a machine and does not need God. Second, human beings are basically good and rational. Third, human reason can design the best approach to human life and organize community. Fourth, science and education can liberate the human race from problems of war, oppression, and disease. Fifth, all religions are the same at their cores, for they are rooted in a common religious consciousness. Together these convictions led to an increasing secularity, which affected the church and its preaching.

Though Enlightenment's rationality gave Christian apologetics a secure place, it also tended to subdue the intuitive and spiritual dimensions of Christian experience. Webber writes of the "dead end street of modernity, which proudly thinks the human is autonomous and the individual mind is the final arbiter of truth."[18] Walker claims that functional rationality caused society to lose the Christian story through "gospel amnesia." Modernity replaced the gospel with its own story that science was all-important.

Lesslie Newbigin's withering analysis of modernity's impact on Christianity argues that modernity privatized the Christian faith, taking it out of the arena of public truth, and that we need to bring it back into focus.[19] He urges Christians to see modern Western culture for what it has become. Rather than thinking we live in a secular society, we must see that it is a pagan society. "Its paganism, having been born out of the rejection of Christianity, is far more resistant to the gospel than the pre-Christian paganism with which cross-cultural missions have been familiar."[20] Western culture needs a missionary movement that is determined by content of faith rather than context of culture. He warns that the traditional church is in much greater peril than it realizes.

Stanley Hauerwas and William Willimon claim that modernity actually "tamed" the church.

> We have come to believe that few books have been a greater hindrance to an accurate assessment of our situation than *Christ and Culture*. . . . Niebuhr failed to describe the various historical or contemporary options for the church. He merely justified what was already there—a church that had ceased to ask the right questions as it went about congratulating itself for transforming the world, not noticing, that in fact the world had tamed the church.[21]

Postmodernity

At some time in the recent past, with its first stirrings visible in the 1960s, postmodernity began to supplant modernity. "Postmodern is a makeshift word we use until we have decided what to name the baby."[22] Modernity's reassuring, overarching set of truths that gave meaning to life, science, and religion has collapsed. Many reasons have been advanced for this disintegration, such as a growing awareness of the limitations of science and rationalism and the brutalities of World War 2 that shattered notions of human progress. In place of modernity's one "big story," which was true for everyone, is postmodernity's claim that anything can be true for anyone—truth is what you make it. There is suspicion toward authoritative answers and absolute truths. There is a new creed: "I feel therefore I am." This postmodern approach to life is hungry for experience and majors in intuition and pragmatism. It glories in personal choosing, in discovering (including spiritual searching), and in its new sense of belonging to a global village.

The influence of postmodernity's pluralism and relativism can be seen everywhere in society. In architecture, art, intellectual life, literature, and popular culture, anything goes—if it feels good to me. Some observers see an increasingly ominous buildup of pressures as postmodernity takes hold. Leonard Sweet graphically likens it to a massive tidal wave:

"A flood tide of a revolution is cutting its swath across our world and is gathering prodigious momentum."[23]

Different generations are caught in its currents: Pre-Boomers (born 1927–45), Boomers (born 1946–64), Post-Boomers or Generation Xers (born 1965–81), and Millennials or Generation Y (born since 1981). Pre-Boomers and Boomers, who are identified with modernity, are often in present church leadership and emphasize rationality and excellence in organization. Generation X is a "hinge generation," born into modernity yet overwhelmed by postmodernity. It tends to be much more experiential, interactive, and pragmatic in outlook, stressing relevance, genuineness, and authenticity. Tensions between generations can be negative and contribute, for example, to so-called "worship wars" between traditional and contemporary music. However, tensions can also provide positive intergenerational creativity. In particular, Millennials, who have known only postmodernity, present a new generational dynamic that Neil Howe and William Strauss view optimistically. They believe Millennials are reversing some of the individualistic and selfish attitudes of Generation X through a commitment to spiritual searching, teamwork, and ecology.[24] There are encouraging signs that this latest generation could make a significant, positive impact.

Because of its amorphous diversity, postmodernity is difficult to describe. Graham Cray summarizes it using three major shifts: from producer to consumer; from industrial to electronic society; from sovereign nation states to globalized world.[25] Together they create a new way of living. "Religious life in postmodern times demands not only to be understood differently, but also to be lived differently."[26] Hunter revisits his list of five Enlightenment convictions in the light of postmodernity. Instead of viewing the universe as a machine, postmodernity shows an openness to mystery, wonder, and transcendence, which provides an almost unprecedented opportunity for the gospel. Rather than the rational being dominant, there has been a move toward the intuitive and the role of imagination. Human reason has clearly not worked out the proper ordering of human society, and utopian dreams of what science and education can bring have been shattered by the realities of increased violence and addiction. As for the conviction that all religions are basically the same, terrorism in the name of religion, most notably on September 11, 2001, has made people less likely to lump all faiths together.[27]

Stanley Grenz recognizes a particular tension experienced by Christians in the face of this culture change because they are so well attuned to modernity and the need to demonstrate faith's credibility and rationality. Preachers have to reject the view that disallows one worldview, for Christ is the center: "He himself is before all things, and in him all things hold together" (Col. 1:17). However, Grenz suggests that the gospel for postmodernity should move in new directions: from focusing on the individual to recognizing the role of the community of faith; from rational certainty alone to an intellectual encounter within human experience; from the dualism of mind and matter to a holistic approach to life and the gospel; from an emphasis on uniformity to a celebration of diversity that focuses on local stories and particulars rather than generals.[28]

Each observer emphasizes different implications of postmodernity. Craig Loscalzo, for example, characterizes its salient features as "the love/hate relationship with technology, skepticism about objectivity, preoccupation with choices, concern for unified communities and the hermeneutic of suspicion."[29] (More on the hermeneutic of suspicion shortly.) Postmodernity has even colored how people write about it. Graham Johnston's *Preaching to a Postmodern World* draws heavily on popular culture, especially movies, to illustrate postmodernity's characteristics. They include a rejection of objective truth, skepticism regarding authority, a crisis of losing one's sense of identity, and the blur of morality.[30]

The growing literature on postmodernity contains many insights, but there is a consensus that postmodern people yearn for experience; authenticity; genuine relationships; holism in worship and life; mystery, wonder, and awe in personal spirituality; and local stories that help make sense of their own stories.

Many have addressed the implications of postmodernity for preaching. In modernity's context, preachers had to deal with the notion that "Christianity is not true." In the relativism of postmodernity ("I feel/know it's true for *me!*), the attack is different: "Christians claim to have the only truth—what arrogance!" The irony of postmodernity is that it has spawned countless spiritual searches while often rejecting Christianity as dogmatic and modern.

Robertson McQuilkin advocates that preachers stand firm against the absolute relativism of postmodernity yet adopt some of its views: the spiritual trumps the material; reality must be experienced; how I feel is more important than what I think; relationships are paramount; hope is in short supply.[31] Ed Stetzer comments, "In the modern context the leader was penalized for transparency. Leaders who shared their struggles frequently regretted it as it became an example in future arguments. In the postmodern era, struggle is more valued."[32] Gene Veith uses paradigm language to describe how preaching needs to change and quotes Leith Anderson: "The old paradigm taught that if you have the right teaching, you will experience God. The new paradigm says that if you experience God, you will have the right teaching."[33]

Johnston argues that preachers need to take a dialogical approach, be inductive, use storytelling, and utilize audiovisuals, drama, and art.[34]

Haddon Robinson, in his preface to the second edition of *Biblical Preaching,* states:

> In the last twenty years, the culture has changed. Television and the computer have influenced the ways we learn and think. Narrative preaching has come into vogue. . . . I have spent a bit more time talking about narrative preaching this time around. Inductive sermons also reflect the influence of storied culture.[35]

Further issues such as preaching's place within electronic worship press upon us. Those who have already encountered the paradox of the new Millennial generation, who want to combine loud worship music with quiet listening to a preacher, know just how complex is the change that is taking place.

In this time of cultural transition, much Western church life sadly appears to be trapped in modernity and increasingly out of touch with a changing world. McQuilkin illustrates this fact with a story about his visit to a small-town Mississippi church. There he met a woman who was celebrating fifty years as church organist. He alluded to the changes she must have seen. With jaw firmly set she replied, "I do not change. If they want Bach and Mendelssohn, well and good. If not they can get themselves another organist." With disarming frankness, McQuilkin draws certain parallels with his preaching, which he likened to "offering Bach pipe organ recitals to an audience wired for sound."[36] Robert Nash describes how the church is an "8 track in a CD world."

> It still swims in the fish bowl of modernity. Traditional churches advocate a carefully constructed and rational system of belief. . . . Worship is well ordered and devoid of spontaneity. . . . The focus of the church is on force-feeding propositional truths about God to an American public that is crying out for an experience with God.[37]

Swimming in an old fishbowl is not an option for preaching.

Orality Shifts

Orality shifts concern how words work and take us to the heart of postmodernity's challenge for preachers. In *Orality and Literacy: The Technologizing of the Word,* Walter Ong analyzes the main periods in the history of words. He calls the earliest period "primary orality," in which people were unfamiliar with writing. Writing, originating with the Sumerians in roughly 3500 B.C., heralded a "technology" that he calls "the most momentous of all human technological inventions."[38] It began to move speech from the oral-aural world to the sensory world of vision. Words could now be seen. In the 1450s, the invention of printing dramatically reinforced the influence of print literacy. Ong believes that more recently electronics have ushered in a period he calls "secondary orality." Notice the repeated use of the word *orality*, which focuses on the role of spoken words and is therefore of particular interest to preachers.

It is convenient, though oversimplified, to divide the history of spoken words into three eras: aural-orality, writing and print, and secondary orality. The early period of aural-orality continued long after the invention of writing, and many of its features were seen up until the invention of printing. Writing and print, of course, continue through the secondary orality era.

Aural-Orality

Aural-orality occurred among people who were not writers and whose communication was through spoken and heard words (the world's population before the advent of print). In this era, words were "sounds" from within a person's "interior consciousness," and these sounded-out words were events in themselves. Hence, the Hebrew word *dabar* means both "word" and "event." The ear was primary to communication because only sound mattered. There was no backup for memory. If people failed to hear and remember, communication failure resulted.

Printing would later aid and abet memory by preserving words on paper and in dictionaries. Prior to such helps, people possessed a small vocabulary and used words carefully so that truths could be remembered. To recall something important, speakers had to "think memorable thoughts." Many techniques were developed to help them remember such as mnemonics, rhythms, and repetition, but the most obvious and far-reaching technique was the story. The "stitching together" of stories, as Ong calls it, was a fundamental way of ensuring that truths were passed on from generation to generation. Inevitably, because aural-orality required speaker and listener(s) to be physically present, the telling of stories created community.

Why does a preacher need to be aware of this era of orality? Doesn't it complicate the already complex task of preaching? Preachers need to be aware of aural-orality's significant role in Jesus' ministry and in much of Scripture itself.

It is a stunning fact that Jesus did not write a book. The "Word became flesh" was incarnated in an aural-oral culture. Of course, there were written manuscripts, especially of the Old Testament, and they were crucial for his ministry's fulfillment. He began by unrolling the scroll (Luke 4:17). However, his entire preaching ministry was oral and had the characteristics of aural-orality. Jesus revealed and communicated memorable thoughts through techniques of aural-orality. He continually admonished, "Let anyone who has ears to hear listen." At the center of Jesus' discipling of others were sounded-out words that created a community of the ear.

Walker argues that aural-orality was profoundly significant for the birth of the Christian faith because oral culture created the most stable of human societies and was the most conducive for the creation of community. It encouraged immediacy in communication, and its techniques, especially the story, enabled people to recall and live the Christian faith. Walker poses some what-if questions about the gospel in other communication cultures.

> If the gospel had come into existence in electronic culture, it is difficult to see how it could have survived intact. Its textuality—for we must assume that the gospel events would have been written down—would have been subject to the manipulation and infinite manoeuvrability of word processing.[39]

Film would have allowed even more distortion of gospel truth, as the propaganda of the Third Reich and the Stalinist era show. "Film can be manipulated by script, camera and editor. This pales into insignificance, however, with the advent of digital recording and the new special effects this makes possible."[40] All this adds up to show "just how crucial oral culture was for establishing the gospel."[41] From the first, God's revelation was profoundly oral.

At the time of Christ's incarnation, the great majority of the population was in a culture of speaking and listening, not of writing. Indeed, it has been calculated that as late as the thirteenth and fourteenth centuries only 10 percent of the population could read and only 2 percent could read effectively.[42] In the thirty years between the resurrection of Christ and the first written records, the good news was told orally. Christ's stories and sayings had to be committed to memory in a culture in which spoken words were disciplined, personal carriers of truth. For the first Christians, words were sounds.

The New Testament reveals telltale signs of orality, such as Paul's use of Timothy as a messenger (1 Cor. 4:17) and the community's role as listeners (1 Thess. 5:27). Some scholars claim that certain books originated as oral proclamations, such as 1 Peter and Hebrews. Greidanus describes some epistles as "long distance sermons"[43] and quotes William Barclay's conjecture that "they were poured out by someone striding up and down a room as he dictated, seeing all the time in his mind's eye the people to whom they were to be sent."[44] Much of the New Testament's diverse language for preaching, as described in chapter 1, reflects this aural-oral culture. The first believers were a community of the ear, and preaching in its many forms was the only way of sounding out words.

Pierre Babin, in *The New Era in Religious Communication*, emphasizes the vital role played by the *medium* of communication within this aural/oral culture.

> The message is not in the words but in the effect produced by the one who is speaking. . . . Modulation is the essence of audiovisual language. . . . Modulation indicates vibration, frequencies which vary in length, intensity, harmonics and other nuances. These vibrations are perceived by our senses and induce emotions, images, even ideas.[45]

Christ's teaching not only concerned information and ideas but also invited hearers into a relationship with him. Babin emphasizes the importance of communal life as the Christian faith was learned through what he calls "immersion." Immersion, which was representative of life until the fifteenth century, was characterized by "the preeminence of communal life, by liturgy and practice, by stories and images, and by the sacred part played by the person teaching." Hearers were drawn into a deep belonging where "there was no gap . . . between the sacred and the profane. The whole of life was bathed in a religious climate."[46] It was a learning experience in which to understand was to participate. Babin was one of the first to call this right-brain communication, which is characteristic of the intuitive, interactive, and experiential nature of aural-orality.

Writing and Print

This second era of communication was initiated by the invention of writing. In contrast to oral speech, which welled up from unconsciousness, writing involved artificial "context-free language." Communication was now possible through read and seen words.

Gutenberg's invention of the printing press in the 1450s had a profound influence as human beings for the first time expressed themselves on paper for mass distribution. Writing became indispensable. Words became precise "things" that could be recorded in indexes, dictionaries, and lists, and science became possible through exact verbalization. The eye was now primary instead of the ear—"Let anyone with eyes to see, see." No physical relationship was necessary between speakers and hearers; individual readers picked up and put down words on paper within their private worlds. Community was no longer essential. Though stories remained vital to communication, they were no longer necessary for a process of memorization.

Babin contrasts the right-brain thinking of aural-orality with the left-brain cerebral form associated with writing and print. Printed doctrinal catechesis could have a logical order and could be memorized from texts with greatly extended vocabularies. Babin makes the judgment that this led to a "more cerebral form of faith. . . . But one day we woke up to the fact that, for the majority of people, the living reality of faith had fled."[47]

Secondary Orality

The third era, secondary orality, is marked by the advent of the electronics revolution. "The electronic transformation of verbal expression has both deepened the commitment of the word to space initiated by writing and intensified by print and has brought consciousness to a new age of secondary orality."[48] Comparing secondary orality with primary orality, Ong stresses that secondary orality is "both remarkably like and remarkably unlike primary orality."[49]

> Like primary orality, secondary orality has generated a strong group sense, for listening to spoken words forms hearers into a group, a true audience, just as reading written or printed texts turns individuals in on themselves. But secondary orality generates a sense for groups immeasurably larger than those of primary oral culture—McLuhan's "global village." We are group minded self-consciously and programmatically.[50]

Modulation, vibrations, and participation in community have returned with two forms of electronic media: the audiovisual, which relates primarily to pleasure and entertainment, and data processing, which involves information and calculation. Babin believes that these two media together have opened up a "new era in religious communication."

> I do not think it is possible to separate an audiovisual form of catechesis, one that appeals to the heart and to human feelings, from a purely notional form, one aimed more precisely at the intellect and reason. This new, combined type of religious education will hereafter be called *stereo catechesis*. . . . The greatest danger threatening faith today, I am convinced, is not the absence of information and firm instruction, but the lack of interest in Jesus Christ and the failure of our hearts to be converted.[51]

Two kinds of language therefore coexist. Conceptual language appeals to intellect and reason and is grounded in writing, print, and data processing. Babin describes it using the following words: abstraction, precision, consciousness, intelligence, clarity, analysis, idea, and a linear relationship of words and logic.[52] In contrast, symbolic language "adds modulation to abstract words."[53] Such language is characterized by the following: knowledge by participation and immersion, image, primacy of experience, music and sound effects, vibration of the voice, unconscious imagery, receptivity and intuition, sensitivity to the spiritual, and evolution by thresholds rather than by linear accomplishment.[54] Babin claims that Jesus' language was primarily symbolic, which affects spirit and heart and moves the body. It is full of "resonances, rhythms, stories, and images which lead to a different kind of mental and emotional behavior."[55] It is transformational more than informational. However, these two languages operate together in stereo form, combining like "two waves, each one carrying with it its own sand."[56]

The electronics revolution has opened up new possibilities for stereo listening and preaching, head and heart, word and image. "Let anyone who has ears to hear and eyes to see, listen and see." Secondary orality has brought a new way of learning, combining both the right brain and the left brain.

It is particularly important to notice the reemergence of story, which "as a technique of knowing was eclipsed in the West . . . with the rise of 'modern' scientific method in the seventeenth century."[57] During modernity, story was often considered an inferior way of knowing, but postmodernity has rehabilitated it. Kevin Bradt prefers to call it "storying" to emphasize that the making of stories is a process of cocreation involving both teller and listeners.[58] For him, such storying is a vital way of knowing.

Words appear to work differently in secondary orality. Jolyon Mitchell emphasizes words' "'spontaneity' and 'conversational casualness' but a spontaneity and casualness that are carefully constructed."[59] This crafted "spontaneity" appeals to all five senses. Multisensory language and story have reemerged as the preferred ways of communicating, painting pictures in words and evoking multisensory experiences.

Television has clearly had a major influence in the electronic era. Michael Rogness stresses its primary role in creating a new kind of audience.[60] It conveys pictures, not concepts; it combines verbal and nonverbal communication; information is conveyed in bytes or impressions rather than sequentially (especially in commercials with fifty images in thirty seconds); our concentration span is shorter (with intermissions every ten to twelve minutes); we listen more passively. Television combines seeing and hearing in ways that contrast remarkably with previous eras of speaking or reading. As a visual medium "the picture and the graphics are the heart of communication, not the words spoken."[61]

Rogness quotes Peter Conrad's blunt assessment: "Television talk is not conversation but a celebration of visibility. . . . Talk on television isn't meant to be listened to."[62]

Tex Sample, in *The Spectacle of Worship in a Wired World,* shows how changes initiated by television have been accelerated by the advent of computers and the Internet. Parents with children in school or college share mutual amazement at how their children's study always seems to be accompanied by loud music, a split monitor with continuous text messaging in one corner, and a DVD playing. Somehow they complete an academic assignment on a remaining scrap of screen. A father recently asked his teenage son what he thought about a particular computer web site and was told, "I just can't read that Dad. It's not moving."[63]

The electronic revolution has especially empowered people with an extraordinary scope for creativity,[64] enabling millions of people to interact, create web pages, do online publishing, and even make films. Often amateur, frivolous, and marked by a lack of control, this communication has what columnist Terry Mattingley calls "fuzzy grammar."[65] Charles Colson gives an example of fuzzy grammar by describing the way in which the film *Titanic* ends. The final scene, in which Rose is lying in bed, shows those who died when the ship sank and the two lovers being reunited. Is it meant to portray a dream, the afterlife, or something else? Its deliberate ambiguity leaves all options open. Colson quotes apologist Ravi Zacharias, who describes a generation that "hears with its eyes and thinks with its feelings."[66]

Sample claims that electronic literacy requires Christians to think about communication in three new ways. First, images require careful reflection. Instead of "seeing is believing," now "we don't see until we first believe."[67] Relationships between culture, language, and image are much more complex in multisensory contexts. Second, there is "sound as beat." "I see what you mean" has given way to "I hear what you say." Rock music in particular has had a great influence on sound as beat, and amplification is part of its power. Babin comments, "For many young people, if they are not shaken by the information, they are not interested in knowing. . . . [They] are affected by the vibration alone."[68] Sample refers to the teenager who rephrased Descartes: "I vibrate therefore I am."[69] Third, visualization concerns not merely viewing the screen in electronic culture but visualizing it in combination with images and sound as never before. Visualization involves a new kind of "wiring" for human beings. Sample describes the changing ratio of senses by quoting a ten-year-old who asks, "Have you *seen* the latest Michael Jackson song?"[70] MTV, with its constant flux of images and sound, is a potent symbol of the new practices that occur when image, sound, and visualization converge. In electronic culture, sensory experiences converge as never before, and "its experience contains its meaning."[71]

Sample argues that the convergence of image, sound as beat, and visualization best happens in "spectacle" and "performance," which create story and community for new generations wired for sound. He pleads for the church to critique electronic culture and see how these new practices of bonding and commitment may work for worship and preaching. "A prophetic church of good news will pitch tent with these emergent formations and practices. But it will also bring its own story, its tradition and its distinctive practices to bear."[72]

Table 2 offers a broad-brush-stroke summary of the major differences between the three eras. Admittedly, there is plenty of scope for disagreement over the details. Still, it is difficult to deny the new era in which preaching must function.

Aural-Orality	Writing and Print	Secondary Orality
Before writing but also affecting a majority of the population before print	Alphabetic letterpress Invention of print (1450s)	Since 1985 Electronic revolution
Aural/oral way of thinking	Literate way of thinking	New ways of thinking
Ear—thought relates to sound	Eye—thought relates to sight and space	Ear and eye—thought relates to space and time
Mono—right brain	Mono—left brain	Stereo—right and left brain, image, beat, and visualization
Story—memorable, mnemonics, rhythms, repetitions	Ideas—conceptual, abstract, analytical, explanation, linear, one-way	Story and ideas—symbolic, image, experiential, modulation, participation, intuitive, holistic, two-way
Language—mobile, warm, personally interactive	Language—inhuman, passive, unresponsive	Language—new self-consciously informal style
Community—group minded because no alternative	Individuality—private world of print	Community—self-conscious global village, spectacle

Table 2. Some Characteristics of the Three Eras of Communication

Hermeneutics

Some readers may be tempted to skip over this last addition to the preacher's vocabulary, but the issue of hermeneutics underlies all that has gone before. Hermeneutics comes from the Greek word *hermeneuō*, which can be translated "say" or "speak" and is found in the New Testament (as in "interpreted" [Luke 24:27] and "translated" [John 1:42]). "Interpretation" is helpful shorthand for hermeneutics, which is "the method and techniques used to make a text understandable in a world different from the one in which the text originated."[73] Hermeneutics has to bridge gaps in time, culture, language, and understanding in order to help people interpret the Bible world for the contemporary one. Gordon Fee and Douglas Stuart warn against simple claims such as "You just have to read the Bible and do what it says,"[74] for readers bring much to the text from their experiences and understanding and inevitably make personal interpretations. Consider debates concerning the role of women in church leadership or the practice of baptism in which scholars line up on both sides. Scripture itself recognizes the need for careful interpretation. For example, 2 Peter 3:16 stresses that Paul's letters contain some things that are difficult to understand and can be distorted, as can other Scripture passages.

Hermeneutics requires attention because it also has undergone some paradigm shifts. F. E. D. Schleiermacher, called the "father of modern hermeneutics," laid its foundations during modernity by arguing that all linguistic symbols should be derived from the way in which understanding itself takes place. He asserted that what is to be understood must, in a sense, already be known. How do you know what the words "brown table" actually mean? You must have some inkling about what the author intends by writing about a table and its brownness. He concluded that you can understand something only if you have a pre-understanding of the author's intention. When you get into an author's mind and context, you will understand. This author-oriented approach was often behind the historical and grammatical focus of traditional preaching. To understand Paul's epistles, for example, you needed to research the grammar of his words; the time, geography, and social conditions in which he wrote; and the relevance of his language to the people then. Modern thinking presumed a large measure of objectivity. As Fee and Stuart put it, "A text cannot mean what it never could have meant to its author or his or her readers."[75]

Hermeneutics, however, has been dramatically affected by paradigm shifts in culture. If the Enlightenment project summed up modernity, then deconstructionism is the centerpiece of postmodernity. Associated with philosopher Jacques Derrida in the 1970s, this theory about language and the phenomenon of understanding claims that words have no objective content. The only reality that words have is what they create in our minds as we use them. Deconstructionists, therefore, can argue that God has no existence independent of language. Words express opinions, each of which has equal validity, for meaning depends on who the listener or reader is.

This philosophical shift encouraged a move away from trying to understand an author's intention to focusing instead on the *reader's* role. Some philosophers emphasize just how much readers bring their own worldviews and interpretations to a text. The recent emergence of feminist or black readings of texts, for example, stems from the conviction that words can be interpreted in a reader's own context rather than by pursuing a pre-understanding of the author's intention. Now a text can mean what it did not mean in its original context.

More recently, focus has moved from both author and reader to the text itself, a move associated with Paul Ricoeur. He warned that readers can too easily project their own ideas into a text, and he outlined a three-stage approach to use when reading a text.[76] Stage 1 is marked by the first naivete. At this stage, readers take the text at its face value. Rather than reading into it, they let it make a literal impact on them. Stage 2 involves a hermeneutics of suspicion. Readers approach the text with a self-critical awareness of how gaps in time, culture, language, and understanding cause them to question the text and wrestle with its language and symbolism. Stage 3 requires a second naivete. Readers recognize that each text has a life of its own and is doing things that are, as Ricoeur puts it, "in front of" the text. Each text has its own world and its own power. Words not only *say* things but also *do* things. Readers have to be open to the text's message as it deals with them. Though they should embrace critical insights, they should also be willing to move beyond them to listen to the text's "voice." As Anthony Thiselton remarks, "In Ricoeur's words, adequate use of suspicion and self criticism in hermeneutics is essential if we are not to worship idols, by projecting our own wishes and images onto revelation."[77]

In practice, biblical preachers are likely to approach Scripture with high commitment to the author's intent yet awareness of both reader and text. Because they believe in Scripture's authority, they will continue to stress the importance of divine authorial intent and to search for a text's original, intended meaning. However, recent emphases in biblical studies on the literary and rhetorical shape of different genres has opened up possibilities of new relationships between reader and text in which texts "signal to the careful reader how they are to be read."[78] And belief in the God-breathedness of Scripture enables preachers to listen not only to what Scripture said and did in the past but also to what it says and does today.

Some work has been undertaken that relates biblical interpretation to Babin's concept of stereo communication—conceptual and symbolic, word and image. Michael Glodo has proposed an evangelical "hermeneutic of imagination" by which to interpret Scripture for postmodernity.[79] Such imagining should be undertaken within constraints of the grammatical-historical method yet do justice to the place of image and word in Scripture. A hermeneutic of imagination pays rigorous attention to authorial intent but also engages with the metaphors and images in Scripture through which we perceive God's transcendent reality.

> The Bible should be able to "out-image" any contemporary imaging, because of the divine character of Scripture and because of God, the end of Scripture. . . . Biblical interpretation for a postmodernist, a-rational age should neither be a choice of word over symbol nor of symbol over word, but rather the proper relation of the two.[80]

The words of didactic and prescriptive material in Scripture require conceptual language. Images in Scripture and poetic and narrative materials require symbolic language. Scripture contains both word and image, necessitating both kinds of language. Glodo calls for an integrative approach in which word informs image and vice versa. Such an approach involves self-conscious reflection on connections between Scripture and the experiences of listeners.

Because the impact of culture change is subtle, preachers can easily and dangerously slip into a casual hermeneutic. I have witnessed preachers who claim high commitment to the authority of Scripture slide into a reader approach in which an entire sermon is a series of personal responses with contemporary illustrations. David defeating Goliath is turned into "How I overcame money problems." Psalm 23 is about "finding stress relief." You know the kind of thing.

A New Era for Preaching?

Many preachers today are confused as they straddle the last two columns of table 2, living in the turmoil of transition like a battered ship pitching wildly in giant waves. Many continue to practice preaching that fits the literacy era, while others struggle to identify new ways within the era of secondary orality.

The place of conceptual language—notional, precise, conscious, analytical, explanation-oriented, and spoken in linear sequence—is assured. It suited the literacy era well and continues in the present era. However, alongside it is symbolic language, which stresses experience, imagination, intuition, and sensitivity.

On September 11, 2001, footage showing two planes flying into New York's World Trade Center and the towers' tragic collapse took watchers to new depths of experiencing reality. Those images deeply united people in trauma. Some observers spoke about the extra power the terrorists gained by the dominance of those horrific images in prime time. Certainly, there had been no comparable worldwide experience before. The global village witnessed it simultaneously.

Watchers needed explanation and analysis, and stations provided experts and interpreters. President George W. Bush and Prime Minister Tony Blair carefully crafted words in set speeches. Yet the spontaneous words and feelings of eyewitnesses, meshing with images, held people captive before television screens for hours on end. Images enabled us all to participate as witnesses in a global experience. Words, images, analysis, and experience interlocked as never before.

Words have God-given power:

> There is nothing more powerful than one person standing up before other people and saying what he or she believes is true. It's more powerful than print, more powerful than television. Nowhere is the person more present than in the spoken word. And people recognize that and respond.[81]

But words now operate in a new reality. The context for 360-degree preaching has changed forever. Incarnational preaching requires boldness in the twenty-first century as preachers stand *under* Scripture and the lordship of Christ and *in* the contemporary, transitioning world to embody God's Word in their words and persons.

5

The Person of the Preacher
and the Power of Scripture

Heinrich K of Frankfurt has been given a 10 month suspended sentence and fined $900 for assaulting a traffic cop. "Here's something for your mouth," shouted Heinrich as he punched the policeman in the face after the cop refused to remove the ticket from his illegally parked vehicle. Heinrich is an anger management consultant.

The Week, 6 November 1999

I have been asked (mischievously I think) why no one has yet produced a fail-safe way of guaranteeing a good sermon. Just imagine the sighs of relief in pulpits and pews if some Dummy's Guide to preaching offered instant success. After all, surgeons can learn to operate on patients successfully; pilots can be trained to fly planes successfully; salespeople can learn to sell effectively. Why not guarantee preachers who can preach successfully?

Unfortunately, such a guarantee is not possible. Any preaching model, even the 360-degree model, is merely an impractical theory unless someone commits to enter its dynamic. It is fantasy preaching unless a preacher dares to let his or her life and words embody God's action. God's empowering of the preaching event necessitates a preacher's willing and costly dedication.

I am convinced that renewed preaching in the twenty-first century will come only through renewed preachers. But personal commitment to 360-degree preaching is demanding, for its elements find their catalyst only in the person of an obedient preacher. Why God chooses *us* to share in a creative partnership when he could communicate in countless other ways remains preaching's great mystery. But he does. Therefore, a preacher's spirituality is necessary for preaching to be authentically prophetic, transformational, and incarnational.

Who Is the Preacher?

Phillips Brooks wrote, "Preaching is the communication of truth by man to men. It has in it two essential elements, truth and personality. Neither of those can it spare and still be preaching."[1] Effective preachers need to reflect on who they are. Each must take seriously issues such as personal communication style, personality typology, gender, and ethnicity.

When David Schlafer invites preachers to "discover their own voices," he suggests that they will be drawn to one way of expressing themselves rather than to others.[2] Some, whom he calls poets, express their experiences of everyday life through *images* that evoke sensory awareness and can lead to deeper insights into God's world. Others, storytellers, are drawn to *narratives*, which make speaker and listeners active participants in a sermon's plot. Listeners are drawn into the story to make their own conclusions. Still others are essayists, most at home with *arguments* that provide explanations through clear, logical presentations. Schlafer urges each preacher to find his or her strongest mode, to develop it, and to have the courage to move beyond its comfort zones.

Recently, I mentioned at a preaching conference that homileticians often leave questions of personality type unaddressed. Immediately afterward, two experienced preachers bounded up to me. One said, "I am an 'E,' and I draw so much of my energy from the congregation that I find it impossible to write out a sermon draft. Writing a sermon beforehand doesn't fit my personality." The other preacher said, "I am an 'I' and am completely different. I cannot conceive of standing in front of people without having a full manuscript." These two preachers were using the popular Myers Briggs Type Indicator (MBTI). "E" refers to extroversion. Such people relate more to the outer world of things, people, and environment; their primary source of interest and energy comes from outside themselves. In contrast, "I" refers to introversion. These people prefer the inner world of ideas, concepts, and feeling. Their energy comes from reflection and study, and after being expended in the outer world, it requires replenishment through quiet time spent alone.

Though oversimplified, this particular distinction does in some way explain different preachers' behaviors.

Proponents, while recognizing the danger of such typology being used to stereotype people, argue that it can increase self-understanding and appreciation of others. Malcolm Goldsmith and Martin Wharton rejoice: "God has created a rich diversity, and the particular characteristics that make us ourselves rather than someone else are all part of the richness of creation." They admonish people: "Recognize and accept and value the gifts and insights that you have; work on understanding just why and how some situations and some people are more difficult to understand and appreciate than others; and learn to value and accept the gifts that others bring."[3] In applying MBTI to religious leadership and preaching, Roy Oswald and O. Kroeger have concluded, for example, that a high "E" brings greater energy but also redundancy and overstatement.[4] "I" is more reflective, has more depth, and is more likely to offer better exegesis with an economy of words. Surprisingly perhaps, many effective preachers in the church's history were introverts who chose to express themselves in public ministry against their personality preference.

Gender issues are also significant. Carol Noren, for example, identifies some characteristics of women preachers.[5] She warns women against reinforcing stereotypes and advises them to examine the nonverbal communication—clothing, posture, facial expressions, and gestures—present in their sermons. Women tend to be more intuitive than informational. When doing biblical interpretation, women and men preachers tend to see different stories. Frequently, women identify with the least powerful and focus on relationship issues. Their syntax also shows a preference for language that fosters relationships.

Henry Mitchell analyzes some distinct characteristics of black preachers such as mannerisms, use of musical tone, call, response and repetition, role-playing, and slow delivery. Black preachers use a significantly lower word count, which Mitchell claims leads to increased levels of congregational comprehension and a sermon's influence.[6] Writing about African American women's preaching, Patricia Gould-Champ contrasts its use of inclusive language, which emphasizes survival, healing, and ministry, with men's preferred focus on church and mission issues. She also comments that women tend to have a more didactic preaching style than do men.[7]

These authors and others offer specialized help, and preachers need to attend to individual needs that require extra attention. However, without diminishing personal uniqueness, all preachers share certain common characteristics that can be illustrated using the three-circles model.

The Three-Circles Model

This model, developed to benefit Christian leaders' spiritual prepara-tion,[8] can be applied to preachers. Its three circles represent knowledge, skills, and character, and their area of overlap represents a preacher's spirituality. Preaching should flow out of these three integrated aspects of a preacher's spirituality. Preaching is an overflow of *who* a preacher is. "The spiritual life . . . is ordinary, everyday life lived in an ever-deepen-ing and loving relationship to God and therefore to one's true or healthy self, all people, and the whole of creation."[9]

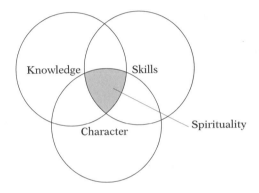

Fig. 3. The Three-Circles Model

These neat three circles obviously oversimplify who a preacher is in several ways. First, they are idealistic. Only Jesus has ever shown perfect balance, integration, and overlap. Realistically, most preachers are represented by woefully lopsided models, with some circles discon-nected or even missing. Some preachers, for example, accumulate a mass of knowledge (large knowledge circle) but demonstrate few skills when selecting material for a clear message (small skills circle). Long-suffering hearers are bombarded by far more information than they ever needed to know.

Second, they oversimplify by focusing on the content of each circle at the expense of their central overlap. Of course, their content does require attention. The circles resemble Aristotle's threefold description of persuasive speech: *logos*, which is the logical appeal of arguments and facts; *pathos*, the emotional appeal; and *ethos*, the ethical appeal of character and integrity. But it is less the constitution of each and more their integration in a Christian preacher's life that is at stake. What matters most is their overlap, which represents the core of a preacher's spirituality.

Third, and most seriously, this model could appear to treat individual preachers in isolation from the dynamics of 360-degree preaching. It could seem that having considered some theological principles of trinitarian preaching we can now put them to one side and move on to the knowledge, skills, and character of a preacher. The truth is these interlocking circles fit in the 360-degree diagram seen earlier, providing a large-scale, close-up view of the preacher, who, along with Scripture, words, God, hearers, and the worship context, plays a role in 360-degree preaching.

As each circle's content is sketched out, preachers should reflect on it to determine their strengths and weaknesses.

Knowledge

Preachers generally feel most at ease in this area because disciplines of study are part of traditional preparation for preaching. Even a modest preacher is likely to have a corner set aside for study and a library of preaching helps. However, three main areas of knowledge need to be developed by preachers: Scripture, theology, and an understanding of the times.

Knowledge of Scripture is a preacher's priority because it is God-breathed to inform and transform. Through it, God initiates 360-degree preaching. Hope for powerful biblical preaching will not be realized unless preachers engage Scripture holistically—using their heads and hearts. The Word written (Scripture), the Word revealed (Jesus Christ), and the Word proclaimed (preaching) are intimately bound together as the Holy Spirit authenticates God's Word of life *to* and *through* preachers. Prophetic preaching requires a balance between technical knowledge, which helps a preacher deal honestly with a text in its context, and spiritual wisdom, which allows a preacher to interpret it truthfully for today.

Second Timothy 2:15 calls for "a worker who has no need to be ashamed, rightly explaining the word of truth." "Rightly explaining" requires serious study in order for a preacher to understand a text's meaning. "Wrongly explaining" takes place through slipshod reading or imported ideas. But rightly explaining also involves not being ashamed. This text confronts a preacher who needs, for example, to avoid profane chatter (v. 16) and to be ready for every good work (v. 21). Scripture has to be read with head and heart, knowledge and wisdom. It requires a preacher's "immersion" into its life.

Second, a preacher's knowledge includes theology—talk about God. Donald English rightly confronts preachers with their theological task in

An Evangelical Theology of Preaching. He defines preaching as "interpreting Scripture in ways that [make] sense to the hearer"[10] and calls preachers to a prophetic task in which they both observe God's transcendence and interpret it for the world. For English, prophetic preaching requires theological content that makes sense of where God is in the world. He likens theology to studying plants in an orderly botanical garden as compared to studying them by walking through a forest characterized by randomness and repetition. He urges preachers to spend time in the theological botanical garden every time Scripture is opened, to ask big questions about who God is and what he is doing.

Third, preachers must understand their times. They need to be keen students, discerning what the people of God should do in changing times. Too many preachers spend over 90 percent of their study on the Bible world and less than 10 percent on the contemporary world. They may have both Bible and newspaper open, but they are steeped in the ancient Near East and have only superficial knowledge about current events. They are more at ease with biblical languages and concepts than with conversations at the dinner table. They are better at describing big problems dramatically, generalizing about human issues, and offering generic solutions than at understanding the nitty-gritty of average people's lives. Unless preachers discern the times and deal with issues associated with culture, paradigm shifts, modernity, postmodernity, orality shifts, and hermeneutics, preaching will not be incarnated in the twenty-first century.

Skills

Fats Waller was once asked to define swing. "If you've got to ask, madam, you ain't got it." We know good communication when it happens to us. What a politician craves, a salesperson yearns for, a teacher requires, so a preacher needs—vitally.

Nothing has higher visibility than a preacher's skills, and hearers may make instant judgments: "He was very good." "I liked her." "That was so boring." When I began preaching as a student in small pastorless churches, I was told only one criterion mattered: "Have you been invited back anywhere? Anyone can be invited once!" A second visit was regarded as a seal of approval.

The skills circle includes matters such as coping with nerves, designing and delivering sermons, and using the voice and body effectively. Some preaching books seem to presume competence in all these areas. For example, many do not mention nervousness at all, yet butterflies in the stomach can create a serious barrier to effective preaching. It is arguable that a measure of nervousness is essential for all good public speaking, for when adrenaline flows, it sharpens alertness and ensures humility. Preaching's awesome task should never come casually. Experienced preachers testify that a dry throat, swollen tongue, and sense of panic can hit at any point in a preaching career. (I will mention nervousness again in a later section on sermon introductions.)

Of the many preaching skills needed, six occupy us here: study, listening, imagination, stereo language, performance, and team building.

Earlier, I mentioned that many preachers are trained to appreciate study disciplines, but maintaining a lifetime of study in busy pastoral lives requires great skill and determination. Fred Craddock urges preachers to view their life of study not as *getting away* from daily work but *getting into* daily work." He recommends practical steps to help preachers establish and maintain realistic routines: study when studying and play when playing, develop an ability to use small units of time, set up a personal library, take advantage of other library facilities, and preserve fruits of study by taking notes. Preachers should explain to their hearers "that time in the study is time spent with the entire congregation and with the community"—it should benefit all.[11] Such study needs realistic time management. James Black describes preaching as "the natural overflow of our religion" and condemns laziness, urges good sleep on Saturday nights, and encourages cultivation of the "homiletical" mind in order to observe daily life as an informed preacher.[12] Claims John Killinger, "There is no profession in which performance depends so much upon the accumulation of insight and information."[13]

A significant part of studying involves listening. "The most important task of any preacher is to become a good listener."[14] As we will see, preachers need to "hear" not only Scripture but also the many voices in culture and the congregation. This involves active listening. A preacher must be attentive and concentrate and reflect on all that surrounds him or her.

Imagination is closely linked to listening. Thomas Troeger claims that imagination can actually be expanded by practice, for its principle is, "We are attentive to what is."[15] In *Imagining the Sermon*, he shows how preachers can develop skills of attentiveness: feel the weight of truth by adopting "the posture and expression of the biblical figure you are describing"; train the ear to catch the power of cadence and imagery; draw parables from life; understand the church's resistance to imagination; dream of new worlds; return to the source—"the One who is praying for us in sighs too deep for words."[16]

At the heart of a sermon's design and delivery lies the skill of using stereo language, which employs both conceptual and symbolic language. Most preachers are drawn to one or the other but must discipline themselves to preach for ears and eyes and to use technology as it complements words with sound and image.

Preaching as performance has gained increasing attention recently. Calvin Morris draws attention to the language of 1 Corinthians 4:9, "God has exhibited us apostles . . . because we have become a spectacle [*theatron*] to the world," and argues that "the preacher cannot avoid being a *theatron,* a public spectacle, for preaching is one of the performing arts."[17] "Unless you present yourself boldly, visibly and audibly before the congregation *and perform* there can be no preaching."[18] He gives instructions for improving performance that include smiling, avoiding reading a sermon, developing timing, and studying the techniques of other professional performers. He calls preachers not to underestimate the importance of entertainment and unflatteringly compares preachers' performances with those of stand-up comics. However, humor in preaching requires great care. David Buttrick has a preacher's rule: "If you are a naturally funny person, your problem will be control; if you are not a naturally funny person do not try."[19] Acceptable humor in preaching depends greatly on a preacher's personality and judgment about appropriateness.

A preacher also needs coaching skills to develop teams so that the wider community is involved in worship and the act of preaching before, during, and after the preaching event. I am convinced that no matter how small a congregation is, involving others brings significant gains. Though the primary tasks of exegesis and sermon preparation remain the preacher's, the preaching process should include others in collaboration. This will be addressed later.

Character

Bishop Quale said, "The art of preaching is to make a preacher and deliver that."[20] Preaching is a character issue. A successful surgeon may be arrogant and selfish, and a skilled airline pilot may be a deceitful philanderer. A writer on ethics may be unethical, and the head of a major charity may be mean-spirited. But no one can preach effectively unless he or she evidently belongs to Christ. "Thus you will know them by their fruits" (Matt. 7:20).

W. E. Sangster describes a preacher's "terrible personalness," referring to the way a preacher confronts a listener with the Creator's awesome claims.[21] This personalness is not just a feature that colors preaching but the very stuff out of which God can speak his Word, for God chooses to incarnate his Word in flesh and his words in a preacher's flesh. Only in Christian preaching are words and Spirit so integrated that the person, the whole person, is wholly important. Message is inseparable from messenger. "The necessity of preaching resides in the fact that when God saves a person through Christ he insists on a living personal encounter with him here and now in the sphere of present personal relationships."[22]

Preaching textbooks often make an assumption that preachers are bound to be persons of integrity. Two circles of knowledge and skills are emphasized, but the third—character—is unexplored. Yet obviously, discussion of a preacher's spirituality involves reflection on character. Like all believers, preachers are public works in progress, jumbles of the good, the bad, and the downright ugly. In character development, these issues matter most: an authentic relationship with God, personal integrity, and relationships with others.

First and foremost, preachers are privileged to live in a genuine relationship with God, belonging as loved children (1 John 3:1–3; 4:7–16). No single fact counts more in a preacher's calling than this security in God's love. Helmut Thielicke warned about a preacher who speaks correct doctrines but does not have an authentic relationship with God. "What comes out will be a paradoxical self-refutation of the message because his existence testifies against it."[23] This can lead to "speaking colorlessly about colors, tonelessly about tones, odorlessly about fragrances."[24] Preachers who are secure in God's love exude positive character.

The old adage holds true: What you are shouts more loudly than what you say. God does not want clever, skillful people disconnected from him. Indeed, a quality relationship with God more than compensates for average knowledge and mediocre skills, which is why so much run-of-the-mill preaching is effective. High-grade techniques cannot substitute for low-grade commitment.

A preacher's character also involves personal integrity, which has many hallmarks. John Stott singles out sincerity, earnestness, courage, and humility.[25] Fred Craddock emphasizes faith, passion, authority, and grace.[26] Elsewhere he writes of the frightening demand of preaching in Luke 2:32 and John 15:22: "Anyone who is a bearer of light is thereby the creator of the possibility of a new kind of darkness."[27] John Westerhoff focuses on four qualities: a willingness to embrace suffering, the practice of silence and solitude, attention to a deep restlessness within, and the need to live so that the image of Christ is seen within.[28]

Today, postmodern hearers particularly seem to value authenticity and vulnerability. Preachers need to be genuine about their spirituality, to be courageous and mature. Jesus' experience with his three closest friends in Gethsemane challenges a leader's willingness to "be real" (Mark 14:33–34). Authentic personal stories connect with both Scripture and hearers. Courage too is vital (Acts 20:27), for prophetic preaching confronts conventional wisdom and secular norms regarding issues such as spending money, leisure, human sexuality, marriage, and divorce. Even more bravery is required to raise questions about justice, racism, and world relief in a narcissistic society. Maturity grows out of consistent discipleship. Through experience and reflection, one learns what it means to be dependent on God. Such maturity rejects simplistic solutions and generic sermon applications. By God's grace and power alone are mature preachers made (Eph. 3:7–9).[29] Preachers never go off duty from maturing. Everything within and around preachers contributes to what is traditionally known as "indirect preparation," a daily weaving together of every experience and insight to form character.

In all this, relationships with others are the litmus test of a preacher's character. "The preacher's first calling is to love. Otherwise the preacher doesn't understand community and has nothing to preach. We must love the community and love the people who belong to the community."[30] Such love moves from close circles of family and friends, through pastoral care of congregation, and beyond to the wider community. Through relationships of trust, people know how much a preacher cares. When John Broadus was asked about the first thing required for effective preaching, he responded, "I should say sympathy; and what is the second, sympathy; and what is the third, sympathy."[31]

Spirituality

As the model's three circles overlap, they form the core of a preacher's spirituality. Gordon Fee reminds us that *pneumatikos* ("spiritual") is a distinctively Pauline word that refers to a relationship with the Holy Spirit. "One is spiritual to the degree that one lives in and walks by the Spirit; in Scripture the word has no other meaning, and no other measurement."[32] Prayer, often hidden in a daily relationship with God, nurtures this living and walking by the Spirit. "The heart of the vocation of preachers and teachers is prayer."[33] Alexander Whyte once warned preachers against attempting flights of prayer in public of which they know nothing in private. Claimed the preacher Robert Murray McCheyne, "The people's greatest need is my personal holiness. . . . A man is what he is on his knees and nothing more."[34]

Each preacher walks a unique spiritual journey. How preachers describe their sense of calling also discloses much about their spirituality. I remember being present when John Stott was asked about the secret to his Christian leadership. With transparent humility, he described his habit over several decades of reading through the Bible at least once each year and how that nourished his life of prayer. Preachers cannot claim before others how vital Scripture is unless it is vital to them. Actually, preachers should not demand spiritual disciplines of others that they do not place upon themselves. Such actions would leave them open to charges of hypocrisy and manipulation.

The three circles are drawn together as a preacher consciously develops competence, credibility, and confidence (see fig. 4). These qualities need to grow through practice and reflection, and each represents an integration of different parts of a preacher's life. Competence marks the overlap between knowledge and skills. It represents a healthy interaction between, on the one hand, Scripture knowledge, theology, and Issachar insights, and, on the other hand, the abilities to study, listen, imagine, use stereo language, and give a sermon of integrity that combines Bible truth with contemporary relevance. Some preachers have knowledge, but it is spoiled by poor delivery; others have an impressive delivery but offer little content. Competent preaching takes a lifetime to develop and can be greatly strengthened by choosing, for example, to collaborate with others.

Fig. 4. Integrating Aspects of the Person of the Preacher

Credibility develops as a preacher integrates skills and character. Clyde Fant defines credibility as "the weight given to the assertions of a speaker and the acceptance accorded them by his hearers."[35] He states that "expertness" is a vital element in credibility, which relates to the extent to which a communicator is *perceived* to be speaking authoritatively. Perceptions are always complex, for they concern how people feel as well as what they understand. Many listeners can sniff out hypocrisy and can tell whether preaching is an overflow or a cover-up. A preacher's authenticity and vulnerability are vital to credibility and arise out of a genuine relationship with God, personal integrity, and healthy relationships with others.

Confidence arises out of an integration of knowledge and character. This is not self-confidence, a dangerous characteristic based on skill that can treat preaching as a form of speech-making or a sales pitch. Rather, this confidence comes through an engagement with Scripture, theology, and contemporary times and a reliance on God's grace. A confident preacher believes in the power of the message and that the preached Word matters.

Crude though these circles and overlaps are, they help to check a preacher's progress. Unbalanced, disconnected circles spell disaster and reveal a lack of competence, credibility, or competence. Circles in balance describe preaching that is prophetic, transformational, and incarnational, preaching that is energized by 360-degree dynamics.

Four Preacher Models

Earlier I noted preaching's diversity in the New Testament and warned against insisting on one size fitting all. But might there be basic kinds of preaching within this diversity? Thomas Long offers four preacher models: herald, pastor, storyteller, and witness.[36] Following his stimulating ideas, I wish to focus on four models, which I describe as teacher preacher, herald preacher, pastor preacher, and narrative preacher.

Teacher Preacher

Teacher preachers give priority to teaching the ideas of Scripture. The related Greek word is *didaskō* ("I teach"). We noted earlier that C. H. Dodd argued for a technical distinction between *kēryssō*, public proclamation to the non-Christian world, and *didaskō*, ethical instruction within the church. This contrast, between kerygmatic preaching to the unchurched and didactic preaching to build up saints, has gone deeply into preaching's literature as well as into preachers' psyches.

Since Dodd's work, the New Testament evidence has been further sifted, and many now argue that *kēryssō* and *didaskō* are used far more interchangeably than Dodd allowed, as seen in references such as Matthew 4:23 and Luke 4:15–16. Acts 28:31 combines the two: "Proclaiming [*kēryssōn*] the kingdom of God and teaching [*didaskōn*] about the Lord Jesus Christ with all boldness and without hindrance." If there was meant to be a significant technical contrast, it would be more obvious.

Though it is unwise to make distinctions on the basis of New Testament word usage, there is nonetheless an obvious contrast in style.

Listeners probably make more judgments based on the differences between preaching and teaching than on any other issue of preaching method. "I call that teaching not preaching," says one. "People need Bible teaching from the pulpit," counters another. Teacher preachers with logical outlines have sometimes been accused of lacking urgency, passion, and warmth. Their supporters claim that teacher preachers are the only ones who provide biblical clarity and produce doctrinally stable congregations.

The teacher preacher dynamic moves *from* Scripture *to* hearers, and its energy resides in God's activity in and through Scripture. Its great strengths are a high view of Scripture and close attention to a text. Ideas from a Bible text lead to sermon ideas that are then preached deductively. This deductive form, which has been well tried and tested in Western culture, begins with a thesis, which is followed by a series of points or sub-theses, each of which is explained, illustrated, and applied to listeners. This method possesses linear logic and coherence and remains the safest and most efficient method of sermon preparation. As John Killinger says, "Every student of preaching ought to master this form. . . . Then if he or she wishes to depart from its use . . . the departure will be a matter of real freedom and not of necessity because the preacher could not manage the traditional form."[37] Its pattern of exegesis, exposition, and application is the bread-and-butter method of preaching.

A master preacher of this style, Stephen Olford, provides the following detailed outline for Romans 12:1–2. He claims that this structure does justice to "textual distinctives behind the truths while stating them in an applicable way":

An authentic call for total commitment
   I. There is an authentic call we must heed
      A. Backed by gospel ministry (12:1a)
      B. Based on divine mercy (12:1a)
      C. Basic to Christian community; "brethren" (12:3ff.)
  II. There is a total commitment we must make
      A. The contents of the sacrificial dedication (12:1b)
      B. The requirements of the sacrificial dedication (12:1b)
      C. The significance of the sacrificial dedication (12:1c)
 III. The radical transformation of our minds (12:2)
      A. The principles of radical transformation (12:2a)
      B. The process of radical transformation (12:2b)
      C. The purpose of radical transformation (12:2c)[38]

In following a text, teacher preachers may be so eager to dissect and present it in a teaching format that they may risk imposing their own standard template to each unique text and treating Scripture as "merely a box of ideas."[39] Craddock is particularly associated with a critique of this deductive format. It announces each point *before* it is developed, often has a weak relationship between the points, has a hortatory tone, and can lose momentum.[40] Much of a preacher's wonder experienced in his or her own journey of discovery in the text may be lost when its outcome is presented in "three heads and nine tails." The old advice "Tell 'em what you are going to tell 'em, then tell 'em, then tell 'em what you've told 'em" is solid but frankly uninteresting. Material should be logically ordered, but does this pattern offer the best way by which people hear and respond?

Earlier I highlighted the importance of understanding orality shifts between modernity and postmodernity. Table 2 links literacy with didactic features, which Pierre Babin called left-brain activity with its potential for the abstract, rational, and linear, as compared with right-brain functions, which are nonverbal, synthetic, concrete, nonrational, and holistic. Teacher preachers are inevitably more left brained in their thinking and more at home with literacy and in modernity. Their congregations have also been schooled in left-brained listening. For such preachers and congregations, the challenges of moving toward a stereo way of ear and eye thinking, conceptual and symbolic language, are particularly acute. Though teaching preaching will continue to have a significant role in the twenty-first century, it will not be enough on its own.

Herald Preacher

Herald preachers give priority to proclaiming God's Word in Scripture. Based on the New Testament word *kēryssō* ("I herald"), herald preachers have a high view of Scripture and of God's presence in the preaching act. Thomas Long describes its dynamic: "The primary movement of preaching is *from* God *through* the herald *to* the hearers."[41] For the herald teacher, preaching's energy resides in God's activity in and through Scripture and through the preaching event itself. Herald preaching's strength lies in the weight given to the power of God's Word and the belief that God himself is speaking in the preaching event. It has been said that in too much preaching God has an inconspicuous role. Not with herald preaching! Though herald preachers rarely operate as though the needs and context of listeners are irrelevant, their primary focus is to hear the Word of Scripture afresh in order to declare it afresh.

While teacher preachers find connections between text and sermon in biblical ideas, herald preachers believe that connections occur through "word-events," convinced that words both *say* and *do*. Preaching's power lies in God's eventful Word. Karl Barth is especially associated with the herald model: "Proclamation is human language in and through which God himself speaks, like a king through the mouth of his herald."[42] Gerhard Eberling emphasizes its word-event character: "The sermon as a sermon is not exposition of the text as past proclamation, but is itself proclamation in the present—and that means, then, that the sermon is the execution of the text."[43]

But the herald preaching dynamic also has weaknesses. Its heavily deductive framework may help a preacher impose his or her *own* three points on a text. Its format can also fail to convey the wonder a preacher experienced in his or her journey of discovery. At worst, herald preaching can be so focused on a text that it ignores the needs of the hearers.

Pastor Preacher

The pastor preacher gives high priority to preaching that is relevant to listeners' needs. Of course, the majority of preachers are also pastors by role, but in contrast to teachers and heralds, the pastor preacher moves *from* hearers back *to* Scripture.

Pastor preachers begin with hearers' needs, or even personal concerns, which then motivate appropriate sermons. This preaching model therefore runs the risk of reducing God's Word to personalized and individualized needs-based messages. Profound scriptural truths can be shrunk to human-sized proportions, and God's transcendence, seen as too demanding or irrelevant, can be marginalized.

This model contrasts significantly with the others we have considered. For teacher and herald, a high view of Scripture means that preaching's energy resides in God's activity in and through Scripture and in the preaching event. Though pastor preachers may also share a high view of Scripture, they feel a greater responsibility to make relevant connections with listeners' needs. Much depends on a pastor's character, integrity, and skills of active listening. Those who practice pastor preaching invariably stress the necessity of quality pastoral relationships.

John Claypool provides an example of a pastor preacher sermon on Genesis 22:1–14 as he reflects on his ten-year-old daughter's death four weeks earlier.[44] He begins by saying that he was drawn to the story of Abraham and Abraham's realization that God was demanding his son of him. "I found myself engulfed in a torrent of emotions identical to that . . . when I first heard the word 'leukemia' spoken about my child." But Abraham returns with his child alive, whereas Claypool finds himself in the darkness of loss. He gives three alternative roads. Two are dead ends: "the road of unquestioning resignation" and "the road of total intellectual understanding." The third is "the road of gratitude." He states, "The whole point in the Abraham saga lies in God's effort to restore men to the right vision of life and a right relationship to it." He concludes by asking his hearers to help him:

> Do not counsel me not to question, and do not attempt to give me any total answer. . . . The greatest thing you can do is to remind me that life is a gift . . . and that the way to handle a gift is to be grateful. . . . As I see it now, there is only one way out of this darkness—the way of gratitude. Will you join me in trying to learn how to travel that way?[45]

Narrative Preacher

The narrative preacher gives high priority to plotting sermons in narrative sequence so that they are both faithful to Scripture and relevant to hearers' listening patterns. Long called one of his models "storyteller," but this name runs the risk of confusing two sorts of sermons.

One kind of sermon contains stories, and storytelling relates to its content. Actually, a large number of preachers commonly use stories as illustrations and applications. Good storytelling appeals to all ages, and teacher, herald, and pastor preachers may all be effective storytellers. The other kind of sermon, properly defined as narrative preaching, uses a story format as the form for the entire sermon. Eugene Lowry uses the analogy of a car trip to make the distinction between content and form.[46] The car itself is the specific content of a biblical story, but the trip is the "event in time" that the car achieves on its journey. For Lowry, sermons should be plotted so that hearers are caught up in sequences of eventfulness. Narrative preachers design sermons to take listeners on journeys, catching them in plots that first present a problem and then offer a resolution that surprises them. Rather than telling individual stories as illustrations, narrative preachers plot an entire sermon in the shape of a single story, often using the narrative sequence of the Scripture passage itself.

The inner dynamic of narrative preaching is composed of two equal movements flowing from opposite directions. One flows from hearing Scripture as God's story and the other from listening to hearers' own stories. As with herald preaching, Scripture's message must be told, yet as with pastor preaching, hearers have a strong influence too.

The strength of narrative preaching lies in the attention given to Scripture's narrative, literary form. Long quotes Edmund Steimle: "If asked for a short definition of preaching, could we do better than *shared story*? . . . Perhaps the image of storyteller can move us toward

. . . a holistic theory of preaching."[47] At its best, such preaching brings high levels of corporate involvement as hearers recognize together that Scripture is their story.

Lowry is famous for his loop design of a narrative sermon with five stages, each characterized by expressive exclamations.[48] The first stage, "oops," upsets the equilibrium of the hearers so that they want to get into the sermon. He invites preachers to look for "trouble" in the text that gives them an "itch." Something is there that raises a problem, and preachers must introduce its conflict or tension so that the "itch becomes theirs." Second, the "ugh" stage analyzes the reason there is a problem and spends time on diagnosis. This is the most lengthy and critical part of the sermon. Lowry gives an illustration of diagnosing the problem of oppression and bigotry. When you ask, "Why would people want to put others down?" the quick answer is pride and arrogance. However, further reflection exposes a mix of motives such as insecurity. In this case, you might conclude, "Self-rejection is the base line underneath the oppressive personality."[49]

This leads to the "aha" stage, which discloses the clue to resolution. This brings the sermon to the one "jigsaw piece" that brings the entire puzzle into focus. Listeners are surprised. This stage pulls the rug out from under them, though first it needed to be laid at the "oops" and "ugh" stages. The "aha" moment marks a radical discontinuity between the gospel and worldly wisdom. The gospel declares the last thing that they would expect to hear. His loop, having gone downward through "oops" and "ugh" suddenly goes upward, "aha," to cross over in a new direction.

Fourth, now on a fresh course, the "whee" stage expresses a new experience of the gospel as it fleshes out good news for human life. After the induction process of the earlier stages, there is deductive proclamation of the gospel. Finally, "yeah" anticipates the consequences. The main climax of preaching is at the "whee" stage, but this last part asks, "What shall we say to this?" because hearers are now in a new situation.

Lowry's central conviction is that sermons are really heard only when they move "from itch to scratch."[50] Yet this loop movement may take various forms. In *How to Preach a Parable,* he offers various options.[51] Simplest is "running the story," which follows the actual flow of a biblical story. "Delaying the story" brings the biblical text into the sermon sequence later in order to resolve a perceived problem. "Suspending the story" begins with the text but suspends its action because of other issues along the way. "Alternating the story" divides the story line into different sorts of material, interspersing text with contemporary references.

Lowry illustrates "suspending the story" with his sermon on Matthew 20:1–16.[52] First, he sets the scene: "It was about a quarter of seven in the morning when the owner of the vineyard went to the marketplace to hire workers for the day." He introduces a note of ambiguity: "One wonders why [the owner] didn't hire all he needed the first time." He tells about the pay time, slowing down the dialogue so that the act of the first workers receiving only as much pay as the last is "unthinkable." This is the "oops" moving to "ugh." He calls for a decision in favor of the workers *against* the owner by using an example of being on a school board that plans to pay a woman less. "Why on earth would Jesus take the side of an unjust owner?" is the trouble in the story, giving the itch. He moves toward the "aha" transition by referring to the rich young ruler in an earlier chapter in Matthew and the shock that Jesus would let such an outstanding prospect get away. Peter asks, "We've left everything to follow you—what do we get?" And the answer? *Cheated.* That's what you get. The kingdom is not a business deal, not a contract, but a covenant.

This is the "aha" moment that reverses the sermon and leads to "whee" and "yeah" as Lowry pursues implications of American bottom-line mentality with its "contracts" and lack of worth. "Jesus was talking about a family covenant. Simon thought it was a business deal." Lowry ends:

> So you see, it doesn't really matter whether the invitation comes at seven, or nine, or noon, or three, or five, or two till. To be invited into the vineyard is to be invited home. Who could ask for anything more?[53]

Narrative preaching fits well with a renewed commitment to literary form in current biblical studies. Joel Green, in his commentary on Luke, argues that a primary ingredient that will lead to certainty for Theophilus is the order of the narrative (Luke 1:1). "For him, the narrative is not the basis of proclamation; rather narration is proclamation." For Luke, an "orderly account" is concerned above all with persuasion. He has "ordered the events of his narrative so as to bring out their significance."[54] Since this kind of preaching is well suited to postmodernity's move to right-brain, symbolic language, it is no surprise to see its popularity among many contemporary preachers.

However, this style of preaching also has weaknesses. As Long notes, not everyone has the same "eureka" moments, and its problem-solving design does not do justice to the richness of the gospel, which cannot be reduced to a single form.[55] Obviously, the more regularly this suspense-driven form is used, the more predictable and contrived it may become. Also, it may sideline nonnarrative parts of Scripture, though, at its best, narrative preaching sees all Scripture in the context of its "big story." Inevitably, Scripture's propositions may more easily be lost in narrative preaching, though Lowry makes room for them at the "whee" stage. Sadly, it must also be admitted that some contemporary preachers have adopted this kind of preaching wholesale with far too little reflection. They have confused telling stories for their own sake with narrative preaching controlled by biblical texts. Sometimes, ironically, storytelling, in trying to avoid dullness, is itself mind-numbing. Paul Wilson says that he has "heard several experienced oral storytellers tell stories that for me verged on boredom. . . . Their language had little sensory appeal."[56]

The Four Models and Scripture

I titled this chapter "The Person of the Preacher and the Power of Scripture." The importance of Scripture's role has been implicit at many points so far, but it is critical to ask how these four preaching models actually relate to Scripture. Nothing is more important in biblical preaching than the way in which preachers understand and use Scripture. Can all these models be called biblical preaching?

Sidney Greidanus provides a good starting point for evaluating the four models using four criteria: biblical content, use of text, length of text, and theme (see table 3).[57]

Categories	Types of Sermons			
Biblical Content	Biblical Sermon			Nonbiblical Sermon
Use of Text	Textual or Expository		Topical-Biblical	Topical-Nonbiblical
Length of Text	Textual Unit	Verse or Clause	Nontextual	Nontextual
Theme	Textual-Thematic	Textual-Multipoint	Biblical-Thematic	Topical-Thematic

Table 3. Basic Classification of Sermons. Taken from Sidney Greidanus, *The Modern Preacher and the Ancient Text: Interpreting and Preaching Biblical Literature* (Grand Rapids: Eerdmans, 1988), 122. Used by permission.

First, under "use of text," he groups "textual" and "expository" together. Often they have been rigidly separated on the basis that textual preaching focuses on one or two verses, while expository preaching deals with a longer Scripture passage. In some circles, it is assumed that the latter, a minimum of one Scripture paragraph (pericopal), is the *only* way to preach biblically. Greidanus argues that these two terms describe preaching from different angles, since both types of sermons are expository *and* textual. Second, in his classification of "theme," he combines thematic preaching and textual preaching into "textual-thematic preaching"—"in which the theme of the sermon is rooted in the text."[58]

For some textual/expository preachers, the category "topical-biblical" preaching is likely to raise their blood pressure. However, there is a world of difference between "biblical-thematic" and the last category "topical-thematic," in which a sermon's content "frequently could have been suggested just as well by a fortune cookie."[59] Francis Rossow argues for rehabilitation of biblical-thematic preaching. He expresses concern that "the gradual development of lectionary/pericopal preaching into a sacred cow" has inhibited this other legitimate form of preaching.[60] Biblical-thematic preaching can be as genuinely biblical as textual-thematic and textual-multipoint sermons. Biblical sermons are not to be judged by their number of Scripture references but by a preacher's humble and daring engagement with a text.

Useful though these criteria are, the four preaching models introduce contrasting dynamics between preachers and Scripture. Teacher preachers react to ideas and propositions in Scripture that can be taught deductively by outlines. Narrative preachers respond to narratives in Scripture that can be preached inductively by stories. But, of course, Scripture does not present either/or choices. It contains ideas and stories, words and images; it provides preachers with a rich variety of propositions and representations, deductive and inductive approaches. It comprises a fertile diversity of genres that should stimulate preachers to explore a range of preaching options.

In an important book, *Preaching and the Literary Forms of the Bible*, Long pleads for attention to be given to texts' literary and rhetorical shape. Just as original writers sought to find the most effective rhetorical forms (as in Luke 1:1), so preachers must be aware of the form of the content and not just the content itself. Different genres of Scripture require different responses. Otherwise preachers treat Scripture as a box of ideas, "simply throwing the text into an exegetical winepress, squeezing out the ideational matter."[61] Scriptural genres are being increasingly analyzed. Gordon Fee and Douglas Stuart, for example, provide a popular account of ten genres in *How to Read the Bible for All Its Worth*.[62]

Mike Graves recognizes roughly thirty "forms" that are smaller literary units found within New Testament genres: aphorisms, miracle stories, vice and virtue lists, poetry and hymns, admonitions, and apocalypse. Identification of biblical genres is not intended to straitjacket sermon forms. Indeed, Graves warns, "One of the biggest limitations of narrative preaching is the tendency to restrict the canon to narrative passages alone."[63] Didactic material may be preached narratively, and narrative material may be preached didactically. Regardless of the approach taken, exegetical humility and integrity are necessary, for "there is no sermon structure or approach to preaching that guarantees biblical content and exegetical accuracy."[64] The distinction between a teacher preacher's exposition and a narrative preacher's story is not as wide as is often supposed. Both are likely to involve deductive and inductive elements.

It is therefore important to conclude that Scripture's diversity of genres legitimates all four models of preachers. Of course, individuals can always treat texts illegitimately. As we have seen, teacher preachers can manipulate texts to impose their own outlines, and pastor preachers can hang a subject on a text as an afterthought. But when considering these four models in the light of Scripture's range of genres, we cannot claim that any one model does justice to all of Scripture. We should avoid battles over style between teacher preachers and narrative preachers or herald preachers and pastor preachers. It is all too easy to place these models in opposition to one another, but the church needs all four. Tension between them is inevitable, for both preachers and congregations will often have strong preferences, but they should be practiced alongside one another as justifiable models for biblical preaching in the twenty-first century.

The flow chart for preaching (fig. 5) shows a diversity of options set before biblical preachers. It is offered not as a classification of preaching types but as a picture of the way in which the types complement one another. Beginning with four types of preacher, the chart shows the crucial role of the preacher as different routes are taken through biblical content, use of text, and sermon form. (I am not concerned with nonbiblical sermons formed in topical-nonbiblical ways.)

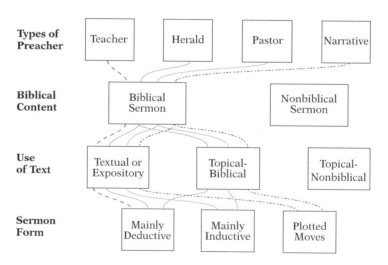

Fig. 5. Basic Flow Chart for Preaching

Three sermon forms summarize the outcomes. "Mainly deductive" encapsulates design forms used by teacher and herald preachers. Exegesis of a text leads to a presentation of ideas and propositions in a deductive structure using outlines and points. However, this form may contain strong inductive elements too. Haddon Robinson, for example, indicates that an expository preacher has to think about the "homiletical idea" and then question how it can be developed deductively, inductively, and through a combination of both.[65]

Since pastor preachers begin with listeners' needs, they use "mainly inductive" sermon forms. This form is also activated whenever a preacher engages a text by asking Fred Craddock's question, "Why not re-create with the congregation the inductive experience of coming to an understanding of the text?"[66] Inductive sermon design, which begins with a problem in the text that hearers readily relate to and works to bring a scriptural resolution, "corresponds to the way people ordinarily experience reality and to the way life's problem-solving activity goes on naturally and casually."[67]

"Plotted moves" refer to various forms of narrative preaching. Alongside Lowry's five-stage loop are many other options. These include the "phenomenological move sermon" associated with David Buttrick, whose main concern is to analyze the way in which sermons work to form faith in hearers, "to describe how *sermons happen in consciousness.*"[68] Rather than sermons being a series of points, he argues for sequences of plotted moves that are carefully crafted. Each move possesses an opening statement, development of the idea, and closure. Since each move takes nearly four minutes, a sermon may comprise five of them so as to give time within the thinking of the congregation "to *form* faith-consciousness."[69]

Henry Mitchell commends "narrative in the black tradition," a popular model that he says resonates with much of Buttrick's theory.[70] Much black preaching is holistic and relational; instead of developing an outline as a "flow of ideas," it pursues a "flow in consciousness" by which preachers "enter the life predicament of the hearers and sense how the sermon will flow in their consciousness."[71] Preachers need to identify a text's "behavioral purpose" and ask, "Am I struggling to get a point across or am I working at a flow in consciousness which will be used to beget trust and change behavior?"[72] Mitchell asserts that congregational empowerment and celebration are the end results, and he warns that one "cannot cerebrate and celebrate at the same time."[73]

The flow chart illustrates several paths open to biblical preachers today. Most teacher preachers follow a straightforward track using Scripture in textual or expository fashion and end up with a mainly deductive sermon form. Herald preachers often follow this same track, though they may also develop the route of topical-biblical use of text. Pastor preachers may develop the topical-biblical use of Scripture in the mainly inductive direction. Narrative preachers, concerned to keep preaching close to the narrative shape and content of Scripture, may employ either the textual/expository or topical-biblical uses, aiming for a plotted moves sermon form.

No one route is exclusive. Preachers in these changing times need to experiment with new ways of preaching that do not depart from biblical preaching but risk new options within it.

6

Preaching
to Changing Times

We cannot content ourselves with business as usual, preaching soothing
sermons to a shrinking number of true believers.

Charles Colson, in Graham Johnston,
Preaching to a Postmodern World

John Holme, age thirty-nine, was a successful salesman as well as an eager
preacher in his village church of Coombe Bissett, Wiltshire, England.
When in 1998 he won a paragliding machine for generating sales of
500,000 pounds, he saw it as a perfect way of spreading God's Word. He
took two training lessons. Then, armed with a megaphone, he took off in
order to "get through to kids on the housing estate. I thought that maybe
if they heard this voice booming out from the sky, they would think it
was God," he joked.

Later in court, prosecution counsel described his hapless flight: "He
set off and seemed to be gaining height, but only at the same rate as
the houses were climbing the hill. This caused him instantaneous fear."
Often flying as low as six feet, he found himself dodging between houses,
trees, and bird tables. Astonished residents said they saw the look of
abject horror on his face. His wife heard the commotion from two miles
away. While negotiating his way through the gardens, he says he saw
heaven, "but as a Christian I would not have been frightened of dying
anyway." Fined for flying too close to a populated area, Mr. Holme com-

mented, "I needed something with credibility. I can't believe I've got a criminal record after this."[1]

Mr. Holme's unusual approach to preaching opened him up to charges of triviality and ridicule in the press, but at least he wanted to make an impact, especially on kids. In his desire to make preaching somehow more credible, imaginative, and bold, he was prepared to take risks. Without endorsing his experiment, I too believe preachers today must take more risks.

Preaching in the twenty-first century means preaching in the midst of change. Lyle Schaller describes three basic options when facing change: to sit back, to plunge in blindly, or to learn from experience so that an anticipatory style of leadership is developed.[2] Some preachers in well-established congregations that are biblically literate and expect traditional preaching can sit back and claim that the effects of culture shift are overstated and that the old ways are the best. Other preachers seem to plunge too quickly into novelty. Instead, preachers need to develop an anticipatory style of leadership in which they learn, listen, and dare to preach afresh. One aspect of such leadership is a preacher's self-awareness of where he or she is in the range of preaching opportunities in the twenty-first century.

A Preaching Spectrum

How can we best sum up preaching in this time of change? The following preaching spectrum draws together some issues raised in the book so far and anticipates the practical work of sermon design in part 2.

Teacher	Herald	Pastor	Narrative
Literacy: left-brained thinking ⟶			Secondary orality: right- and left-brained thinking
Ideas ⟶			Ideas and stories
Formal language ⟶			Informal language
Linear, outlines, points ⟶			Journey of discovery
Epistles, law ⟶			Narrative, parables
Essayist ⟶			Poet, storyteller
Solo effort ⟶			Team effort
Mainly Deductive ⟶		**Mainly Inductive** ⟶	**Plotted**
Modernity ⟶			**Postmodernity**

Fig. 6. Spectrum of Preaching Possibilities

Across the top of the spectrum are the four models of preachers described in the last chapter. At the bottom a line represents the shift from modernity to postmodernity. Based on orality shifts (tables 2 and 3), the left side is characterized by literacy: left-brained thinking that is conceptual, analytical, linear, and explanatory. This type of preaching uses ideas and is mainly deductive. At the other end of the spectrum is secondary orality: right- and left-brained thinking that is symbolic, experiential, image-oriented, and holistic. This type of preaching uses ideas *and* stories and is plotted. Whereas modernity's language style tends to be formal and passive, postmodernity's language style is self-consciously informal—deliberately conversational. Modernity encourages deductive communication with outlines, points, and subpoints, while postmodernity encourages mainly inductive approaches that take hearers on journeys of discovery.

In terms of biblical genres, the mainly deductive approach is closely identified with preaching the epistles and other didactic parts of Scripture, while the mainly inductive approach relates to narrative sections and especially parables. Many other details can be placed on this spectrum such as David Schlafer's three categories of preachers: essayist, poet, and storyteller. The more preachers collaborate with others, the more they move across the spectrum from solo to team effort.

We should note that shifts across this spectrum correspond to recent preaching history, as shown in Lucy Rose's analysis of twentieth-century preaching. Traditional preaching was dominant in the first half of the century; kerygmatic preaching was strong in the 1960s and 1970s; transformational preaching has occurred since the 1980s.[3] It is remarkable how closely each correlates with the four models: teaching preaching with traditional, herald preaching with kerygmatic, and pastor and narrative preaching with transformational.

Traditional preaching focused on transmitting ideas and was intent on "getting the message across," with John Broadus's *On the Preparation and Delivery of Sermons*[4] standard fare in most U.S. seminaries. Kerygmatic preaching, which regarded each sermon as an event in which God speaks a saving word, owed much to Karl Barth, though the thinking of C. H. Dodd and R. Bultmann was also influential, notably the "new hermeneutic" with its stress on the performative power of words and the Word in Christ. H. Grady Davis's *Design for Preaching,*[5] published in 1958, marked its innovation. Transformational preaching also uses terms such as *event* and *encounter* and is especially concerned that "a sermon . . . be an experience that transforms the worshipers."[6] This type of preaching emerged in the 1980s, building on the work of Davis and R. E. C. Browne but particularly linked with the breakthrough book of Fred Craddock, *As One without Authority.*[7]

Paul Wilson claims:

Not since the Middle Ages or the Reformation have such mighty winds swept the homiletical highlands. Theorists now speak of propositional and narrative preaching; of deductive and inductive sermons; of different cultural understandings of preaching . . . of the pericope and various kinds of criticism (historical, redaction, form, sociological, literary, canonical, rhetorical, etc.); of the role of a reader's experience; of changes in worship; of ways of thought being altered by mass media and computer technology.[8]

Divisions such as those between propositional and narrative preaching have contributed to a larger distinction between a "new homiletic" and the "old homiletic." "New" relates to postmodernity, secondary orality, and electronic literacy, whereas "old" is connected to modernity and literacy. Within modernity, the same range of styles held for three hundred years: expository (preaching on a long Scripture passage, generally a paragraph), textual (preaching on a short Scripture passage), and thematic (preaching on a topic or theme).[9] In contrast, postmodernity seems to offer a bewildering variety. Eugene Lowry identifies six models, some of which were encountered in the last chapter: inductive sermon, story sermon, narrative sermon, transconscious African American sermon, phenomenological sermon, and conversational-episodal sermon.[10] Though some of these have long histories, together they have a new identity and are called the "new homiletic."

As I previously expressed disquiet about battles between the four kinds of preachers, so I am also uneasy about inflaming conflict between the old homiletic and the new homiletic. Some perceive them to be in mortal combat, with "exposition" and "story" facing each other across barricades. But both the old homiletic and the new homiletic have been in danger of mistreating story. On the one hand, the old homiletic, with its points and outlines, can atomize story, reducing something living to alliterative headings that appeal to left-brained people. But on the other hand, those employing the new homiletic can be so obsessed with story form that they lose sight of what the gospel means. Boykin Sanders warns that preoccupation with either biblical exegesis or narrative theology means "the major focus becomes how preaching is done rather than what is preached . . . the gospel."[11] For the old and the new homiletic, Scripture is *the* story that needs exposing.

Engagement with Scripture's story calls for renewed confidence in the message and the dynamics of biblical preaching. It also calls for a wider definition of much expository preaching and a deeper textual commitment of much narrative preaching. Harold Bryson, in *Expository Preaching*, argues for an eclectic understanding of expository preaching drawn from a wide range of etymological, morphological, and substantive definitions. He settles for "the art of preaching a series of sermons, either consecutive or selective, from a Bible book."[12] He claims that

> the *message* of preaching is far more important than the *method* of preaching. The issue in a sermon is not *how* God's truth is exposed but *if* God's truth is exposed. Biblical truth in a sermon can be exposed either explicitly with a deductive approach or implicitly with an inductive approach. *The manner does not matter but the message does.*[13]

Traditional preaching—teaching and heralding—remains the main player along the spectrum. In her plea for "other voices at the homiletical table," Rose sees traditional theory as a major voice because "many of its central claims remain dominant and normative in other understandings of preaching."[14] Its methods of exegesis and sermon writing remain the most efficient means of sermon preparation. In an increasingly secular/pagan society, teacher preachers will continue to have an important role in presenting the Christian story and doctrine.

Some preachers have expressed reservations about the long-term effectiveness of the new homiletic with its inductive and narrative approaches. "The newer approaches to preaching are exciting and imaginative, but they do not yet have a proven record of being able to encourage the biblical literacy and theological depth necessary to sustain Christian identity, community and mission."[15] Even some who strongly advocate "thinking in story" agree that didactic preaching "will not die completely in a post-literate world." Richard Jensen gives three reasons: Much of Scripture is didactic in nature, requiring the best teaching techniques; certain audiences will always be at home in a literate environment; and all people have times when they need "teachable moments."[16] Yet mounting evidence suggests that narrative preaching deeply engages contemporary hearers.

A thoughtful member of the church where I am interim preacher said to me recently, "I am confused when I listen to preaching. Personally I am much more at home with old-style, linear, verse-by-verse exposition, but I admit it can easily bore me. Newer narrative preaching can be lively and connect with me, but I really do not know what to make of it."

Many share in that confusion yet urge preachers to find biblically responsible ways forward. Robert Webber warns:

> Throughout history Christians have always struggled to incarnate the faith in each particular culture. Consequently a style of Christianity successful in one era changes as another era begins. Those who remain committed to the old style of faith subsequently freeze that style in the particular culture in which it originated.[17]

Preachers cannot continue as though the third era of communication has not dawned, yet how do they continue?

Fresh Commitment

Earlier chapters highlighted significant issues such as the power of Scripture, words, God, hearers, and the preacher; story, orality, stereo language, holistic worship, and teamwork. These aspects converge into four main challenges for twenty-first-century preachers: engage Scripture holistically, experience renewed spirituality, express through word and image, and experiment beyond comfort zones.

Engage Scripture Holistically

As the Holy Spirit first breathed Scripture into existence, so he continually breathes through its ideas, stories, words, and images. Whatever challenges cultural transition may create, Scripture remains more than equal to them. It never falls behind as inappropriate or outdated. Though he asserts that television has created new audiences who think in different ways, Michael Rogness finds Scripture more than capable of responding. Preachers need to "create concrete pictures in the minds of their listeners. Long before television, the Hebrews used pictorial language. They thought in metaphor and image."[18]

Though Scripture remains the strongest resource, unless preachers engage it holistically, they will miss some of its power in this time of cultural change and communication shift. For many preachers that means new preaching behavior. Cerebral, flat, and lifeless Scripture reading causes sick preaching. Today, preachers must be immersed with heart and head, with the right brain as well as the left, with stories as well as ideas so that Scripture comes alive within their message. Many seminary students find this approach difficult. Many are predisposed by academic discipline to a literate way of thinking (the middle column of table 2). Scripture reading often seems to result in outlines, points, ideas, and propositions. But secondary orality necessitates commitment to Scripture with the heart as well as the head. Throughout preaching's history, effective preachers have always responded holistically to Scripture, but in the twenty-first century this need has become imperative.

Holistic engagement with Scripture fuses prayer with Bible study. "In praying we dwell with; in studying we dig into. . . . In praying we treat the text dynamically and relate it directly to our life story; in studying we dissect the text and look for abstract meaning."[19] Study and prayer belong together as preachers open themselves to Scripture's power. My colleague Roland Kuhl says that he used to pray, "Lord, open the Word to me." Now he prays, "Lord, open me to your Word." Part 2 advocates the use of *lectio divina*, "sacred reading," as one way by which preachers can ensure holistic engagement.

Holistic engagement with Scripture also means living its story. It is a truism that Jesus is the world's greatest storyteller. Though he used other teaching methods, his vibrant stories were most characteristic (Matt. 13:34). Yet, of course, far more than the stories he told, he himself is the story. "Although Jesus as a figure of history is the object of the story, he is also, as God's Word, the author of the story. . . . Following him in faith is to be drawn into God's story which then becomes our own."[20]

Stories have power. "Each act of storying creates a 'brave new story-world' that enfolds all previous tellings and tellers, listenings and listeners within it."[21] Narrative was instinctive in the era of aural-orality, and the significance of story has been reaffirmed in postmodernity. Narrative in Scripture is not some kind of "soft option" that serious biblical preachers should reject in favor of solid propositions. Story is a God-given way for serious biblical preachers to experience truth. G. Robert Jacks urges, "*Submerge your personality* to become a servant of God's Word. *Do* read Scripture with imagination. If it's a story, let the drama come alive. . . . *See it happening.*"[22] Scripture tells *the* story for the world, and Christ invites hearers to live it in him. Over two-thirds of Scripture is actually narrative in genre, but all its teachings, laws, prophecy, poetry, and dreams relate to the greatest story ever told, of God working out his mission through his Son and his people. Mike Graves provides a helpful metaphor of preaching as a symphony in which a preacher enters the "mood" and the "movement" of Scripture as if participating in a music concert.[23]

All four kinds of preachers need to have a holistic engagement with Scripture. They must see it, think it, feel it, and live it. They must taste and see that the Lord is good. Postmodernity does not raise issues that need different answers. They need preachers who have experienced Bible reality. The golden rule for preachers remains: First, open Scripture and experience God's Word for yourself. If it does not come alive to preachers' heads and hearts, to their eyes, ears, and senses, it is unlikely to come alive to listeners. There are no quick fixes and no shortcuts. Scripture must be loved, obeyed, and lived. Rather than being shrunk to manageable bits, it needs to overwhelm those who dare to engage it.

Experience Renewed Spirituality

Spiritual authenticity occurs when a preacher's personal walk with God enables public worship to flow from private worship with words that are "congruous with their actions whether they are in the pulpit, at the office, on the phone, at the hospital, at the grocery stores among friends or in their own homes—especially in their own homes."[24] In contrast, shallow spirituality leads to shallow preaching.

I have already warned that the 360-degree preaching model is merely theory unless preachers have the courage to enter its dynamic, sharing in communion with Father, Son, and Holy Spirit. No part of a preacher's life falls outside the influence of God's love and power.

I confess that my own spiritual life came alive several years after I had begun ministry when I experienced the power of "joining in prayer." Up until that point I had suffered from "self-starting prayer," which frequently resembled an attempt to start a car with a suspect battery on a cold winter's morning. Sometimes it spluttered to life, but more often it did not, in spite of my coaxing. When I began to experience the liberation of joining in prayer with the interceding Christ, I found a new spirituality open to me (Rom. 8:34; Heb. 7:25). At every point of my life, waking, sleeping, working, driving, playing, I became aware that my Lord prays for me and invites me to join with him all the time. Living in response to this continuous intercession has profoundly changed my approach to everything, especially to preaching.

At a preaching conference one minister spoke frankly in the final plenary session: "Most of the time I am so tired from all the visiting, caring, and organizing of the parish that I confess I can only get through by plagiarizing my sermons from bits and pieces I stitch together. I do know how to preach properly, but I just don't have the time most weeks." Many beleagued preachers will react with sympathy, but the vision of 360-degree preaching calls for renewed spiritual commitment that trusts God's grace and believes nothing is more important than living and preaching his Word.

Hearers recognize spiritual authenticity in a preacher. Just a glimpse may be enough. Dean Inge once commented, "It does not seem to me that clever books and brilliant sermons have done so much for me as those chance glimpses into character far above my own."[25] A preacher's spirituality matters more than he or she will ever know. It is "a fragrance from life to life" (2 Cor. 2:16).

Express through Word and Image

Key to many challenges associated with shifts in communication is the language preachers use. We noted that stereo language combines conceptual language and symbolic language (table 2). Unfortunately, many preachers trained in literate ways of preaching have missed out on such language. Unless preachers learn to speak in new ways, they will fail in the new age.

The obvious starting point for developing a new language, a task that is within the reach of all preachers, is a renewed commitment to the importance of words as images. Several authors have stressed this need by referring to television, film, and radio. Michael Rogness states, "We need language with the rich texture of imagery—metaphor, simile, story, zippy adjectives and verbs."[26] Paul Wilson chooses movie making as an analogy for preaching: "If preaching is to reach youth and teenagers, especially, it needs an approach like this movie making idea."[27] He suggests that preachers compose sermons as if for a movie script. Again, stress is placed on creating pictures in the minds of listeners.

In his radio research, Jolyon Mitchell found parallels for preaching. He asserts that preachers should learn from the multisensory language used by effective U.S. and U.K. religious broadcasters. "There is a need to develop a re-newed or re-formed language that draws less upon abstract theological concepts and more upon the art of making pictures with words."[28] He quotes Patricia Wilson-Katsner's definition of "imagery," which includes "the whole physical and sensory dimension of the world portrayed in the sermon."[29] Mitchell pleads for preachers to use language that is relational and holistic.

But will words, even when carefully crafted, be enough by themselves today? Symbolic language involves participation, image, music, and sound, in addition to the human voice. How are preachers to respond to claims that we have entered the age of vibration? Music videos provide the best illustration as songs vibrate ears and rapid images from every angle vibrate eyes. As one writer says, "For many young people, if they are not shaken by the information, they are not interested in knowing."[30]

The rubicon facing twenty-first-century preachers can be bluntly stated: Can they avoid new technology? Can they continue to use words only, or do words need to be complemented in new ways? I am convinced that new technologies are unavoidable, and, as occurred with printing in the fifteenth century, they are rapidly being assimilated to form new textures of communication. Technology has transformed the possibilities for stereo language.

I agree with Tex Sample's assessment of secondary orality: "Electronic culture is not simply some reprise of orality."[31] We have moved into a new multisensory culture that integrates image, beat, and visualization in ways never experienced before. Preachers need to realize that generations are "wired" differently and that for them multisensory events convey meaning through holistic experience. As Lori Carrell states, "Technology can provoke our awareness of the dynamism of words spoken."[32]

The new wave of preachers experimenting with PowerPoint, video imaging, and interactive drama indicates some attempts to take the electronic era seriously. Of course, such attempts are often pursued without much reflection or skill. PowerPoint, for example, is particularly vulnerable to being used as an extension of older, literate ways of thinking. PowerPoint slides with three points and lumps of text are merely sophisticated overhead projection acetates. They are likely to irritate and distract rather than help, especially among those for whom electronic communication is second nature.

Rather, preachers need new ways of thinking. Renewed spirituality and holistic engagement with Scripture should lead to new expression that involves symbol, image, experience, modulation, participation, and intuition (table 2). Electronic technology is misunderstood when treated as a fashionable, superficial means to spruce up tired, lifeless language. Instead of offering quick fixes to pep up presentations, it invites a new way of communicating.

Electronic technology has to become as much a part of our church experience as pipe organ technology. Moderns may disagree, seeing electronics as a passing fad (while preferring pipe organs!). They may argue that spoken words themselves can powerfully create multisensory images. Why go to all this extra effort and expense? Yet we stand on the threshold of possibilities. In too many churches, new technology has been invested in music but not in preaching. Preaching should not be an afterthought, occupying unimaginative slots in worship services. As authentic worship offers its best to God in stereo language, preaching should be at its heart.

Understandably, many preachers will quail from this challenge. Many will share my confessed technological limitations and resent the costs in time and money. Why can't preachers just learn to use words better and be done with it? Of course, no one doubts that words as images remain crucial to the preaching task. Biblical preaching that uses multisensory language will always outdistance PowerPoint presentations that employ flat, lifeless language. Technology offers no panacea. In fact, it can diminish words and even compromise the Word of God when video clips, stories, and drama reduce Scripture to a passing reference.

Preachers can "become so intent on their own cleverness that style supersedes substance."[33]

However, we live in a time of communication shift that pushes preaching toward responsible uses of technology. Over one million PowerPoint presentations are made each day in the United States. Young people learn and live with an acceptance of technology that is second nature. Just as churches once spent money and energy on pipe organs, today they need to make a fresh commitment to new ways of communicating to ensure that God's Word is clearly heard.

Experiment beyond Comfort Zones

The word *experiment* can sound threatening, but these days of change demand a willingness from preachers to do new things. H. Beecher Hicks startled preachers in a workshop I attended by declaring, "Decide to do something different."[34] Traditional foundations in prayer and Bible study need to be well laid first, as I will show in part 2, but changing times require a willingness to experiment.

Experienced preachers quickly make ruts with reassuring patterns of beginnings, endings, and length. You know the kind of comments: "I always begin with a topical story," says one. "I always begin with the Scripture text," says another. "I usually preach for forty minutes." "I preach for twenty-five minutes." When asked why, most answer that it is what they and their hearers are used to! For the gospel's sake in changing times, preachers and hearers cannot take refuge behind convenient and comfortable habits. No style is sacrosanct and off-limits for change. Each sermon has many possibilities, and each preacher has a spectrum to move along. Teacher preachers, for example, could try narrative preaching. Quite possibly, some members of a literate congregation may initially condemn it as nonbiblical, but others (especially young people) will respond positively.

Preachers face a much more radical area for experimentation when it comes to leadership styles in preaching. Thomas Bandy contrasts the "modern" solo professional minister with the postmodern "coach" who takes responsibility for mentoring teams.[35] Though at times his criticisms of traditional ministry are harsh, he is right to focus on the contemporary role of "coaching teams." In contrast with traditional roles for clergy and laity, a coach and a team have such unity that "the distinction between who is leading and who is following at any given moment is impossible to make."[36] Yet a coach brings "a mission attitude, a work ethic, a variable game plan and a winning faith."[37] So, too, preaching should never be seen as a solo effort. Effective preaching has a community dynamic as preacher and hearers respond to God's returning Word.

Collaborative preaching has been gaining attention lately. John McClure charts its beginnings in Browne Barr's 1963 Lyman Beecher Lectures and traces its development through the work of John Killinger, Reuel Howe, Clyde Reid, Don Wardlaw, and others.[38] He makes a plea for the "round table pulpit" where leadership and preaching meet. Instead of "dialogue sermons," which involve other people in their delivery, he commends a process by which a single preacher "includes the actual language and dynamics of collaborative conversation on biblical texts, theology, and life."[39]

Donald Coggan argues from the apostle Paul's activity in *dialegomai* (Acts 17:17; 18:4; 19:8, 24–25) that preachers should encourage dialogues that are "prospective" in preparation and "retrospective" in reflection.[40] He suggests drawing together a group of hearers: "The purpose of the meetings is, first and last, the sharing of the gifts of the members of the group for the building up of the Body of Christ. Preacher and members of the congregation meet to ensure that that part of the weekly worship which is preaching shall steadily become a worthier offering to Almighty God."[41] Though the preacher retains primary responsibility, others share in the process of writing the sermon.

Some preachers have practiced working with groups to good effect. David Mains experimented successfully in Circle Church, Chicago,[42] and David Schlafer advocates using a "preaching discernment group," which he defines as "a community of *covenant* listeners in *Spirit*-ed conversation."[43]

In limited ways, I have practiced group work in my own ministry. In my preaching classes, students work through their preaching tasks, such as exegesis, interpretation, and sermon design, in small groups so that they experience accountability. Doctoral students in the ACTS program[44] have the responsibility to set up parish groups to whom they are responsible. These small groups of five to seven people form cross sections of the congregation and are intimately involved in planning and evaluating each preaching event. While students comment on the extra work involved, they agree emphatically that such groups are invaluable, transforming preaching into a corporate experience.

Technology's increasing role not only necessitates collaboration but also offers strategic opportunities for young people. "It is no secret that those most influenced by electronic culture participate in church at far lower levels than those of previous generations."[45] Some see the church's future life jeopardized as young people bypass it in search of other spiritualities. "Any church can determine whether or not it will survive into the twenty-first century by estimating how many people are involved in it between the ages of fifteen and thirty-two."[46] Collaborating in the use of technology in worship and preaching enables young people to be involved at the heart of church life. Too often the church woefully underestimates the valuable energy and creativity of young people, expressed elsewhere through word, image, and sound. They are an untapped reservoir of resourcefulness at this time of cultural change. With their enthusiasm for teamwork, they are new allies for preachers, and they urgently need encouragement as partners in the task of communicating the gospel today.

Michael Slaughter gives a detailed description of teams he has developed for "designing worship celebrations for a post-literate age."[47] He argues that five ministerial mind-sets have to change. First, the "lone ranger mentality" has to be replaced by ministry teams. Senior ministers cannot do postmodern ministry by themselves, but they can develop teams that can do it together. Second, the clearly defined job description has to give way to flexibility in teamwork. Third, long-range planning has to cede to short-term rapid response. Fourth, seminary training has to be seen as no longer essential. Key team members can emerge from within the church. Finally, a mind-set that assumes that a committee or staff group is the same as a team misses out on essential differences. While committees evaluate, approve, and delegate, a team dreams, develops, and deploys.

Experimentation requires much of a preacher's vision, time, and courage. Some of us languish within our comfort zones. Len Wilson lays some blame on seminary preaching classes, which he says have become "exercises in exegesis and analysis that often bypass a narrative focus in electronic storytelling and cultural literacy."[48] Perhaps there is some truth here. However, rather than apportioning blame, let's state that the future lies in new generations of preachers who have eyes wide open to the challenges of the twenty-first century and give their best within preaching's 360-degree dynamic.

Preachers who engage Scripture holistically, experience renewed spirituality, commit to the use of word and image, and are willing to experiment beyond their comfort zones are on fire for God. Part 2 lays practical foundations for such effective preachers, positioning them for the future that lies ahead.

Part 2

Preaching Opportunities

7

The Preaching Swim

Images are a way to explore realities that cannot be fully investigated or explored by objective study or measurement.

Donald E. Messer, *Contemporary Images of Christian Ministry*

What picture most appeals to you in regard to preaching? Eugene Lowry, who depicts preaching as *plot*, has collected some suggestions:

We not only have [H. Grady] Davis's *tree* and [Fred] Craddock's *trip*, but also R. E. C. Browne's *gesture*, Tom Troeger's *music of speech*, David Buttrick's *move*, Henry Mitchell's *celebration*, Lucy Rose's *conversation*, David Schlafer's *play*, and Paul Scott Wilson's *spark of imagination*.[1]

I encourage my students to develop imaginative models or images to portray preaching. One wrote this:

Preaching is sort of like painting a picture. There is something you have seen. It is most outstanding—beautiful in a startling and breathtaking way. Everything inside you wants to capture it on canvas so that it can be shared with others. Painting requires paying attention to the details of what you see and imagining how to shape it on the canvas. Each color is lovingly chosen. Every brush stroke brings the scene closer to being alive. And finally comes the time for the unveiling—the scary, humbling, and joyous sharing of the beautiful grace of God.

In the past, I have pictured the preaching event as a ski-jump[2] and a mountain climb. But I have long been searching for an image that resonates with the 360-degree preaching model and embodies the weekly journey from text to sermon.

Proposing a Model

When a seminary invited me in the mid-nineties to lecture on how I preach each week, I was forced to reflect honestly on what I had actually been doing each week for twenty years. (I commend not waiting twenty years before undertaking this revealing exercise!) I realized that my weekly practice involved a "journey" through a sequence of actions that involved not only study and technique but also my relationship with God. Actually, what mattered most in this process was not me trying to be fresh and original but God drawing me into discovering more of him and his Word, inviting me to live in its power, and encouraging me to work hard with him.

As I thought about how best to describe this journey, I eventually focused on the picture of a "preaching swim." Perhaps my Baptist background attracts me to water, though I confess I am a weak swimmer and feel acute anxiety when in too deep, especially when buffeted by waves and crosscurrents. I am reminded of my call to preach with its sense of being plunged into something that would always be uncomfortably too deep. Any text about preaching overwhelms when its challenge is taken seriously, such as, "We are ambassadors for Christ, since God is making his appeal through us" (2 Cor. 5:20). C. W. Koller regarded this as perhaps the New Testament's most important text for ministers.[3]

A swimming manual advises teachers to think back to their first experience with water so that they do not take the strangeness of water for granted. It lists disturbing features for new swimmers: pressure on the body; the way in which water's density affects breathing and heart rate; buoyancy; and changes in vision, hearing, touch, and smell. First-time swimmers also experience a fear of drowning.[4] Similarly, new preachers may feel disoriented when immersed in Scripture and preaching responsibilities for the first time.

The "preaching swim" model visualizes swimming down a river. It begins with immersion into a flow at the river's source. The river gathers strength as it widens and deepens, bringing life and health to people on its banks. Each week as I take my preaching journey, I live in the flowing power of God's Word to bring it to my hearers in fresh ways. "I am about to do a new thing; now it springs forth, do you not perceive it? I will make a way in the wilderness and rivers in the desert" (Isa. 43:19).

Sometimes early explorers such as Lewis and Clark traced rivers back to their sources and thereby opened up continents. Preachers move in the other direction, beginning at a bubbling source in God's Word that flows out, creating new channels, deepening and impacting lives of individuals, communities, and nations.

Scripture's references to springs and rivers resonate with life and energy. In dry deserts, rivers represent life. "On every lofty mountain and every high hill there will be brooks running with water" (Isa. 30:25); "The LORD in majesty will be for us a place of broad rivers and streams" (Isa. 33:21); "I will open rivers on the bare heights" (Isa. 41:18); "He will come like a pent-up stream that the wind of the LORD drives on" (Isa. 59:19). Jesus offers living water, which "will become in them a spring of water gushing up to eternal life" (John 4:14). John 7:37–38 contains the promise, "Out of a believer's heart shall flow rivers of living water," which is linked with the work of the Holy Spirit.

Ezekiel 47 traces the prophet's progress into the river—ankle-deep, waist-deep, and then deep enough to swim. The river flowing from the temple teems with life, offering fresh water instead of salt water so that "everything will live where the river goes" (v. 9). Scripture's last chapter (Revelation 22) visualizes this river filled with the water of life, which nourishes fruit and trees for the healing of the nations.

Water may be a cause for praise (Pss. 36:8; 46:4), but its energy can also be destructive, causing fears of being overwhelmed (Pss. 42:7; 69:1–2, 15).

There are other evocative references. James 3:11 likens the tongue to a spring and warns about it being a source of fresh or brackish water. Baptism speaks of immersion and identification with Christ (1 Peter 3:21).

The swimming down a river metaphor seems to encapsulate much that is important for preaching. Most importantly, it conveys God's energy and movement in the preaching process. In the ancient Near East's dry and thirsty lands, water represented the mystery of God providing resources and energy for life. In a parched world that longs for an authentic word from God, flowing water speaks of surging good news as the Triune God initiates, sustains, and empowers the preacher's task. We preach because God commands it, empowers it, and blesses it. Preaching continues to owe its power to a preacher's immersion in the deeper currents and tides of God's Word. At its best, preaching is a pulse-racing, people-changing, community-developing, history-forging adventure.

Often, preaching metaphors seem to place most of the responsibility for preaching on preachers' shoulders, as though everything depends on their understanding, techniques, and energy. In this model, a preacher's prime responsibility is to be immersed in the dynamics of trinitarian preaching. The preaching swim keeps preachers focused on God's energy and movement.

In discussing the preaching swim with a swimming coach, he emphasized the uniqueness of swimming's physical movements. On land we operate by Newton's law: For every action there is a reaction. Since many movements take place against immovable objects, such as the ground, they tend to be piston-like. However, water is a viscous medium and offers only minimal resistance before moving in the direction of a force. In water, therefore, piston movements are highly inefficient. Rather, swimmers need to make "sweeping" movements, finding "still water" against which they can exert resistance. Thrashing about gets one nowhere. This is evocative language for considering the role of a preacher's spirituality in the preaching process. Listening, waiting, and obeying achieve much more than thrashing about.

The preaching swim also emphasizes personal commitment. Though traveling by boat is much safer and faster, preachers must jump in for their own swim. Copied sermons and generic outlines encourage cloning of others' preaching experiences. God wants preachers who are compelled by authentic commitment to his Word and passionate commitment to interpret its good news for *their* hearers. To the question "To preach or not to preach?" the only answer should be, "You cannot stop us." As Peter and John said, "We cannot keep from speaking about what we have seen and heard" (Acts 4:20).

Personal styles will vary. All swimmers have a natural stroke style and often take to one stroke more than another. One may prefer the backstroke, another the crawl; some like gentle breaststrokes, while others take to extravagant butterfly action. God honors preachers who make their own strokes with honesty, hard work, love for their people, and passion for the lost. God works through preachers who offer their best.

Serious swimming requires high levels of fitness and preparedness; so does serious preaching. Preachers need to be fit in body, mind, and spirit. They need to immerse their entire life in God's work. Christians should be used to this tension of working hard within God's work. "Work out your salvation with fear and trembling; for it is God who is at work in you, enabling you both to will and to work for his good pleasure" (Phil. 2:12–13). Preachers who opt to stay on dry land or paddle in the shallows have misunderstood this principle.

Swimming can also be dangerous, and preaching too involves a sense of danger. Complacency can be deadly when swimming; underwater currents, riptides, and undertows can catch the unwary and cause drowning. Complacency is also dangerous when preaching. Trivializing, manipulating, misleading, and downright hypocrisy have eternal consequences.

Jesus reserved his most critical condemnation for professional religious people who presumed their "rightness" (Matt. 23:2–4, 13–15). Martin Luther said, "I have often been afraid and awed to think that I have to preach before God's face of his great majesty and divine being."[5]

D. Martyn Lloyd-Jones, a great British preacher, commented that he had preached a good sermon only twice in his life, and both times he had been asleep. "I still remember the awful feeling of disappointment, on both occasions, when I found I was only dreaming. If only I could preach like that in the pulpit when I was awake."[6] The most effective preachers rightly remain dissatisfied with their best efforts and feel inadequate to the next occasion. As Thomas Long warns, "Preaching is a wild river, wide and deep," and preachers have to "navigate its currents."[7]

The image of preaching as swimming in a river can also be used to describe the cultural context. Streams and rivers have a profound long-term influence on their environments. Sourced in high places by springs, rainfall, and snowfall, they begin to move downward, joining other tributaries, deepening, and widening. They encounter obstacles, fall over sheer rock faces, and tumble through narrow gorges and over massive boulders. A river's power, which allows it to surge, overwhelm, and burst its banks, demands continuing respect. Over time, the imprint rivers leave on the land can be breathtaking. With climatic change or shifts in sea level, they can create spectacular environments. When standing on the edge of the Grand Canyon, it is difficult to imagine that rivers created this landscape, yet they did. Rivers shape environments and bring life to inhabitants living on their banks. When preachers swim in God's news, they belong to the contemporary world with its new, rough terrain of postmodernity. Their swim interacts with culture as they engage Scripture and interpret it for their hearers. Over time the flow of God's truth through preachers should impact the entire environment.

The preaching swim moves from source to destination, providing a model of sermon preparation as a progression of phases. For convenience, the preaching swim process will be described by a number of stages containing various phases. Yet in reality, the process involves being churned backward and forward by surges, crosscurrents, and obstacles. After all, preachers move toward nothing less than fresh encounters with God. And God's Word does not return empty.

One further aspect of the preaching swim should be stressed—its fellowship. Each preacher is responsible for being immersed within the dynamic of God's Word but never as a solo act. Many others swim alongside. William Willimon reminds preachers that they belong to the community of the baptized,[8] for many are on the Christian journey. In David Schlafer's language, preachers have "preaching parents" and "enter into a procession of other voices,"[9] especially through Bible commentaries and other study aids. And as already noted, preachers can intentionally develop preaching teamwork by inviting others to swim alongside. Preaching support groups, even in the smallest church settings, can benefit preachers immensely.

The preaching swim, therefore, illustrates several important aspects of the act of preaching: God's energy and movement, personal commitment, fitness and preparedness, inadequacy and danger, cultural context, progression of phases, and fellowship. I invite you in these next few chapters to visualize preaching as swimming in a river.

An Overview of the Weekly "Swim"

Though a preacher's lifelong journey could be described as a marathon swim, the preaching swim applies to the short-term weekly process of preparing a sermon. There are five stages within the preaching swim that contain thirteen phases (see appendix A for a full outline). Its first two stages belong close together because they both involve immersion and listening.

Stage 1: Immerse in Scripture

Immersion sums up the challenge of engaging Scripture holistically. Immersion involves a learning experience in which understanding means participation. It requires preachers to be open to Scripture—to feel its pulse, sense its mood, and prayerfully enter a Bible passage in its context by listening with heads and hearts, right brain as well as left. Preachers cannot do this secondhand or at a safe distance. Rather than standing on a riverbank to fish for ideas, they need to plunge in to Scripture's flow to experience its story and its power. This immersion is listening in the *past* tense. God's words and images in Scripture breathe with creative potency as God shares himself, and preachers need skill and sensitivity to hear his message in its original context.

Traditionally, this stage is called "exegesis," and it lays the vital groundwork for biblical preaching. Listening in the past tense involves asking questions such as What happened in this text? What did this mean to the first hearers? What did it say? and What did it do?

Stage 2: Interpret for Today

Stage 2 closely parallels exegesis and can be described as listening in the *present* tense. As preachers immerse themselves in Scripture, they need to keep in mind an understanding of their own times. They need to listen to several voices within the contemporary world. Scripture's voice is primary, but the voices of congregation, culture, preacher, and worship are also present. To interpret a text for today, preachers need to ask, What does it say now? What does it do now? What is its mood and movement? A preacher summarizes the outcome of this interpretation process by completing the following sentence: "By the grace of God, what this sermon will say is . . . and what this sermon will do is . . ." This is called the "main impact" of the preaching event. Some call this stage "hermeneutics" (though this term properly includes the entire process of exegesis as well as interpretation).

Stage 3: Design the Sermon

Once a preacher has sharpened a sermon's main impact, he or she must design its content into a sermon that will adequately carry its message. At this stage, preachers find themselves somewhere along the sermon spectrum between traditional deductive design and plotted inductive narrative design (fig. 6). The most difficult part of any communication is not what to say but how to say it, and preachers must work at both. This stage is called "homiletics" and involves designing a sermon that says and does the same things the biblical text says and does. Twenty-first-century hearers have to be engaged just as convincingly as the first hearers were.

Stage 4: Deliver the Sermon

Delivering the sermon requires yet another range of skills and disciplines. Incarnational preaching concerns the person of the preacher—spirituality, voice, and body. Authentic messages come from authentic messengers, represented by integrated circles of knowledge, skill, and character. Consider Francis of Assisi's startling advice: "Go and preach the gospel. If you have to, use words." Many other factors also weigh in alongside words for effective preaching. We have noted that technology invites new ways of combining word, image, and sound. Today, trinitarian preaching occurs within an electronic context, and twenty-first-century preachers have a responsibility to pursue new opportunities for delivering sermons—offering the timeless message in timely ways.

Stage 5: Experience the Outcomes

Figure 7 shows that 360-degree preaching involves action *after* the delivery as well as before. Preaching as a God-event moves individuals and communities forward in responsive living. God's Word will not return empty because it empowers both preacher and hearers to live differently. Sermons are not conversation pieces to tickle gray matter but God's springboards for action in kingdom life. Preachers *and* hearers should expect to be different. Hearers should say, "By the grace of God, what the preacher said to me is . . . and what he calls me to do is . . ."

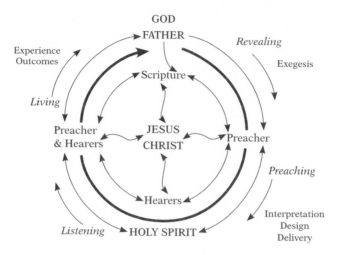

Fig. 7. Preaching Stages within the 360-Degree Dynamic

Figure 8 provides a profile of the preaching swim. None of the five phases should be omitted from each weekly swim. Shortcuts are tempting for busy preachers, but they imperil genuine outcomes by disconnecting parts of the 360-degree model.

Before we consider each of these phases in turn (chaps. 8–12), three practical matters need attention: sermon triggers, preaching support groups, and developing a system.

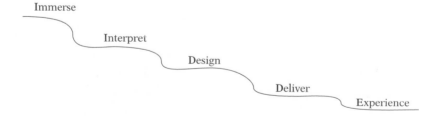

Fig. 8. Profile of the Preaching Swim

Triggers for Preaching Relevance

A "trigger" is that which causes a sermon to be born, the reason for its conception and delivery. Just why did a preacher choose that particular text or theme rather than another—why did he or she jump into that particular flowing stream?

Many imponderables contribute to trinitarian preaching's wonder and mystery. Any discussion about triggers, therefore, must avoid the suggestion that somehow preachers mechanically initiate the preaching event. I have some Post-its on my desk that advertise a marketing firm. The heading says, "Marketeers make it happen." Never should it be "Pulpiteers make it happen" because only God can make things happen. Yet God can use several triggers: textual, liturgical, pastoral, individual, doctrinal, social, and missional.

Textual Triggers

Textual triggers initiate sermons through the order of chapters and verses within biblical texts. When preaching through 1 John, for example, the first sermon might focus on 1 John 1:1–4; the next sermon will be triggered by 1 John 1:5 (probably verses 5–10). Of course, the prior question still has to be asked: Why 1 John? This will likely be answered by the purpose of the overall preaching plan devised for the congregation.

Textual triggers provide valuable discipline by tightly constraining preachers. They safeguard against artificial starting and ending points, though printed divisions and headings of chapters and verses can sometimes mislead preachers. First Corinthians 13, for example, is often preached as a stand-alone chapter, beginning with 1 Corinthians 12:31b. But its call to the "most excellent way" makes sense only in the context of a church contesting hierarchies of spiritual gifts.

Those privileged to preach in one community regularly can know the joyful discipline of preaching through entire books as the biblical writers intended them to be heard and read. I vividly recall reaching 2 Corinthians 8 and preaching three consecutive sermons with the titles "Giving 'til It Thrills: Part 1" (8:1–7); "Giving 'til It Thrills: Part 2" (8:8–15); and "Hallelujah! This Series on Giving Is Nearly Over!" (8:16–24; 9:12–15). By the third week I could have said (though I didn't), "Don't blame me; it's the way Scripture is written!"

The dangers of textual triggers are equally obvious. What can be worse than a lazy preacher plodding through a book verse by verse while relying on favorite commentary notes? Sequential preaching of this kind can also miss an occasion's special needs. The set passage for the Sunday after September 11, 2001, for example, may not have been appropriate for a congregation swollen by visitors sharing in the shock of the terrorist attacks on New York and Washington, D.C.

Textual triggers have always been popular in certain preaching traditions, but it is interesting to note new calls for verse-by-verse preaching because of declining biblical literacy.[10]

Liturgical Triggers

Most preachers heed the Christian year's high points with special services at Christmas and Easter. However, liturgical triggers concern preaching that is based on lectionary readings throughout the year.

Lectionary preaching also disciplines preachers by placing them within a comprehensive plan that draws themes from the whole range of Scripture and juxtaposes readings from the Old Testament and the New Testament. "The cycle of the Christian year and the 'givens' of the lectionary in worship signal the community as other than some kind of private entrepreneurship. . . . The Bible is at the core, not as a *resource* but as *source*."[11]

As with textual triggers, there are some disadvantages. Some preachers express frustration about preaching on set passages that do not always have obvious connections. Set passages can also be inflexible in the face of sudden needs, and they inhibit a preacher from pursuing a sequence of textually triggered sermons.

Pastoral Triggers

Most preachers have pastoral roles, and nothing grounds preaching in hearers' lives more than healthy pastoral relationships. But this trigger refers to specific pastoral needs in the community that initiate sermons. Perhaps a church community has been rocked by tragic bereavement or split through personality conflict, and gaping wounds need a word of healing or rebuke or both.

Pastoral triggers require great care. Pastoral preaching requires courage to face issues biblically, humility to remain vulnerable in a crisis, and confidentiality. A Christlike leader should deal with issues of power and control in a manner different from the way the world handles them.

Individual Triggers

Sometimes sermons are initiated by a preacher's individual choice. Such a choice may mean that a sermon theme or text has so convicted a preacher that he or she knows God is dealing directly with him or her. *This* message *has* to be preached. The sermon has gripped and preached to the preacher first. Such moments of disclosure may come within private devotions, in Christian fellowship, or out of the blue. Sometimes preachers appear to be on fire with a word that is radiant in their words, faces, and conviction. "Within me there is something like a burning fire shut up in my bones" (Jer. 20:9). Hearers recognize reality whenever preachers speak of what they really know.

However, individual triggers may also be negative. Preachers may choose to preach a particular sermon for any number of personal reasons or based on less than pure motives. Itinerant preachers face the danger of making careers with "star sermons." "Successful" sermons may be repeated for no other reason than that they keep going well. Thoughtless repetition for a preacher's own convenience or for ready applause entirely misses the cost and power of 360-degree preaching.

Doctrinal Triggers

Doctrinal triggers concern systematic doctrinal teaching series. James Black challenges preachers, "Keep near to the big controlling truths."[12] Doctrinal triggers may lead to consecutive sermons on doctrines concerning the person of the Holy Spirit, theology of worship, on being the church, the atonement, or the last things. Such doctrinal teaching series are likely to draw texts from a variety of biblical books.

While providing solid thematic teaching, continuous doctrinal preaching can run the risk of becoming too cerebral. Preachers who use doctrinal triggers can also organize Scripture around preferred topics and miss the wider counsel of Scripture.

Social Triggers

Occasionally, a significant event will trigger a particular sermon. Such sermons were traditionally called topical sermons. In contrast to pastoral triggers, which come primarily from within a preacher's community, social triggers result from national or international events. I have already mentioned the significance of the Sunday following the terrorist attacks of September 11. Many preachers suspended their plans and prepared entirely new sermons as this tragedy gripped society.

Mass media's global influence ensures that the majority of hearers will be aware of the latest news. A television program or a major headline may provide the starting point for a sermon. Often such sermons will need to wrestle with ethical issues and may require skills in defending the Christian faith. Such sermons are known as apologetics.

While social triggers lead to sermons of high relevance, there is always the danger of assessing Scripture in terms of topical appropriateness. Though human needs must be addressed, Scripture's primary revelation is of God's character and action, which are essential for salvation and discipleship. Those who practice topical quarrying for texts may fail to practice the disciplines of textual and liturgical preaching.

Missional Triggers

W. E. Sangster claimed, "Few Protestant preachers would contest the statement that a biblical basis and an evangelical purpose should characterize the majority of sermons."[13] However, many sermons are aimed at faithful attendees on the inside rather than seekers on the outside. Sermons triggered by missional concern for the latter call for response in faith and action. Sangster called this "preaching for a verdict." Such preaching requires both boldness and sensitivity and sometimes addresses particular groups who have not yet come to faith in Christ. The twenty-first century desperately needs missional cross-cultural preaching that reaches the lost and energizes the found for witness and service. Preachers who are committed to seeker services, in which it is assumed that nonbelievers are always present, often base their sermons on missional triggers.

Sermons based on missional triggers rightly present the gospel for a response. Holding out the gift of salvation is the primary task of preaching. Yet preachers also have a responsibility to make disciples and to help believers grow and develop beyond their initial faith response. Missional sermons need to be complemented by sustained textual preaching and doctrinal preaching.

Preachers looking at this list of triggers will be able to identify which category they usually fall into. The majority probably use textual or liturgical triggers. Over a period of thirty-five years I have deliberately preached sermons triggered by every category and have experienced many positive experiences within each.

Forming a Preaching Support Group

The previous chapter challenged twenty-first-century preachers to experiment beyond comfort zones and, among other issues, referred to collaborative preaching models. What does this mean in practice? Basically it means that others should always be involved in the preaching swim. At the very least, preachers need the encouragement and advice of a close friend or spouse and should operate with basic accountability to another trusted leader. Mentoring relationships are embedded in Scripture, such as Jesus with the Twelve (Mark 3:7), Barnabas with Saul (Acts 9:27), and Paul with Timothy (1 Tim. 1:18). Preachers cannot help but be leaders. Even preaching that is slightly tinged with prophetic, transformational, and incarnational qualities cannot avoid leading others. But the challenge to "coach" teams is an art and a science that makes special demands of preachers. It requires leadership with high levels of competence, security in relationships, the ability to grow trust, and sacrificial investment in time.

John McClure describes his development of collaborative preaching as a long-term exercise in leadership.[14] A group of ten people meet with him once a week for one and a half hours for a time of feedback/feedforward (ten minutes), engaging the biblical text (twenty minutes), and engaging one another (sixty minutes). This is followed by his own review. He explains how one such group operates in the life of the community for a set period, to be followed by another group, so that over several years all who wish to do so have taken part in "roundtable preaching."

Other models include David Schlafer's "preaching discernment group," which meets before, during, or after the preaching event.[15] Schlafer sees parallels with the Council at Jerusalem (Acts 15) as participants meet before the preaching event to name images, issues, actions, tensions, and questions present in or directly connected with the Scripture text. During this process the preacher contributes but does not control the discussion. While the sermon is preached, the listeners' first task is to describe in their own words what they hear the preacher say. Afterward, the group reflects on a series of questions such as What did we hear and see in the sermon just preached? and Where is this sermon taking us? Schlafer provides detailed questions to be asked at each stage by the preaching discernment group. Donald Coggan emphasizes how such a group needs to be united and prayerful as it provides a source of strength for the preacher.[16]

Michael Slaughter describes in detail the Ginghamsberg church's weekly timetable.[17] Beginning each Wednesday morning at 8:00 A.M., the celebration team meets, including the creative coordinator, technical coordinator, communications director, multimedia director, band leader, and lead pastor. Between 8:00 and 8:30, they prayerfully review the previous weekend's worship experience. Between 8:30 and 10:00, the pastor introduces the "seed idea," which the team works with as together they identify "seeker themes." The team develops elements of design between 10:00 and 11:00 and between 11:00 and 12:00 plans its structure. At 12:00, when the structure is agreed upon, the coordinators work on the different tasks involved with smaller teams. On Friday the group comes together at 11:30 for an hour-long rehearsal, and it meets again on Saturday at 2:00 before the first of five services, beginning on Saturday at 5:30.

Though Slaughter's heavy technical preparation remains the exception, an increasing number of preachers are involved with others in regular group planning and preparation of worship services. Every one admits that large amounts of time need to be invested but champions the value of collaboration. Most, having experienced the fruits of teamwork, would not choose to return to lone-ranger mode.

Teamwork does not diminish an individual preacher's responsibility but enhances it. Individuals are called and gifted to "swim" and to be the persons God uses in the speaking/listening/seeing/doing event to form Christ-shaped individuals and communities. However, teamwork boosts the process, especially at stage 2 (interpret for today), stage 3 (design), as well as stage 5 (experience the outcomes). Twenty-first-century preaching can only benefit from such collaboration.

Developing a Doable System

In whatever ways the preaching swim is undertaken and teams are involved, all preachers should develop a system by which they record their progress. Just as preachers need to, in Schlafer's words, "find their own voice as preachers," so too they need to hone their own methodology.

Some approaches are conventional. Richard Bewes, for example, describes his system:

> The Bible is there, open in front of me. I then get a large piece of paper.
> . . . Then I draw a line down the length of the page, somewhat to the right
> of center. The wider left hand section is reserved for my jottings on the
> *meaning* of the text or passage; the right is given over to stories and such
> illustrations as may occur to me during my preparation.[18]

Paul Wilson devised his four-page model as a theological exercise but recognizes that a preacher might literally use four pages, each comprising a quarter of the preparation work involved through successive days in the week.[19] Some preachers think visually and sketch out preaching plans diagrammatically. Others are adept at conceptualizing their preparation without any need to write or draw. One preacher I spoke to recently said that he prepares by "thinking into PowerPoint slides," linking together images and words. When teams are involved, progress needs to be recorded carefully. At the delivery stage, preachers may use memory or various sized pages, cards, Post-it notes, or PowerPoint slides.

Certain kinds of preaching may require specific methodologies. Joseph Webb, in *Preaching without Notes*, argues for memorization and says that the decision to preach without notes should be made *before* sermon preparation. He methodically records findings and thoughts from Scripture, but as the sermon outline form develops, he spends much time memorizing its sequences and content. "The 'emotional' disciplines of sermon preparation will be different, since what happens in the hours leading up to the sermon delivery will be altered significantly in order to preach without notes."[20]

Each preacher should develop a workable system that allows both discipline and flexibility. I often begin conventionally with paper, not unlike Bewes's pattern above, which enables me to scribble down my responses and to think through possibilities. I end up with a couple sheets full of ideas and images underlined, circled, and connected. For me, this is the best way to monitor the brainstorming and Spirit-storming process. Soon after this, however, I turn on my computer and start clarifying these scribbles by writing a stereo draft. More on these practical matters as we turn to the next chapters.

8

Stage 1:
Immerse in Scripture

Read aloud; read as if for the first time; look and listen for something you haven't seen or heard before; don't use commentaries too quickly.

A Guide to Improving Your Preaching, tape 1

Biblical preaching always gives Scripture first place as God's prime way of evoking his alternative reality. God-breathed Scripture, within the 360-degree model, initiates effective preaching. In today's culture, nothing matters more than preachers engaging Scripture holistically with heads and hearts—immersing themselves in Scripture's life and flow. The section on engaging Scripture holistically (in chap. 6) stressed the importance of fusing prayer with Bible study and story with ideas. Now this must be fleshed out in practice. What postmodern listeners need is not less Bible but more lived-out Bible, not worked-up sermons but worked-out sermons.

To help illustrate the practical process of sermon preparation, I need to choose a text to focus on. Inevitably, making such a choice then limits by its content and genre. However, the practical stages that I will illustrate by working with one passage are relevant to all others. Hopefully, what is lost in variety will be compensated for by depth. I will use the short, familiar passage Luke 15:1–7. This lost sheep story is set within a chapter of "lost stories" that seems to resonate with postmodern listeners.

The first stage of the preaching swim is called exegesis. From the Greek *exegeomai* (see, for example, Luke 24:35; John 1:18; Acts 10:8; 14:21; 15:12), it means "leading out of what is there." In John 1:18, Christ exegeted the Father to human beings—he "led out the meaning of" God to us. For preachers, exegesis is "a systematic plan for coming to understand a biblical text."[1] Its dangerous opposite is eisegesis, which "puts into Scripture what is not there" as preachers bring their own views and applications to a Scripture passage and use it for their own purposes.

Exegesis is listening in the past tense (stage 1), and it belongs closely to the next stage of listening in the present tense (stage 2). David Schlafer claims that preaching is more listening than speaking. "The spoken word of the sermon is both an orchestration of, and a response to, the many voices to which good preachers are constantly listening."[2] In exegesis, listening to Scripture's voice is all-important both to hear God's Word clearly and to avoid eisegesis. Yet even at this first stage, preachers do not come to Scripture neutrally, as though they can dissect a text without involving their own personalities, experiences, and context.

As I turn to Luke 15:1–7, I cannot help but look at it with *my* heart and *my* mind. My spiritual state, my relationship with God and my hearers, my prior knowledge, and my urgency about preaching all contribute to my exegesis. I remember a preacher saying, "No one in the urban Western world could ever find a story about sheep relevant." I may have many such voices in my mind, but exegesis requires that I intentionally commit myself to the discipline of carefully and systematically seeking the text's meaning. Though I carry a jumble of personal issues into the process, and maybe even a possible bias, I must be diligent and methodical so that God speaks a fresh word to me.

Primary Sources First

For good reason, students join my seminary preaching classes only after they have completed their courses in Old and New Testament studies and theology. Why? Because exegesis requires preachers to offer the best of what they know of themselves to the best of what they know of the text without consulting commentaries. Preachers need to practice a personal listening to God's Word in the belief that the same Spirit who breathed Scripture into existence continues to give it life.

Tragically, many seminary-trained preachers view exegesis as an academically inclined exercise intended to display scholarship and research. Instead of spending time alone listening to Scripture, they regurgitate other scholarly opinions. Open Scripture is bypassed in favor of commentary helps. Of course, commentaries, at best, are written by gifted people intent on helping readers discover the riches of God's Word. In no way do I wish to disparage commentators' ministry in God's service. Yet too many preachers seem frightened to practice a belief in a speaking God who meets them in Scripture. They dive too quickly into historical-grammatical research and see "waiting on God" as suspiciously pietistic and vulnerable to eisegesis. Why delay the hard work of discovering a text's meaning when it is presumed to be available only through others' sound scholarship?

As preachers study Scripture in depth, their scholarship should not displace listening to God. In some exegesis classes, students are encouraged to compile lists of initial observations *before* they conduct research. An Old Testament colleague, for example, uses O. H. Steck's pattern of exegesis, which begins with questions such as What feelings, reactions, and associations does the text call forth in me (inviting/repulsive; happy/sad)? What does the text say that is new? Familiar? What jumps out at me? Disturbs me?[3]

Let me emphasize my belief in the importance of rigorous sound scholarship, knowledge of biblical languages, and a commitment to textual studies. Training should provide knowledge about Scripture's historical and geographical issues, the overall story of God's revelation, and significant theological issues. Greek and Hebrew language skills can especially help preachers immerse themselves within texts. But this study can also run preachers along a narrow cerebral track and damage possibilities of holistic exegesis. Using commentaries at the outset can diminish personal immersion in a text and lead preachers to treat Scripture as something to be read about or thought about through *other* people's thoughts rather than something to be encountered directly as God-breathed words to all their senses.

Therefore, preaching exegesis must combine prayer with study. Eugene Peterson translates Psalm 40:6 as "ears Thou has dug for me"[4] to emphasize the importance of listening. He calls for "contemplative exegesis" that involves "opening our interiors to these revealing sounds and submitting our lives to the story these words tell in order to be shaped by them. This involves a poet's respect for words and a lover's responsiveness to words."[5] Gordon Fee sees "listening to the Spirit" as the exegete's ultimate task, which is "to hear the text in such a way that it leads the reader/hearer into the worship of God and into conformity to God and his ways."[6]

Such immersion makes scholarship subservient. What a preacher initially lacks in detailed knowledge about a passage's genre, history, and theology will be more than compensated for by a quality relationship with God-breathed Scripture. Of course, commentary work is always necessary later, but failure to engage Scripture personally in the beginning can fatally flaw preaching exegesis.

The exegesis process has three phases:

Phase 1: Prayerfully read Scripture aloud
Phase 2: Listen and investigate
Phase 3: Check out investigations

Phase 1: Prayerfully Read Scripture Aloud

The preaching swim begins with reading the Scripture passage aloud to oneself. One practical method of combining prayer with Scripture that is being rediscovered by some contemporary evangelicals is called *lectio divina* (literally, "divine reading"). Practiced in the church since the fourth century, it was also adopted by Protestant leaders such as John Calvin and by the Puritans. Those who advocate its use "reflect a confidence in the power of God to speak through nothing but a naked reading of Scripture that would make an inerrantist blush!"[7] It deepens preachers' spiritual engagement without compromising the careful work of exegesis.

Lectio divina involves four steps. First, reading *(lectio)* requires the savoring of the Word—"taste and see that the LORD is good" (Ps. 34:8). At this stage, slow reading aloud seems especially appropriate. We have already noted Scripture's orality and seen how the oral tradition helped to form relationships and community (1 Cor. 4:17; Col. 4:16; 1 Thess. 5:27). Hearing reaches more of a person than simply reading. So a preacher should first sound out the passage in its context. As David Day claims, "God has something to say through this particular passage which he has chosen not to say in any other way."[8]

Second, meditation *(meditatio)* enables a preacher to enter more fully into a text, to visualize its story, to dwell in its words and images, to open up all the senses to God's action in it. The same Holy Spirit who first breathed on the text breathes still. Third, through prayer *(oratio)* a preacher continues in conversation with God, consciously focusing on him and his particular word in the Scripture passage. Fourth, contemplation *(contemplatio)* is the willingness to wait and open the mind and heart to receive and experience God's grace. Only when preachers make room for God to speak to them will they be in a position to pass on his message to others.

This prayer process requires time and patience. Preachers must avoid quick fixes and pursuing the first preachable words that grab their attention. The entire Scripture passage deserves space, time, and visualization. There are few worse moments for a preacher than to hear a passage read in the worship service before the sermon and to be struck by something significant in the text for the first time.

In phase 1, preachers respond to a text of Scripture as though they have never heard it before. Consciously, they open themselves to new surprises, new challenges, and new experiences. Like plunging into a powerful stream's energy and flow, preachers have to immerse themselves in the passage's words, images, and story. First-person experience is essential for a preacher's swim.

In terms of listening, opening Scripture is like entering the middle of a conversation. Set in historical and cultural contexts, these conversations bear witness to God's speaking and action. Unfortunately, it is often easier to interrupt a conversation than to attend patiently to what the other person is saying. But in reading Scripture, preachers are hearing God's story and his revelation, not airing their own views and opinions. They never reach a point when they can stop listening, no matter how well they think they know what a passage is saying.

Applying *lectio divina* to Luke 15:1–7, for example, allows me to experience the circumstances, the mood, and the movement of the parable of the lost sheep. Slow reading *(lectio)* allows me to enter the conversation as welcome "sinners" gather and Pharisees and teachers of the law mutter (v. 1–2). The stinging rebuke of verse 2 bites hard. I listen as Jesus tells the parable to *me* in the crowd. As I spend time visualizing its drama *(meditatio),* I sense both love and hostility around Jesus. Jesus' identification jumps out at me: "Suppose one of *you* has a hundred sheep." Jesus is looking at the Pharisees. I am surprised by the proportions—one hundred sheep and one lost; the risk—ninety-nine left in the wilderness and the search for the lost one, which could be anywhere; the joy—"joyfully" he puts the found sheep on his shoulders, goes home, and invites friends to rejoice with him (v. 5–6). I am hit by the extraordinary implications of joy in heaven over one act of repentance. Is there irony about those "who need no repentance" (v. 7)? I take time to sense the tension, power, shock, and wonder.

I also need to make space to pray *(oratio),* focusing on what God is saying to sinners, mutterers, shepherds, lost sheep, found sheep, and friends of the shepherd. The last stage is *contemplatio*—I wait to receive God's grace. I make room for silence. This text has become a personal event enabling a fresh experience of God's grace in action.

Lectio divina is one of many ways by which preachers can slow down and experience Scripture. Other methods include reading several different Bible versions, writing your own paraphrase, and imagining appropriate music. In whatever ways prayerful imagination is applied, the end of phase 1 should bring a preacher to a deeper awareness of how God has spoken and acted in this text. Throughout, the golden rule is: First, open Scripture and experience God's Word for yourself. Don't rush to a commentary. Savor God-breathed Scripture personally. Nothing can substitute for this immersion in the text that helps you to see, hear, touch, taste, smell, and above all pray with fresh eyes.

Barbara Brown Taylor, in her sermon on Luke 15:1–7, clearly engaged personally:

> We love these stories because we imagine ourselves on the receiving end of them. I listen to the parable of the lost sheep and it is about *me*. I am the poor, tuckered-out lamb, draped across my dear redeemer's shoulders so full of gratitude and relief that I vow never to wander away from him again.[9]

In another sermon, K. M. Yates comments, "These leaders had an ugly spirit. It must have cast quite a chill over the sensitive soul of the Lord Jesus."[10] These are signs that these preachers immersed themselves in the text.

Phase 2: Listen and Investigate

Opening Scripture to swim in its flow and engage in its conversation involves preachers in investigation. Any good conversation requires interaction, participation, receptivity, and intuition, which are many of the qualities of symbolic language. You can always tell when someone is engaged with another by his or her questioning and posture. Glazed eyes and monosyllables are a dead giveaway that a person is not actively involved. Quality exegesis depends on knowledge gained through participation and immersion. Its outcome is not just bytes of information to be transmitted but inspiration to be expressed through image, picture, symbol, and words. Above all, it involves transformation as new realities are awakened. This is the source for "the evoking of an alternative community that knows it is about different things in different ways."[11]

So with all that preachers are and have, they listen and investigate a text's reality and power, swimming in its currents. Committed exegetes explore both with an openness, like curious children awakened to something they do not know yet, and with mature reflection that discerns what God may be saying.

Exegetes need to investigate from two perspectives. First, a wide-screen perspective takes in an entire passage and its wider settings within the Bible and its time and culture. This perspective helps preachers see the big movements of divine and human action. Second, a close-up view examines the details, contents, and form of a particular passage.

Wide-Screen Perspective

In investigating the large movements of God's grace in action, preachers need to ask some standard questions.

Why this text? This recalls the issue of sermon triggers. Why is it important to deal with this particular Scripture passage on this occasion? Among the set lectionary texts, is this the appropriate one to focus on? Is there a pastoral, social, or missional motive? Am I choosing it because it is easier on me as an individual? My choice of Luke 15:1–7 was an individual choice.

How is it written? Earlier we noted the significance of literary genres. Bible writers "chose and arranged language not only for content but for impact."[12] Obviously, it makes a difference whether a text is a story, poetry, a set of laws, or another form. Preachers need to be aware of the form of the content and not just the content itself. For example, Gordon Fee and Douglas Stuart describe three levels of narrative in the Old Testament: the top level, which concerns God's universal plan; the middle level, which centers on the nation of Israel; and the bottom level, which focuses on individual stories. Responsible exegetes must investigate what God is saying and doing in a story.

Some preachers stress the role of genre. Mike Graves calls for "form sensitive preaching."[13] He likens sermon preparation to listening to music, noting both textual mood ("the state of mind or feelings that the text evokes") and textual movement ("its progression, structural pattern, or division of thought"). He divides the four major New Testament genres—Gospels, acts, epistles, and apocalypse—into smaller literary units called forms.

Parables are one such form in which Jesus used metaphors or similes drawn from life. Jesus told parables vividly, with skillful attention to small details, but often left the endings open so that listeners were forced to make their own application. Graves argues that sermons on parables should attempt to say and do the same thing, creating mood by using contemporary, concrete stories that produce a similar reaction. However, he recognizes the danger of trying to copy a genre in preaching. A parable does not necessarily *have* to be preached as a contemporary story, nor does a narrative passage require a narrative sermon. Genre identification is a useful tool, but it should not be a prison for preachers. Since Luke 15:1–7 has a narrative introduction and contains a parable, it is important to listen to its mood and movement.

From the perspective of oral interpretation, G. Robert Jacks offers an analysis of how different types of Scripture passages affect readers. "Some can be called *vital* (e.g., story passages), some *mental* (like Paul's letters), and some *empathic* (such as the Psalms)."[14] Vital passages are a slice of life, and action moves the delivery. Mental passages are dominated by thoughts and appeal to the mind, and ideas move the delivery. Empathic passages appeal to the heart, and feeling moves the delivery.[15] According to these criteria, Luke 15:1–7 is a vital passage in which action moves the delivery.

Where does the passage begin and end? The answer to this question is not always obvious. Divisions of chapters and verses sometimes separate what should be kept together. For Luke 15:1–7, the division between chapters 14 and 15 may conceal an important connection. Chapter 14 concludes with challenges to outright commitment and a call to be good salt: "Let anyone with ears to hear listen!" (Luke 14:35). But then 15:1 reveals that tax collectors and sinners are actually the ones who come near to listen. By beginning at 15:1, you can miss the shock and horror that these lowest life forms, detested by religious leaders, are the very ones who use their ears to listen.

Sometimes preachers are tempted to stop short in a passage. For example, preachers often finish with the mission call of Isaiah 6:8 and completely omit the tough commission (vv. 9–12) and its crucial realism. While stopping at verse 8 makes for much easier preaching, doing so creates considerably less scriptural integrity.

Though Luke 15:1–7 can obviously stand alone, it may also form a doublet with verses 8–10 (linked by the word *or*), complementing aspects such as male and female, country and town, outside and inside. Both stories make the same point. Further, the well-known story of the prodigal son is third in sequence so that the "muttering" of verse 2 provides the context for all three parables. Actually, the story of the prodigal son seems to be more about the older brother, which is no surprise in light of Luke 15:1.

How does the passage fit its context? Asking where a Scripture text begins and ends should also help place it within its context. How significant is the bigger picture? In class, I give my students a picture of a stout tree branch and ask them to imagine its context. Enjoyable debate ensues, with strong opinions about which way should be up and how it relates to the rest of the tree. There are gasps when I reveal that it comes from a picture of a giant Australian Boab tree that has distinctively swollen branches and a huge girth that dwarfs people beneath it. The picture they saw occupies only a tiny fraction in the top right-hand corner. Most students have not seen this unusual tree before. In their imaginations, they were searching for something familiar, when all the time something utterly unfamiliar was in front of them. This activity illustrates how each part of Scripture grew out of a much bigger story and may be dramatically different from a person's usual experience.

What relationship does Luke 15:1–7 have to its context? It forms part of a larger chunk of stories in chapters 15–19 that Jesus told as conflict escalated during the last week of his life. As Jesus continued to associate with the riff-raff, there was mounting condemnation. Luke 15 appears to be a significant part of accelerating conflict.

What is important about the passage's theology and historical setting? Even before consulting commentaries, trained preachers should raise questions about a text's original circumstances—its time and place and especially what God is doing in it. Each preacher has the responsibility to bring his or her "knowledge circle" to bear and ask how God reveals himself and what he is doing in a text. Throughout phases 1 and 2, preachers must keep praying, "Lord, open *me* to your Word" as they conduct personal theological reflection.

Luke 15:1–7 seems to emphasize that God cares about outcasts. God is revealed as a risk-taking God who takes the initiative to search for the lost and then welcomes them and rejoices when they are found. Yet repentance is also tied in. What is significant about those who repent and righteous people who do not need to? At the end, there is striking confidence in the way Jesus speaks of God's joy. A preacher might also recall an Old Testament background in which shepherds and sheep are mentioned, as in Psalm 23 and Ezekiel 34. Other references may also come to mind, such as Jesus' claims about shepherding (John 10). At this phase, commentaries are no substitute for a preacher's own prayerful immersion.

Close-up Perspective

The act of reading out loud often uncovers details unnoticed before. These moments of disclosure may prove highly significant and need close attention. At this point, no question is off-limits. Thomas Long suggests various approaches when using a close-up perspective.[16] Write a paraphrase. Stand in the shoes of each of the characters. Ask about unusual details. Why, for example, does Mark say the grass is green in Mark 6:39? Does the text have a center of gravity—a main thought around which all other thoughts are gathered? Is there conflict either in the text or behind it? Frequently, conflict in a text helps to explain and interpret it. Questions can be asked through the "eyes" of different characters within a text.

Luke 15:1–7 is packed with tension as tax collectors and sinners gather around Jesus, and the Pharisees and teachers of the law mutter complaints. Why do they criticize him for "eating with them"? When Jesus tells the story of the lost sheep, can you picture the contrasting faces of the two groups? Descriptions such as "wilderness," "on his shoulders," "friends and neighbors" jump out. The sudden twist that equates being found with repentance is surprising, as is the comment about the ninety-nine who do not need to repent. Are there really people who do not need to repent, or is this irony in the face of self-righteous critics? With imagination, I can see details as this event unfolds and hear anger as well as applause at the end.

Focus and Function

Two definitive questions now become essential to investigating a text. They ask about the "saying" and the "doing" of the text and sum up the heart of sermon preparation in all its stages and phases. In exegesis (stage 1), these questions ask about the text in its original setting: What *did* it say? and What *did* it do? At the next stage—stage 2, interpret for today—they will be posed in the present tense: What does it say *now?* and What does it do *now?*

Long calls these two questions "focus" and "function." "Focus" describes what a passage says and "function" what it does. For Long, these are "compass settings" so that "what the biblical text intends to say and do . . . becomes what the preacher hopes to say and do."[17] While Long emphasizes the use of focus and function at the later interpretation and design stages, they can be used at the very beginning.

After employing wide-screen and close-up perspectives, a preacher needs to identify the focus of a passage. The focus of Luke 15:1–7 could be stated in various ways. For example:

Jesus warned self-righteous religious people that God rejoices when lost sinners are found.

Jesus called lost tax collectors and sinners to repentance with much rejoicing in heaven.

Jesus showed that God goes out of his way to bring lost people to himself.

Jesus emphasized that God's love reaches out to individuals.

Though it is tempting to ask which of these is the correct, best, or soundest focus, the truth is they *all* express biblically justifiable meanings of the passage. No preacher can claim to express the *total* meaning of a passage.

Inspired Scripture continues to breathe, and preachers may express its multifaceted truth differently yet honestly in their preaching.

This leads to the question about function: What did the passage do? We noted that words are never mere neutral carriers of information, for they possess power to do things as well as to say things. This is especially true of God-breathed Scripture. Its language reveals what happened in the recorded event and also evokes a response today. In Luke 15:1–7, the words did at least two things: *rebuked* complacent religious people who resented that Jesus was spending time with outsiders and *encouraged* tax collectors and sinners to experience God, who loves outsiders. There were two dramatically different functions depending on where a person was in the crowd.

Preachers must always ask both what a text said and what it did. Often outcomes are implicit, as in Luke 15:1–7, in which we sense both the rebuke of the Pharisees and teachers of the law and the profound encouragement for anyone identifying with the lost sheep.

My immersion into Luke 15:1–7 has increasingly drawn me to reflect on the contrast between the grumbling, joyless religious critics and the joy emphasized in verses 5, 6, and 7. Actually, in spite of its beginning, an amazing joy pulses through the entire text. I particularly feel the "sting" of verse 7 when Jesus contrasts the one and the ninety-nine. My preliminary focus is: Jesus warned self-righteous religious people about missing God's joy. During my *lectio divina* exercise, it crossed my mind that we rarely see Jesus smiling. Yet this story, in spite of the tense setting in which it was told, seems a likely context for a smiling Christ who provides unforgettable insight into sublime divine joy. God is joyful about repentance. So my preliminary function is: Jesus rebuked complacent, joyless religious people about missing God's joy. However, I have also been gripped by this story's evangelistic power: It is such wonderful good news for sinners.

Phase 3: Check Out Investigations

I cannot minimize the spiritual daring demanded by phases 1 and 2. Many preachers will find it almost intolerable to go through them without open commentaries at hand. Their training has emphasized scholarship's resources, and they feel vulnerable without them. I can imagine reactions such as, "How do I know I haven't made big mistakes because of wrong assumptions?" "My preaching text is much more complex than Luke 15:1–7—it has *English* words I do not understand, never mind theological implications I cannot fathom." "You are encouraging me to flirt with eisegesis!"

Phase 3 is the vital safeguard to a preacher's immersion into Scripture. After preachers have prayerfully given time to a text, their work and preliminary focus and function must be checked rigorously. A preacher always swims in company with others, and many have already written commentaries after studying a text in depth. The issues that seemed vital to a preacher now need checking, correcting, and expanding. Sometimes commentaries will confirm initial exegesis and deepen its implications. At other times, however, they will expose important connections with other Scripture texts that were missed or show that a preacher has overstated something or has misunderstood the text.

Preachers therefore need to develop their "skills circle" throughout their preaching journeys. They should take great care to acquire biblical and theological resources that can be used to check and deepen their sermons. Often when I am immersed in the study of a particular biblical book or theme for a sermon series, I will visit a good theological bookstore and spend considerable time browsing in the relevant section before adding to my library. I look for commentaries with a high view of Scripture that have grappled with a text's original language and form and have dealt with difficult issues. Usually, my checking process involves at least five or six contrasting commentaries written from different backgrounds and experiences.

Preachers need to develop theological libraries that, in addition to commentaries, include books on Old Testament and New Testament background and reference books such as dictionaries, atlases, and concordances. Resources on CD-ROMs and the Internet are also helpful. Theological and doctrinal books should feature prominently so that dealing with great issues of faith, such as the person of Jesus Christ, the Holy Spirit, the atonement, and the Trinity, is part of a preacher's main diet. It is always helpful to read trusted authors who have wrestled with topics of controversy and modern thought as well as Christian history and mission.

Phase 3 requires concentration. Large amounts of interesting (and sometimes contradictory) material can potentially overwhelm a preacher. In regard to Luke 15:1–7, commentators discuss Pharisaic regulations that banned them from table fellowship with those considered sinful, what is meant by the ninety-nine righteous who need no repentance, and shepherding practices and sizes of flocks during this time.

Based on their investigations, the commentators explain the story's main point in various ways. I. H. Marshall: "The joy which is experienced by a person who recovers what he has lost . . . is a reflection of the joy felt by God when he recovers what he has lost."[18] Joel Green: "The accent of parable and appropriation is on the *consequence* of recovery, the necessity of celebration that follows restoration."[19] Norval Geldenhuys emphasizes that the shepherd's risk-taking points to Christ's work of redemption on the cross, and the joy of the shepherd confronts critics, who should rejoice instead of criticize.[20] Robert Tannehill underlines verse 7's theme of Lukan repentance, which is "more an experience of being found by a concerned seeker than the product of human effort. And its public sign is joy at the gift of new life rather than doleful remorse."[21] Fred Craddock comments, "These texts were written not simply out of historical interest in the religious community surrounding Jesus but primarily because these texts addressed a church with the problems herein associated with Pharisees."[22]

These comments interact with my own exegesis, helping me to deepen or correct my own insights.

So Take the Risk

It may still seem impertinent to emphasize personal immersion in a text, diving in at the deep end, *before* reading commentaries. Yet what I dare to practice as a preacher is based on a conviction that God empowers me through an open Bible within his 360-degree dynamic. Prayerful exegesis (with or without *lectio divina*'s exercises) always requires personal commitment and spiritual courage. Phases 1 and 2 may easily occupy one or two hours or more. But I testify that the more time I spend here, the more I am alive within God's 360-degree dynamic. Whenever I allow busyness and panic to send me straight to commentaries, the sermon always loses life and authenticity. Of course, I cannot prepare without benefiting from others' scholarship in phase 3.

I keep track of my investigations by using sheets of paper. In the left column, I respond prayerfully to the text, verse by verse. In the right column, I note questions, answers, and insights that seem significant and that surprised or troubled me. I try to address the entire range of questions in phases 1 and 2, and my jottings record my progress. Then in phase 3 my work is affirmed, rejected, or redirected before I begin stage 2.

9

Stage 2:
Interpret for Today

Haddon Robinson winsomely recalls a disastrous sermon he once preached on John 14. He did his homework, but

> five minutes into the sermon, I knew I was in trouble. At the ten minutes mark people were falling asleep. One man sitting near the front began to snore. Worse he didn't disturb anyone! No one was listening. Even today, whenever I talk about that morning, I still get an awful feeling in the pit of my stomach.[1]

What went wrong? He says he spent the entire sermon wrestling with tough theological issues. It was all valid teaching material, but it did not speak to his audience's life questions. Preaching involves both sound exegesis *leading out* from the text, expressed in biblical terms and theological language, and a main impact *leading to* the hearers, expressed in accessible language and attention-grabbing images.

SW? and YBH?

Two questions confront preachers as they move from exegesis toward their hearers. SW? asks, So what? of preaching. Older, well-behaved churchgoers do not often ask this, being polite and having sometimes stoically endured lifetimes of listening to near pointlessness. But those not yet committed in faith, especially younger people, can ask pointedly at the end of a sermon, "I gave you my time—so what?" A common complaint about much current preaching is that it spends over 90 percent of the time in the Bible world and less than 10 percent in the contemporary world. People make comments such as, "Why did the preacher spend so long going over what we already knew?" "Frankly, it didn't seem relevant to me." "It had solid subject matter, but it never took off." "It was just so predictable and flat."

YBH? asks, Yes, but how? A sermon may be delivered with great passion but leave hearers wondering how any of it applies practically. Some preachers seem to be more effective at calling for the first steps of repentance and faith (perhaps by giving an invitation) than at subsequent applications for lifelong discipleship. Genuine application often requires courage from preachers. As Bryan Chapell writes, "Preachers know instinctively what makes application the most difficult part of preaching—the rejection we invite by being specific."[2] He calls this specific point of application the "breaking point," when the preaching "turns" to affect the congregation. Hearers can opt out during vague principles but are less able to dodge practical consequences. As preachers move on from exegesis, they need to be alert to the responses that God is calling for today. The Holy Spirit is the great applier of God's Word, but he needs consecrated, bold preachers who know and love their hearers in order to sharpen his specific challenges.

The lack of YBH? in many sermons is all too transparent. David Mains goes so far as to say that while many hearers can tell you what a sermon subject was, 80 percent of hearers are unable to tell you what response the preacher was looking for. Thought-provoking and biblically sound sermons can still end in midair with no practical outcome. Mains believes that the primary reason for this 80-percent failure is that biblical preachers want to remain textual, but since the "how to" is often not obvious in the text, they fail to give it due attention.[3]

It is not that the Bible is boring or irrelevant. Far from it! But when a preacher treats a biblical text in a vacuum, sealed off from contemporary questions and concerns, hearers can feel disconnected and unmoved. Unless a preacher deals critically with contemporary life, a text's application can seem like an afterthought or, worse, can appear utterly trivial. This in turn makes the text seem even more distant and less important. Preachers must listen not only in the past tense but also in the present tense.

Unavoidable Hermeneutics

Earlier, hermeneutics was defined as "the method and techniques used to make a text understandable in a world different from the one in which the text originated."[4] Hermeneutics answers the SW? question. Gaps have to be bridged not only between the Bible world and the present but also within the text itself. Great care must be taken with even the most apparently straightforward text.

In Luke 15:1–7, for example, the text's meaning is inextricably bound up with its meaning to Luke and to his first readers. Contrast Luke's setting with that of Matthew (18:1–14), who placed this story in a different context about leaders restoring erring people. Different emphases are made as the story is written for different situations. Biblical preachers with a commitment to a high view of Scripture will continue to stress the importance of divine intention and also to recognize the role of human authorial intention—what did Jesus mean and Luke convey in Luke 15:1–7?

Biblical preachers also need to acknowledge how much they bring to texts based on their personalities and experiences. Influential voices can be both negative and positive. But preachers live in a hermeneutical community of faith in which voices may be heard and understood by the Holy Spirit's interpretative power. Interpretation of Scripture involves the Triune God of grace working in preachers, who bring to a text all that they are—their experiences, culture, prior understanding, senses, and imagination—in order to listen in the present tense.

Listening in the Present Tense

David Schlafer lists five voices that may influence preachers: Scripture, the preacher, the congregation, the cultural environment, and worship. Of course, they are not of equal value, as if they have voting rights and can join ranks to outvote Scripture. Any suggestion that voices can temper or overwhelm Scripture must be rejected. Scripture's voice is the dominant one, and nothing must compromise or dilute it.

However, employing the other voices reflects the preacher's stance *under* the lordship of Christ yet *within* contemporary culture. The notion of five voices alerts preachers to communication complications in changing culture and safeguards preaching from simplism. Some of the voices, especially that of culture, may seek to contradict and deny the primary voice of Scripture, while others may resonate with it, sensitizing and deepening its message. "The spoken word of the sermon is both an orchestration of, and a response to, the many voices to which good preachers are constantly listening."[5] Schlafer calls this "sacred conversation." Michael Glodo invites preachers to develop the "hermeneutic of imagination," which, rooted in rigorous exegesis, maintains a balance between unrestrained imagination and truth's freedom.

> "Taking every thought captive to Christ" (2 Cor. 10:5) should restrain our autonomous imagination. But approaching the Bible under the freedom of the truth (John 8:32) should also be a fantastically liberating experience, imaginative faculties included.[6]

Stage 2 seeks to answer the question, What's the main thing God wants to say and do through the preaching today? What, by the grace of God, is going to be the sermon's main impact? Robinson claims that "sermons seldom fail because they have too many ideas; more often they fail because they deal with too many unrelated ideas."[7] Too often preachers heap up points rather than simplifying and clarifying them. Their sermons sound like buzzing, random conversations without a distinctive message sounding through. One thing has to drive the entire preaching event.

Robinson calls this one thing the "big idea." Others refer to it as the central idea, central proposition, theme, thesis statement, subject, master idea, or main thought. I prefer to call it the "main impact." Terms such as idea, central idea, proposition, or thesis statement sound too cerebral, as though they are concepts for the head alone. Instead, I want to emphasize that both head and heart are involved, for Scripture both *says* and *does* through its focus and function. The word *impact* accentuates a text's eventfulness and nowness. A text both declares truth and evokes a response in experience and behavior.

Stage 2 comprises three phases:

Phase 4: Listen now
Phase 5: Sharpen the main impact
Phase 6: Throw in possibilities

Phase 4: Listen Now

Listen Now—to Scripture

Scripture's voice is of paramount importance, and all others are heard in relationship to it. Having listened to what the text said and did in the Bible world, preachers now listen to what it says and does in the twenty-first century. Having investigated the original context through exegesis, preachers now explore similar questions in their contemporary context. To use the swimming analogy, preachers now focus on the way in which the flowing river may impact its surrounding landscape.

Some of the wide-screen and close-up questions can be asked again about the text in relation to the contemporary world. How is it written? now asks about the passage from a twenty-first-century experience. Are there parallel ways of expression that resonate today? What corresponding issues can be found in hearers' lives, and how can the text's theological issues be heard in faithful ways?

How do close-up insights, such as those parts of the text that "surprise" or "trouble," relate today? What responses from different characters are relevant? What images and metaphors grab attention? The most important questions are What do you hear this word of God *say now?* What does it *do now?* The focus and function identified in exegesis (stage 1) are essential to interpretation in the present tense (stage 2).

What a text does has a great influence on a preacher as he or she seeks to be sensitive to its flow, mood, and movement. As Fred Craddock describes it:

> A mother talking to a child is not just saying; she is doing, as is a physician at a bedside, a comedian before an audience, a politician before a crowd, friends over dinner and a preacher in a pulpit. As things are being said, persons are informing, correcting, encouraging, confessing, celebrating, covenanting, punishing, confirming, debating or persuading.[8]

David Day provides a range of options concerning what a Scripture text might do: foster an attitude, correct an error, provoke a disclosure, encourage the dispirited, and celebrate the truth.[9] All these and more happen in Scripture.

As Luke 15:1–7 demonstrates, there are generally more than one focus and function, and preachers need to be alert to the possibilities. In a recent class exercise with this passage, students identified the following as they worked through stage 2:

Saying	Doing
God's call to repentance	Challenges people to faith/repentance
God's extravagant joy	Encourages celebration
God loves sinners	Challenges those who feel unloved
God's concern for individuals	Personalizes evangelistic challenge
God's concern for the lost	Corrects error of the self-satisfied
God's rebuke of the self-righteous	Rebukes those who look down on outsiders

In my personal exegesis and commentary work on Luke 15:1–7, my preliminary focus and function were: Jesus warned self-righteous religious people about missing God's joy, and Jesus rebuked complacent, joyless religious people about missing God's joy. Now, as I listen in the present tense, I recognize myself and many of my hearers in the Pharisees' role. I reflect how we, like them, can miss out on the truest kind of joy—the "being found by God" type of joy. The first hearers would have followed the logic of verses 3–6 and been mystified by and angered at the sudden twist as Jesus tells them that they are missing out. I am also impressed at how this apparently simple story remains subversive dynamite today as it conveys revolutionary joy. It urgently calls religious people not to miss the joy. Somehow, my eventual sermon needs to inculcate joy.

While several foci and functions may be genuine outcomes of exegesis and interpretation, eisegesis continues to lurk dangerously, offering false possibilities of foci and functions. For example, eisegesis might concentrate on the neglect of ninety-nine sheep because the shepherd puts all his energy into finding the one that is lost. Its focus: God's priority is the lost, not the found. Function: rebuke a church organization that concentrates on the found! This presumption about the fate of the ninety-nine would miss the story's purpose. Commentaries would show this to be an unsafe option.

As Scripture's voice is more clearly defined by determining the passage's focus and function, preachers also need to listen to four other voices.

Listen Now—to the Preacher

As we have seen, the person of the preacher is pivotal for preaching. Incarnational preaching uses words in flesh. Each preacher, with a unique swimming style and an individual journey through exegesis and interpretation, brings his or her own gifts and personality mix. The three circles that connect knowledge, skills, and character are like preaching fingerprints. At best, a preacher's spirituality can be transparent so that the gospel can be seen, but at worst, it can conceal God's message beneath ego, laziness, and prejudice. As David Schlafer describes it:

> Temperament, educational and vocational experience, family history, special interests, secret sins, unresolved resentments, unhealed wounds, fond hopes and faint ambitions—all these add color to what the preacher says and what the congregation hears.[10]

In *Your Way with God's Word*, Schlafer describes a preacher's voice as his or her "signature" that develops and modifies over time.[11] He invites preachers to discover their own voices through examining aspects such as language, culture, personal relationships, and faith communities. He asks them to determine if they are poets (preferring images), storytellers (preferring stories), or essayists (preferring arguments). He invites them to consider their "preaching parents" and how past wounds, joys, and fears may have affected them. Schlafer also calls for theological reflection about their experiences of God. He argues that only when preachers know where they are comfortable can they reach beyond their comfort zone.

Preachers need to use creativity, constrained by rigorous exegesis, as they work out possibilities for a sermon's focus and function. Scripture's rich images invite the "hermeneutic of imagination." Thomas Troeger claims that imagination is a skill that preachers can develop by being attentive to what is.[12] "If we examine the imaginative work of artists and poets, we discover that they have drawn the raw materials of their creativity from close observation."[13] He likens these observations to having video replays in our heads that "become receptive to the Holy Spirit, who works upon our consciousness through patterns of association and juxtaposition."[14] David Day comments, "The connection between the ancient text and the contemporary world is not procedural but poetic, not mechanical but metaphorical. I have to bring something of myself to the text."[15] Yet this bringing of myself requires acute self-awareness and submission to God.

As I prepare to preach on Luke 15:1–7, I am increasingly aware that this story challenges my own personality and perspectives. Which side appeals to me most—the "grumbling righteous" or the "found sinner"? Though I prefer the latter, honesty compels me to recognize that I might be on the other side. And when it comes to joy, can I truthfully say I have experienced joy of any kind recently? What biblical images resonate with me and why? Am I in danger of overemphasizing something? Which part is difficult for me, and am I trying to avoid it? Have I prayed and reflected enough? Has my study been rigorous enough, or are the pressures of getting a sermon written forcing my hand?

Listen Now—to the Congregation

Schlafer warns that listening to the voice of the congregation is not about deciding how to say what people want to hear or do not want to hear. Rather, it involves trying to address people with realism—as and where they really are. It involves wrestling with SW? and YBH? questions.

Such listening can be reinforced in several ways. First, there is the pastoral relationship between preacher and congregation. From this privileged position preachers can hear their community's heartbeat. No other profession is as involved in critical moments of joy and sorrow. Fred Craddock warns preachers against patronizing hearers by making presumptions. He suggests that they should sometimes deliberately distance themselves by asking what they do *not* know about their hearers. "The audience for this sermon next Sunday will be men, women, young people and children whom I do not know. Their lives and experiences are totally their own, unrelated to who I am and what I do." He recommends writing down what is not known to ensure respectful treatment so that afterward "even strangers will likely say to the preacher, 'You understand us quite well.'"[16]

Second, preachers can engage in research. Wide expanses of a congregation's activity can be alien to a preacher's experience. For example, workplace issues rarely surface in many sermons. Mark Greene writes of national research in Britain that shows that Christian workers feel unsupported by the church. "47% say that the teaching and preaching they receive is irrelevant to their daily lives."[17] A personal poll of Christians revealed that half had never heard a single sermon on work, and 75 percent had never been taught a biblical view of work or vocation. Preachers who are oblivious to workers' issues cannot relate Scripture to them. Greene calls preachers to preach with "worker's eyes"—to experience the daily work of congregational members by visiting them and listening.

Third, there is the empathetic approach. Some preachers try to assemble a group in their imagination to represent different perceptions and experiences. With empathetic imagination a preacher can attempt to see through different eyes: single parent, teenager, college student, married person, childless couple, single person, and so on.

Fourth, preachers can formalize listening by meeting with small groups who bring reflections, concerns, and interests into dialogue. Several ways of collaborating were identified at the end of chapter 7. Practitioners of this method often express initial surprise at the variety of voices and the range of feelings, including frustration and alienation, anxiety and tension, celebration and optimism. This process costs much in time and energy but proves invaluable in sermon preparation.

In my last pastorate, I worked with a group in this way and marveled at members' eager responsiveness to my exegesis and interpretation and their creativity. Eventually, drama, testimony, song, recitations, and pictures were interwoven with the spoken word. The group's purpose was not primarily to provide illustrations and applications (though often they did). Rather, the members offered a richer variety of responses than I was capable of as a solo preacher. My own listening to Scripture became much more sensitive through listening with them. Schlafer comments on his experience of this process: "While the organizational development, images and sentence constructions of the sermon were my own, the meaning had come forth from the shared dialogue of the community."[18]

Some of the observations I have shared concerning Luke 15:1–7 emerged from small group interactions in a preaching class. Some students focused on the text's joy, while others heard it as sober rebuke of their own attitudes. Listening with them revealed Scripture's multidimensional challenges.

Listen Now—to the Cultural Environment

Popular culture wears many faces that are indicative of deeper issues. Preachers need to listen within their cultural environments so that Scripture's voice can be heard clearly and relevantly.

Each church possesses its own "cultural mix." Rick Ezell suggests a way in which local churches can identify their target audience.[19] In his Naperville church, he created the profile of "Naperville Norman and Nancy" by closely examining geography, demographics, values, as well as spiritual data. Such research enables preachers to lock on to their target audience and therefore fire the "right arrows."

Generational differences are also readily apparent in popular culture. In *The Three-Eared Preacher*, Mark Greene devised a congregational questionnaire that focused on these differences.[20] Questions included: What magazines do you read? What radio programs do you listen to? About how many hours of TV do you watch a day? What are your three most popular TV programs? Small groups containing representatives of the various generations can ensure greater sensitivity to the voices within culture.

Generational differences also reveal deeper issues of culture shift and orality. The Millennials (born 1981–present) have known only postmodernity and are characterized by the following features: They yearn for experience; authenticity; genuine relationships; holism in worship and in life; mystery, wonder, and awe in personal spirituality; and local stories that make sense of their own stories. Many of these characteristics relate to secondary orality, in which stereo communication fuses conceptual language and symbolic language.

Preachers have to stay in touch with culture in order to develop insights about the times. Bill Hybels lists his weekly reading: *Time, Newsweek, U.S. News & World Report, Forbes,* and *Business Week.* Every day he reads the *Chicago Tribune* (*USA Today* when he travels) and watches at least two TV news programs. "When I say, 'On *Nightline* two nights ago, Ted Koppel was talking with . . .' [the listener] says to himself, *I saw that! I wonder if he felt the same way about that as I did?* and he stays with me."[21]

Only when preachers stay alert to the world, in which God's Word has to be heard, can there be incarnational preaching. If they fail to discern the spirit of contemporary culture, they become false prophets; if they fail to speak words heard in contemporary culture, they become irrelevant prophets.

As I prepared to preach on Luke 15:1–7, a news event about nine miners trapped in Pennsylvania captured the nation's attention. Many said that rescue was impossible, but after seventy-seven hours, on July 28, 2002, the nine miners were pulled from a rescue shaft. One miner, Blaine Mayhugh, was interviewed on the *Late Show with David Letterman* wearing a shirt that said, "God has blessed us—9 out of 9." The president called for prayers of thanks to God. The television images and happy outcome spoke volumes to me about spiritual issues of rescue and redemption. I realized that this event could be of value in my sermon on Luke 15:1–7.

Listen Now—to Worship

Preaching belongs within the worshiping community as it progresses from Advent to Christmas, Epiphany to Easter, Trinity to Pentecost. Themes and moods develop along the journey of the Christian year that can greatly influence sermon preparation.

Preachers also need to be sensitive to the rhythm of worship's ebb and flow—through praise, penitence, Scripture reading, intercession, offering, and communion. Some worship planning teams prepare the weekly liturgy and share a common vision and aim with the preacher. David Peacock says that such teams should ask, What do we want to give God the opportunity to accomplish in this service? He lists some of these different outcomes:

> Praise, understanding, inspiration, spiritual and practical help for the next week, unchurched encouraged to return, confession, communion, heart response to God's love, greater awareness of needs of others, commitment, recommitment, intimacy, the immediacy of God's presence, filling and empowering of the Holy Spirit, healing: physical and spiritual, correction and rebuke, teaching and learning.[22]

Peacock claims that between one and three of these outcomes will usually be appropriate for each Sunday.

Different worship contexts can be visualized for a sermon on Luke 15:1–7. I could develop the lectionary's complementary readings: Deuteronomy 4:15–24 and 2 Corinthians 1:12–22.[23] A multigenerational family worship service might provide an opportunity for a lost/found drama. If worship concludes with communion, the theme of table fellowship could be emphasized.

Phase 5: Sharpen the Main Impact

Sermons should always have one good idea. Throughout stage 2, there has been one purpose in listening to different voices: What does God want to say and do through the preaching today? What is the main impact of the sermon going to be? Preaching must convey vital truth if it is to evoke an alternative reality. Such preaching needs a clear objective.

Phase 5 crystallizes this main impact. Clarifying what should be said and done in a sermon is one of the preacher's most difficult tasks. Yet it is the most critical exercise for effectiveness. Nothing is more urgent than identifying the one thing that matters for the sermon. This determines its design and outcome.

Preachers line up to testify how difficult this undertaking is. John Jowett, a Congregational British preacher of the nineteenth century, confessed, "I have a conviction that no sermon is ready for preaching, not ready for writing out, until we can express its theme in a short pregnant sentence as clear as a crystal. I find the getting of that sentence is the hardest, the most exacting, and the most fruitful labor in my study."[24] Richard Bewes says, "This is the hardest part of the preparation, understanding the elusive 'one thing' that God is saying in this passage, and will be saying through your talk in a few days' time. At times you will become desperate in your inability to see the passage straight, and you will find yourself on your knees praying, pleading, scanning; then taking a break to clear your head."[25] As Charles Simeon reputably said, "Any fool can make simple things complex, but it takes a wise person to make complex things simple." Actually, it takes a wise person with the help of the Holy Spirit.

The Holy Spirit has been involved at every stage so far in the 360-degree preaching model. He was instrumental in exegesis and interpretation, and he continues to have prime responsibility in this clarifying process, especially by "internalizing" God's message for a preacher. Nothing substitutes for this personal experience of God's Word that makes it urgent within. Preaching should burn in a preacher's bones first. It is a burning *in*, not a burn *out*. Burnout happens when a preacher attempts spiritual fireworks without the Spirit. Burn in is when a preacher so attends to the Word that he or she comes alive within it. An unmistakable inner reality accompanies the Spirit's work in preachers' lives. The Spirit convicts a preacher of Christ's cleansing, forgiving, reconciling work and of the message's significance. He inspires imagination to break mediocrity's shackles as light gleams on the Word rather than on the preacher. Through the work of the Holy Spirit a preacher grasps the import that "we do not proclaim ourselves; we proclaim Jesus Christ as Lord and ourselves as your slaves for Jesus' sake" (2 Cor. 4:5).

The Holy Spirit is the sermon designer par excellence. As James Forbes describes his experience:

> Sometimes it is so exciting to have the Spirit guiding me as I prepare to preach that I have to stand up and walk around a little bit because it is so hot, so intense, when the anointing brings the collaborator into the process of "getting the sermon out."[26]

Though a sermon's main impact can be expressed in many different ways, a preacher must work within God's dynamic for *one* of these ways to be effective. Throughout it is the Holy Spirit who convinces preachers that their messages are spiritually significant and motivates their highest commitment. He chastens laziness by driving preachers to try again and again. He frees preachers to be their own persons by grace. He enables risk-taking—with less paddling in the shallows and more venturing into deeper places. He works to lessen preachers' natural ways with words and to increase God's way with words. He sensitizes preachers to love their hearers. First Corinthians 13:1–3 warns that a gifted church, in spite of its impressive ranking of leaders, apostles, prophets, and teachers, only makes noise unless there is love.

Supremely, the Holy Spirit inspires homiletical risk-taking—a daring to preach fresh words never heard in the same way before. The Spirit never despises or excuses hard work and always invites preachers to be willing to say and do new things in his strength. He gifts preachers to kindle interest and commitment in hearers. Helmut Thielicke condemned preachers' self-protection: "This passion to safeguard ourselves is not inspired by the Holy Spirit, it is based merely upon fleshly anxiety."[27] Indeed, Thielicke described Spurgeon as "the shepherd who was content to allow his robe . . . to be torn to tatters by thorns and sharp stones as he clambered after the lost sheep."[28]

The Holy Spirit has first place in design. As I enter phase 5, I recommit myself in prayer to his work as collaborator. I imagine, as I am carried along in the flow, that the Paraclete comes alongside me, deepening my understanding and enriching my imagination by adding images, words, and events. He guides me toward a single, all-encompassing impact that will embrace all secondary points, illustrations, and applications.

At the conclusion of phase 5, a preacher should be able to fill in the blanks in this sentence: By the grace of God, what this sermon will say is . . . and what it will do is . . . This sentence acts as the focal point for sermon design and delivery.

Defining the main impact is pivotal for all that follows. Encapsulating the Scripture text's focus and function profoundly influences how a sermon will be designed so that it has the *same* focus and function. Thomas Long originally used these terms, *focus* and *function*, for this express purpose. He defined *focus* as a "concise description of the central, controlling and unifying theme of the sermon" and *function* as "a description of what the preacher hopes the sermon will create or cause to happen for the hearers. It names the hoped for change."[29]

My preparation on Luke 15:1–7, through phases 1 to 5, has resulted in a focus and function that can now be expressed by a main impact: By the grace of God, what this sermon will say is that religious people had better not miss God's rescue joy, and what it will do is invite hearers to experience God's joy in being rescued.

Phase 6: Throw In Possibilities

Once the main impact is clear, the preaching swim goes into a critical phase much like entering whitewater rapids or plunging over a waterfall into a whirlpool. Every new sermon is a fresh swim in different crosscurrents and undertows through which a preacher needs to move to let a particular text be heard. What should be included? Still immersed in Scripture and hearing many voices around, a preacher encounters thoughts and images while talking with others, driving, reading a newspaper, watching TV, seeing a movie, listening to music, or just walking the dog.

I call this the throw in possibilities phase (more respectably called generative thinking).[30] All kinds of ideas bubble out of the main impact as preachers swim through churning currents of ideas. Each preacher's swirl of ideas, images, and applications is highly individualistic. Nobody else has ever been in exactly the same situation—this is going to be a fresh word to a new time. The way in which people's creative juices flow is also personal. Some people need quiet and paper; others need noise and action. Stroking the cat, relaxing with children, gardening, making bread, brainstorming with others in groups, or listening to loud music—preachers need to foster whichever creative process works best for them.

Mark Galli and Craig Larson suggest that preachers can cultivate the right frame of mind for spontaneity. Factors contributing to healthy creativity include a strong sense of mission, a dread of repetition (creative people are "repetiphobes"), joy, curiosity, and wonder.[31] These elements flow out of a preacher's interconnected three-circle spirituality, which interprets insights from the many voices of congregation, culture, worship, and experience. You can never predict outcomes as the Holy Spirit orchestrates these voices within and around a preacher. Given enough time and prayer, creativity can be profoundly stimulated as the Holy Spirit opens eyes to happenings that are from God, brings to mind other Scripture passages, and testifies to significant truths.

As noted earlier, a failed listener makes an uninteresting preacher, and gifted preachers are characterized by an irrepressible curiosity and interest in all they see. All effective preachers are good observers and realize the patience and self-control required to note details of observations immediately after they occur. A conversation at a checkout counter, a story at the hairdresser, a smile that transformed a situation, or a glimpse of something wonderful in personal devotions must be captured, or it will be lost.

Recording observations, therefore, requires a disciplined system. In common with many communicators, I keep a succession of notebooks in which I record observations, conversations, moments of human experience, and unlocked memories. Whenever something strikes me as potentially significant, I record it, without knowing if it will ever be used. Newspapers, magazines, books, television, movies, and plays are also sources of ideas. I cut out stories in newspapers and magazines and store them loosely and chronologically in boxes. Every time I open notebooks and files, they spark memories, weave images, and stimulate connections. Periodically, I wade through cuttings and weed out those that have lost their freshness. More methodical preachers develop systems to record their resources such as a card index system or in computer files. Each preacher needs to find a method that works for him or her.

In addition to personal collections of preaching materials, there are many ready-made resources, especially compilations of sermons and illustrations on-line. For busy preachers, such resources can provide genuine help, but only *after* they have completed exegesis and interpretation. Preachers should never substitute these resources for their own observations and experiences, which, rooted in their own communities, have a ring of realism that is often missing from other resources.

As I look at the ideas that have surfaced in regard to Luke 15:1–7, I keep the main impact in the forefront of my mind. I keep asking, What is truly important among these many ideas? I jot down key references such as Isaiah 53:6, which is about stray sheep, and Psalm 1:5, which is about sinners not being welcome among the righteous. I find that certain ideas have grown in significance among my notes: Jesus is in conflict with religious people; Jesus has table fellowship with sinners; God searches for and finds human beings; there is joy in heaven over one repenting sinner; those who do not repent miss out on the joy.

I especially need to emphasize that God's rescue is the most important thing in our lives. Luke 15:1–7 has sparked thoughts about rescue stories. I write some down, including my own. As I reflect on it, I wonder whether I have forgotten its joy. Could it connect with the text in a worthy way? What about other rescue stories of people I know? How might contemporary religious people miss joy? What are the kingdom implications when people think they are righteous?

Many other ideas swirl around me as I work, travel, shop, see films, and listen to music. Lance Armstrong, a cancer survivor, has just won his fourth Tour de France cycling title, and having just read his autobiography, *It's Not about the Bike,* I wonder whether his act of overcoming adversity and his joy in winning could somehow be a counter plot to Luke 15.

Galli and Larson offer six categories of what they call "prime receivers" that provide material for preachers: true stories, fictional stories, generic experiences, images, quotes, and facts. The Lance Armstrong story fits into the first category. Generic experiences might include "feeling lost stories"—who among us hasn't experienced the desolation of a child separated from his or her parents? Images connect through TV, video, and film.

This part of the preaching swim occupies much of my week, and nothing is off-limits as a potential contribution. I am caught in the flow of God's Word for the contemporary world. As scribbles fill the page, I move to the next stage.

10

Stage 3:
Design the Sermon

> When you have finished your sermon, not a person in your congregation
> should be unable to tell you, distinctly, what you have done; but when
> you begin your sermon, no person ought to be able to tell you what you
> are going to do.
>
> Ward Beecher, quoted in James Black, *Mystery of Preaching*

If you take a thousand preachers and give them each the same Bible text,
keep them from collusion and plagiarism, allow them to simmer with
the Holy Spirit for several hours, and then encourage them to deliver
their sermons to their congregations in their usual styles, what will the
result be? Nothing less than a thousand different sermons, each varying
in terms of content, length, style, and apparent outcomes.

Why so many? Because, baldly stated, each of these preachers has a
different personality, experience, and gifting; each has engaged Scripture within a different context; each has responded to culture shift and
orality change differently; and each has designed a sermon for his or her
own listeners. Each comes to the design stage in a unique way. Each is
at a different point on the sermon spectrum (fig. 6). This is the wonder
of sermon design—every passage has the potential to come alive with a
different shape, color, texture, and outcome.

Like the dry bones in Ezekiel's vision (Ezekiel 37), the bones of a message need God's breath to assemble them, to cover them with flesh, and
to energize them. All the hard work of exegesis and interpretation ushers
in a new happening. A sermon has to be born. This design stage perplexes

my students more than any other part of sermon preparation. Often they complain, "I've done my Bible work and had thoughts about a sermon, but I just don't know how to plan it—to get illustrations, to make an application, or to come up with a gripping introduction. How can I come up with something to say on Sunday?" That is the cry at the heart of stage 3.

This idea of sermon uniqueness sounds frightening to any cautious preacher. It implies risk-taking, swimming further out than ever before, daring to do something new. Yet it is the possibility of uniqueness in sermon design that most demonstrates 360-degree preaching. Preaching empowered by Father, Son, and Holy Spirit has the potential to impact people unlike any other form of communication. It comes alive because God connects it, breathes on it, and enables it to transform particular people at particular times and places. The same occurrences will never recur, and within them, truly, anything might happen.

Some people express concern about emphasizing the uniqueness of design, worried that preaching may become an artsy-crafty, people-pleasing exercise rather than a telling of the gospel as it is. After all, the command in 2 Timothy 4:1–3 seems straightforward. Why not just do it?

In John 12:49, Jesus with a loud voice makes an extraordinary claim: "For I did not speak of my own accord, but the Father who sent me commanded me *what* to say and *how* to say it" (NIV, emphasis added). Jesus describes his own speaking mission: "The Father who sent me commanded me what to say." Yet he makes a further distinction—"and *how* to say it." A preacher immediately recognizes the difference between the content—the what—and the way in which it is communicated—the how.

Both content and design matter to the Lord. Christian preachers sometimes appear to spend most of their energies on the what, as though how they present the message is so effortless it requires little thought. Just do your Bible work, sprinkle it with active language, spice it up with lively illustrations and applications, and smile! David Day warns about expecting a "preachable message [to] pop out, like toast from a toaster into our hands."[1] John 12:49 reinforces how different these two parts of preaching are. A sermon's how always calls for acute understanding of where people are in culture. When culture is in transition, preaching design is even more vital.

Homiletics Defined

Technically labeled "homiletics," this design stage has been defined in a variety of ways. "It is the science of which preaching is the art and the sermon is the finished product."[2] "The art and science of saying the same thing that the text of Scripture says."[3] "The study of sermon preparation, thus establishing an unbreakable link between the sermon and a right understanding of the meaning of the text on which it is based."[4] However it is defined, homiletics marks a distinct process in preaching. Whereas stages 1 and 2 concentrated on arriving at the message—what to say—homiletics moves into the process of how to say it. It is as though, after being immersed in the text and having come through waterfalls, rapids, and whirlpools, the preacher comes upon several river branches, and he or she needs to pursue one of them.

Fred Craddock suggests that all preachers should have this statement on their desks: "The task of sermon preparation is this: the process of arriving at something to say is to be distinguished from the process of determining how to say it."[5] He claims that many dull and unimaginative sermons are caused by a preacher failing to understand that these two tasks cannot be collapsed into a single process.

Sermon Structure

Sermon design involves three elements: content, structure, and delivery. Already we have seen how content develops as a preacher listens to various voices and a sermon's main impact stimulates a wide range of possibilities. Inevitably, content influences structure just as structure affects content; delivery has an effect on both. Consideration of sermon delivery will be delayed until the next chapter, when some of its implications for design will become obvious.

Sermons are no different from other forms of public speech in their need for structure so that hearers can sense order and progression. Thomas Long defines sermon form as "an organizational plan for deciding what kinds of things will be said and done in a sermon and in what sequence."[6] Arguing that such a plan is about forming communication rather than shaping information, he further defines it as "a plan for the experience of listening, not just an arrangement of data."[7]

Earlier I stated that several sermon forms are legitimate for biblical preachers and illustrated some sermon options on a preaching spectrum (fig. 6). In the design stage, a preacher chooses which options along the spectrum best fit the sermon (fig. 9). Much depends on the Scripture text's genre and on the person of the preacher. Is it going to be a mainly deductive, mainly inductive, or narrative sermon? Will it use technology to dramatize images?

Long claims, "It has become increasingly clear that a sermon's form should grow out of the shape of the gospel being proclaimed as well

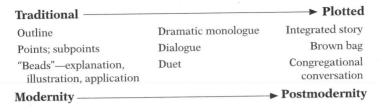

Fig. 9. Spectrum of Sermon Designs

as out of the listening patterns of those who will hear the sermon."[8] Many sermon forms are possible along the spectrum, beginning with mainly deductive and concluding with plotted forms. Murray Frick illustrates several possibilities.[9] The dramatic monologue allows for personal identification with a character, such as the innkeeper in the Christmas story. The dialogue sermon involves a conversation between two speakers, which he illustrates with a dialogue between a burdened preacher and God. The duet sermon involves two readers in which one begins with a question, passage, or poem, and the other responds with a related or contrasting piece. His example contrasts readings from Job with Elie Wiesel's *Night*. The letter from home is styled on Garrison Keillor's hometown stereotypes. Frick tells the story of the widow's mite (Mark 12:38–44) in this style. The brown bag sermon involves members of the congregation writing down questions to which a preacher can respond on the spot or prepare for other occasions. The congregational conversation invites participation that can be spontaneous.

Some of these types are becoming more common. Bryan Wilkerson gives a good example of dramatic monologue when he narrates Luke 2:1–20 in the first person as a shepherd.[10] He begins:

> "Whoa-oa-oa-o. Would you look at those stars! There's Orion, and the Pleiades, a shooting star . . . and another one! Aah, I will never get tired of looking at the night sky."

As the shepherd describes his circumstances, listeners are led to reflect on Christmas in new ways that surprise with their depth of content.

Tim Stratford describes how his congregation has learned to cocreate preaching with him. Sometimes a sermon contains preplanned questions and answers from the congregation, but other times the hearers help create the sermon event. In a Passion Day sermon on Mark 10, in which Jesus goes to Jerusalem for sacrifice, Stratford begins by asking what sorts of sacrifices his hearers have made. Stratford reflects positively on how "there was no more incarnational entry into Passiontide than what this occasion offered."[11]

It is also appropriate to add various uses of illustrations and applications along this spectrum. Traditional sermons often provide an illustration for each point. These sermons resemble beads threaded together, each of which takes the form of explanation, illustration, or application. Mainly deductive sermons can also be divided into two parts: first the doctrine and second its application.

As preachers move across the spectrum, inductive and plotted sermons integrate applications into their very shapes and patterns. Perhaps preachers use "hook" sentences to keep high levels of interest and make passing references to contemporary events or familiar images. Sentences that begin with "Did you see . . .?" or "Have you noticed . . .?" grab attention and bring hearers into the preaching event. In narrative sermons, applications occur throughout a story, perhaps a retelling of a Bible story, which has its own power to influence listeners as they make it their own story.

Long provides a useful summary of some stock sermon forms:

1. If this . . . then this . . . then this—the logical building of steps suited to teachers.
2. This is true in this way . . . in this way . . . and also in this way . . . and in this other way—when the central claim needs to be heard in different ways.
3. This is the problem, this is the response of the gospel, and these are the implications—the classic pastor preacher's structure sometimes called the problem-solution form.
4. This is the promise of the gospel, and here is how we may live out that promise—begins with the claims of the text and suits herald preachers.
5. This is the historical situation in the text, and these are the meanings for us now—a dialogue between the Bible world and the contemporary world.
6. Here is a prevailing view, but here is the claim of the gospel—this has similarities with the Lowry loop in which hearers' equilibrium is upset.
7. Here is a story—which offers a variety of narrative forms.[12]

Paul Wilson offers another way of summarizing different forms by depicting their "profiles" as they move to and fro between text and contemporary world.[13] He calls the main impact the central idea. Above it he places the biblical text and beneath it our situation.

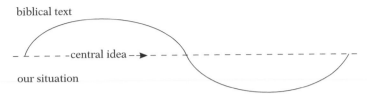

1. Move once into the biblical text and then apply it to our situation. This is a standard form of exegesis followed by application.

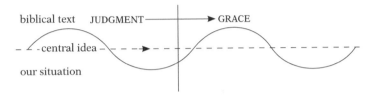

2. Move twice into the biblical text and twice into our situation. Wilson suggests that this is particularly appropriate when developing themes of judgment and grace. First, there is judgment in Scripture and then in our situation, followed by a similar pattern with grace.

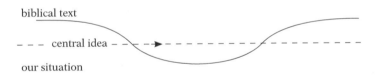

3. Move partly into the biblical text at the beginning of the sermon and complete the treatment of the text at the end. Here the contemporary situation is the filling in a sandwich, with the text forming the outer parts.

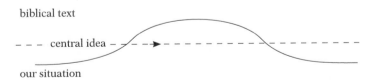

4. Move from an experience in our situation to the biblical text and conclude with an experience in light of the text. This is the typical inductive sermon that begins with the listeners' situation, moves to Scripture, and finally returns to the hearers.

5. Move several times between the text and our situation. Preachers should not include too many switches, but a number can add dynamism to preaching.

This brief examination of structure provides a framework by which to consider the four phases involved in sermon design:

Phase 7: Choose the sermon form
Phase 8: Throw out possibilities
Phase 9: Write a stereo draft
Phase 10: Test for impact

Phase 7: Choose the Sermon Form

In this phase, a preacher commits to a particular form for *this* sermon. Which possibility best communicates the exegesis and interpretation?

Beginner preachers must avoid the temptation to overcomplicate design and delivery with too much experimentation. The design process is complicated enough. Preachers first need to master didactic preaching. Teacher preachers decide on main headings that will do justice to the text's main impact. The design is conventional and orderly, containing a few main divisions (three is a popular number) and subdivisions, all placed in logical sequence. Each section supports the main impact and is proportionate to the other parts of the sermon, providing a sense of progression and movement. Illustrative material is added to the structural framework once the outline has been secured.

The traditional form's strength lies in its attention to rigorous exegesis and its user-friendly nature. Haddon Robinson's classic, *Biblical Preaching,* suggests working with the "homiletical idea" (similar to the main impact) in these steps:

While thinking about the homiletical idea, ask yourself how this idea should be handled to accomplish your purpose.

Having decided how the idea must be developed to accomplish your purpose, outline the sermon.

Fill in the outline with supporting materials that explain, prove, apply, or amplify the points.[14]

Robinson provides an example in Joseph Stowell's sermon on the three parables in Luke 15. The homiletical big idea is: "Indifference toward lost people is changed by a correction that produces a compassion that acts." His sermon is called "Who Cares?" and has the following outline:

    I. Careless corrections: Religious people do not care about the lost because of cultural and theological biases that lead them to a false perception of their own correctness.
      A. Culturally, religious people in Jesus' day believed it was not proper for them to associate with tax collectors and sinners.
      B. Theologically, religious people believed God loves "good guys" and hates "bad guys."
      C. We are not exempt from having our concern for the lost victimized by the same cultural and theological dynamics.
    II. A divine correction: Jesus corrects us by demonstrating that a holy and righteous God cares for and seeks after sinners.
      A. Lost people are a loss to God.
      B. Lost people have worth and value to God.
      C. Lost people left to themselves are helpless and hopeless.
      D. When lost people are recovered, heaven rejoices.
   III. Applied compassion: If we share God's compassion, we will act in compassion toward the lost.
      A. We will repent of our prejudice against sinners.
      B. We will own the task of evangelism.
      C. We will leave our comfort zone to seek the lost.[15]

Stowell's introduction "tells them what he's going to tell them," and through constant questions and everyday illustrations, he keeps hearers interested. He concludes:

The crowd around Christ on that day in Luke 15 must have felt he cared for them. I wonder if the world around me, those who are lost, sense that I am that someone who cares? People need the Lord.[16]

All who are called to be preachers need to practice as teacher preachers first. No preacher should move along the preaching spectrum without having developed basic outlining skills. Musicians need to master scales on instruments and read music fluently before they tackle dazzling heights of virtuoso performance. Artists have to master basic techniques of representation before they can become impressionistic. The mainly deductive form, with its outline and points, is the method of ensuring that exegesis is central and that a sermon stays close to the text, giving clarity to the message's purpose.

Next along the spectrum is the herald preacher. Jeremiah Wright demonstrates aspects of the herald model by linking Luke 15:1–7 with Isaiah 53:1–6 in a sermon called "The Good Shepherd."[17] He begins with a series of examples of how "Jesus talked very differently" and engages the congregation in the tension caused by "church folk" today acting as the Pharisees did in response to Jesus' different talk. The heart of the sermon identifies how "all we like sheep" get lost.

1. How do sheep get lost? Sheep can see only six feet ahead, so they get lost six feet at a time. He explains how people get lost little by little—by missing worship, reading the Bible less, engaging in a little gossip—until they are far away.
2. Sheep have no ability to find their way back. You cannot find your way back to the Good Shepherd.
3. You are lost, but God is looking for you.

He concludes by giving a powerful call to respond to the Lord, who "loves you back into his fold."

As preachers grow in experience and better understand culture shift, they will be motivated to use other sermon forms. The models of pastor and narrative preacher are more inductive in style.

Barbara Brown Taylor uses the narrative form in her sermon on Luke 15:1–7 called "The Lost and Found Department."[18] At the beginning, she stresses how "we love these stories because we imagine ourselves on the receiving end of them." She wonders out loud why the Pharisees "choke on their rage" and describes how offended they are at Jesus' treating sinners like special cases, "which is as good as condoning their behavior and thereby robs them of their motivation to do better. . . . All they have to do is wander off from the flock, pursuing their own whims, and the good shepherd will go off after them. It is not only bad shepherding; it is bad pastoral care. It is bad theology. . . . What about the good people? What about us?"[19]

She reaches a turning point. The parable is not actually about lost sheep but about good shepherds.

> Repentance is not the issue, but rejoicing; the plot is not about amend- ing our evil ways but about seeking, sweeping, finding, rejoicing. . . . It is about questioning the idea that there are certain conditions the lost must

meet before they are eligible to be found. . . . It's about discovering the joy of finding.[20]

Then Taylor develops an extended story about a ten-day wilderness hike she shared with fifteen people, one of whom, Pat, was unpleasant and uncooperative. When Pat was lost for eight hours, the trip leader set off to find her. She describes the joyful welcome Pat received. "We were too glad to have her back. Imagining her out there in the dark, we had all felt more than a little lost ourselves, so finding her was as good as being found."[21] The next day Pat was up first, now part of the flock. Perhaps the welcome had made all the difference.

In conclusion, Taylor says how difficult it is not to judge those who seem to capitalize on staying lost and how much she is tempted to concentrate on "good" people.

> Then I hear someone behind me who calls me by my name, and big brown hands grab me by the scruff of the neck, hauling me through the air and laying me across a pair of shoulders that smell of sweet grace and sunshine and home, and I am so surprised, and so relieved to be found that my heart feels like it is being broken into, broken open, while way off somewhere I hear the riotous sound of the angels rejoicing.[22]

If defining the main impact is the most difficult part of sermon preparation, then deciding on the sermon form is a close second. My work on Luke 15:1–7 has raised all kinds of possibilities, and I can see various design shapes. For example, I have two headings in my notes that do justice to the main impact and would result in a sermon with two parts: (1) God says, "Rejoice with me." (2) The sinner says, "Rejoice with me." This could convey much of my exegesis and interpretation. However, I also feel Jesus' parable challenging me to adopt a narrative approach, perhaps beginning with a modern rescue story with a dynamic of joy that might be transmitted to hearers. Eventually, I am drawn to a narrative form, though as yet I do not have the sermon's final pattern.

Should I begin with the passage's context of conflict, with the parable itself, or perhaps with a contemporary story? I try various possibilities to see how they might open up hearers to the parable and its joy. Since my main impact focuses on how easy it is to miss God's rescue joy, I need to make rescue joy palpable to my listeners. Because this is a familiar story, I need to express it in a fresh way.

Because the miners' story has grown in importance throughout my reflections, I eventually decide to begin with that. It raises the stakes about joy in rescue from the outset. I also plan a section on how Jesus told stories, for I need to alert my hearers to the special use Jesus made of parables. This lays foundations for emphasizing the passage's context of conflict and how Jesus provokes personal identification within the story. I know the main impact, joy in rescue, will become a spiritual challenge for hearers as the sermon moves to its conclusion. Before I write the sermon, however, I must move through phase 8.

Phase 8: Throw Out Possibilities

Complementing throw in possibilities, which generated a number of ideas at phase 6, is throw out possibilities (sometimes called evaluative thinking). At this phase, a preacher must employ disciplined thinking to select, edit, censor, and clarify. Many potentially good thoughts need to be rejected to ensure that the main impact is heard clearly.

The larger the number of possibilities, the greater the need to prune, subtract, and divide them. Creativity always results in too many ideas, images, metaphors, and stories. Preachers must identify the most appropriate possibilities and place them in the best sequence, and they must ruthlessly throw out the rest.

At this phase, the Holy Spirit continues to have a key role. After stimulating the creative ferment of generative thinking, he then wields a red pencil, helping preachers to cut out everything that confuses the main impact and obscures its thrust. He disapproves of quick fixes and sees through false motives. Creative people rarely enjoy losing good ideas and fight against wastage. But clarity and simplicity are essential for effective sermons, and they will never emerge without bold editing. Good preaching is characterized by what is not said almost as much as by what is said. Powerful sermons arise from courageous editing.

At phase 6, my preparation of Luke 15:1–7 was greatly enriched by generative thinking. But as a narrative structure begins to develop, I need to discern the best possibilities and reject the rest. Of the many reactions to the parable, I feel keenly the shock that it *wasn't* a happy ending for the ninety-nine who missed the joy. Yet above everything else, the redounding joy of God's rescue is palpable. Some of the stories I had thrown in need to be kept, especially the miners' amazing rescue. Others, such as the Lance Armstrong story, cannot be used this time. The phrase "God's rescue joy" seems apposite, but several other ideas need axing. This process of honing the sermon design is further helped by the next two phases.

Phase 9: Write a Stereo Draft

Though a few people seem capable of organizing a sermon in their minds, the majority of preachers need to put something down on paper. Part 1 of this book stressed the way in which people today respond with eyes and ears, needing both conceptual and symbolic language. Therefore, to avoid falling into an essay/lecture style, my script must have a clear structure, written both for the eye and the ear, emerging out of my holistic engagement with the text. At this phase of preparation, I turn to my computer to create such a script, which I call a stereo draft.

Writing a stereo draft is therefore paradoxical. It must be written as though it is not written! We have to learn to write the way we talk. Scripts do not just convey information but embrace symbolic language. For listeners, who have only one opportunity to catch the point, language, image, and metaphors must capture them in stereo.

David Day notes that when a piece is written for the ear and not just the eye, vocabulary moves down a level or two and becomes colloquial; sentences become shorter, and there are more of them; and direct speech pushes out third-person description.[23] Because few of us are used to writing in this way, it takes a great deal of practice. Yet once the stereo technique is mastered, it provides a powerful tool, ensuring that preachers have a good balance between active language and conversational ease, what Jolyon Mitchell calls a contrived casualness—"a spontaneity and casualness that are carefully constructed."[24] He calls preachers to paint word images with multisensory language that affects taste, touch, and smell. Clyde Fant warns about two "pulpit dialects." "Upper garble" strives for inflated grand language and "loses humanity in divinity"; "lower garble" "speaks to no one in particular about nothing in particular . . . [and] vaporizes each statement into a forcelessness."[25] People do not want to be preached at, nor do they want a vague conversation.

G. Robert Jacks shows how traditional rules of written grammar for the eye have to be broken and provides examples of rewrites so that people can better listen by ear. If you cannot hear yourself saying it, don't. His fifty rules include advice such as:

Advice 10: Remove unnecessary or assumable information and get to the point.

Advice 18: Avoid the "literary sound."

Advice 20: Avoid clichés.

Advice 22: Give us stories—from life, if possible.

Advice 45: Consider first person (we, I) rather than second person (you)
             for a positive tone.
Advice 49: Preach like Jesus—show more than you tell.[26]

A prime technique for writing a stereo draft is called testing for impact, which is the next phase in the preaching swim.

Phase 10: Test for Impact

Books on communication generally stress a stage called "rehearsal" when speakers try out a speech. This is not what phase 10 is about. It is not about a preacher learning finished lines but rather about shaping the lines themselves. Phase 10 forms part of the process of writing a stereo draft that requires preachers to hear their own words so that they write the way they talk, not the way they write. The best way to ensure that a sermon will impact hearers' eyes and ears is for preachers to preach to themselves, collaborating with the Holy Spirit.

When a preacher begins preaching a sermon to himself or herself, with the congregation in mind, the words come together differently. A vital phrase jumps out that was not originally in the script. Or what first seemed alive on paper comes across as boring. Words change order and emphasis. A particular heading that seemed to be the way to sum up a section is not gripping. It is clumsy off the tongue and too predictable. Frankly, some important parts of the script may just not work. Even more significantly, a preacher may find that entire sections need to be deleted or reordered. No written script, however skillfully organized, survives this test intact.

By testing a sermon aloud, preachers become their own listeners and experience their sermons. If parts are unclear to the preacher, they will be dull to listeners. With experience, preachers gain a sense of how best to pace sermons and to use repetitions and pauses to maximum effect. Perhaps a phrase can act as an echo at several points. Only through this process can a preacher create a genuine stereo script.

Phase 10 reveals much about my stereo draft on Luke 15:1–7. My introductory story needs shortening, and its joy needs emphasizing. A sentence hits me vividly: "When Jesus tells a story, it is always deeper, and you need to listen to its ending." This was not in my original writing, but I sense its potential for repetition. In my first draft, I concluded with three rescue stories: mine, yours, and the church's. In testing for sound, I discover a need to reverse the last two so that I end with yours. Many other alterations occur, larger and smaller, each one improving the sermon.

Beginnings and Endings

Two parts of a sermon draft are particularly important: the beginning and the ending. Like a moviemaker, dramatist, or novelist, a preacher should know the power of a good beginning. From the first words, hearers should expect that something significant is about to happen. Thomas Long claims that sermon beginnings should promise something of what is about to follow and express its value; language and tone should create fair expectations and lead directly to the sermon's next step.[27]

A sermon's first sentence or two deserves intense preparation. Is the introduction too predictable, trivial, patronizing, or just plain dull? Perhaps it is too sensational or too interesting, sending listeners off in a hundred different directions. Getting the beginning right is essential for at least two reasons.

First, a strong beginning provides a fixed point of seriousness. It immediately shows that a preacher is prepared and earnest. First sentences reveal a sermon's serious intention and invite hearers to sit up and take notice. "This matters to the preacher. I must find out more."

Second, a strong beginning helps a preacher cope with nervousness. Public speaking is often accompanied by nervousness, especially for inexperienced speakers. Butterflies in the stomach are always worst at the beginning of a speech and can rapidly settle down once it is underway. This early clutch of nerves emphasizes the importance of how a preacher begins. In some worship contexts, a preacher first prays, while in others there is an informal greeting or a word of thanks. After those first words, however, a preacher should pause before delivering the carefully chosen first sentences. Starting well settles nerves as listeners appreciate genuine preparation; their attentiveness in turn helps a preacher to grow in confidence.

Sermon endings also require attention. Traditional conclusions often summarize a sermon's main points and perhaps give an application or a final challenge to act on the message. Richard Bewes recommends this approach and suggests that a preacher allude to an earlier illustration, use a story or event in human experience, or end with a quotation.[28] In contrast, Paul Wilson condemns such endings: "If we think that the congregation will not grasp our meaning before the conclusion, it is time to rewrite the sermon, not write a summary." He warns preachers to avoid endings such as posed questions that are unlikely to be answered or remembered and quotations or personal testimony that "will leave a congregation with a consciousness of the preacher rather than the gospel." Rather, he commends endings that use simple, direct, concrete language.[29]

Endings clearly depend much on sermon design and on the person of the preacher. I tend to leave the ending's exact wording open, relying on God's empowering. Tying endings down can sometimes straitjacket God's outcomes. Of course, I have a general idea of what should be said, but I have often found specificity and intensity in my final words that can be explained only by the grace of God.

I recognize how dangerous this advice is. Some preachers lack the ability to bring a sermon to a timely closure. I recall one preacher confessing his failure to stop: "I just couldn't find a right place to finish but went on and on!" Long-winded conclusions are deadly to human spirit. A preacher with this tendency owes it to his or her listeners to nail down conclusions beforehand.

Advantages of a Stereo Draft

Stereo drafts have many advantages for preachers. First, they help preachers edit sequences to discover how ideas and images best flow together. Second, they capture stereo language. Through stereo drafts preachers can develop powerful and memorable expressions for ear and eye.

Third, they help with timekeeping. One of my doctoral students commented, "I try to get my sermon down to two thousand words on my computer. Then I know I've got about twenty minutes' worth at my pace of delivery." Of course, sermon length greatly depends on congregational expectations. But whatever the hearers' expectations, a stereo draft enables a preacher to quit *before* his or her hearers do.

A fourth advantage involves using technology for delivery. Testing for effect can make multimedia presentations immensely powerful. I can recall several occasions when words, images, and sound combined so effectively that the sermons are still clear in my memory. When a PowerPoint presentation has not been tested, however, the images can be merely irritating or distracting. A businessman said to me, "I have been trained professionally to use PowerPoint sparingly, where less is more—not like my preacher!" For technology to be effective, stereo thinking in stereo draft is essential.

Keeping in the Swim

During the throw in process, many ideas, stories, and possibilities were added in note form. The process of writing a stereo draft fleshes out the possibilities that survived the throw out phase. Their details must now be thoroughly researched, and language must be honed.

My sermon on Luke 15:1–7 begins with the Pennsylvania miners' rescue story, and I must attempt to tell it as grippingly as the press has done. Since the drama began, I have kept newspaper clippings from several sources *(Chicago Tribune, USA Today,* and *Wall Street Journal)* and made notes from TV programs. Stereo writing requires pertinent facts, real personalities, and believable description. In testing for impact, I decide to use the *Chicago Tribune* editorial on the rescue, and I need an accurate quotation. This tightening of the stereo script is moving me toward the preaching swim's fourth stage: delivery.

11

Stage 4:
Deliver the Sermon

All tasks completed. All targets met. All systems fully established, up and running. All preparation completed. All pigs fed and ready to fly.

a wall plaque

Delivering a sermon raises many issues that require attention long before that critical moment when a preacher stands in front of hearers. Many delivery modes are possible, and preachers need to decide which option to use.

Sermon Delivery Modes

The last chapter noted that three elements interact to influence sermon design: content, structure, and delivery. Having already considered content and structure, it is now vital to see how delivery affects sermon design. Another spectrum illustrates various delivery possibilities open to preachers. Note how the role of memory correlates with different styles represented in the diagram.

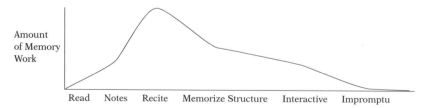

Fig. 10. Spectrum of Sermon Delivery

Delivery mode is often a highly personal matter for preachers, and preferences can change over time and within different situations. Some preachers are committed to reading full manuscripts, others to preaching without notes. New technology has influenced some preachers, such as my colleague who "thinks" his sermon into a limited number of Power-Point slides. Others work with teams to offer drama and video. Let's briefly consider six methods of delivery.

Reading a manuscript. At one end of the spectrum lie those preachers who write full manuscripts and then read them word for word. Read scripts guarantee vital language, graceful style, completeness of thought, and confidence before a congregation. Jonathan Edwards's early preaching remains an outstanding example of this form. But being tied to a script usually limits eye contact and can turn preaching into a lecture rather than a living encounter. Inevitably, teacher preachers with a cerebral style are much more likely to need full manuscripts. Minimal memory work is required for this method.

Using notes from a full manuscript. For this method, preachers first write a full manuscript, which provides confidence regarding a sermon's structure and content, and then summarize it by making a few notes (perhaps on cards). These notes include headings, important phrases, quotations, and reminders of illustrations. This method builds on disciplined preparation and attempts to provide some liberty in regard to eye contact and spontaneity. Yet its dependency on paper can still be a barrier. Of course, much more memory work is needed to recall details from a full manuscript.

Reciting a manuscript. Popular during the nineteenth century, memorizing a full manuscript results in tight, vivid language and maximum eye contact. Its gravest disadvantage, however, relates to the large amounts of time that are gobbled up by memorizing a script and the consequent danger of giving a head performance rather than one from the heart. A person who memorizes a sermon can all too often appear to be reading off an imaginary television prompter. Supposedly spontaneous, this method can easily distract with its unnaturalness. This delivery method inevitably requires the highest amount of memorization.

Memorizing the structure. This is my preferred method. Even though I have preached for well over thirty years, I generally write a full stereo draft, which allows me to test for impact and feel confident in its vital language, graceful style, completeness of thought, and ability to engage hearers. But as it is tested and continues to be shaped, its overall structure and certain key expressions eventually become so familiar that I can deliver the sermon without a script or notes. This method does not require total recitation. Of course, certain sequences and phrases should be memorized, such as the introduction and key points, but much is left open, giving preachers flexibility to respond to the Spirit's prompting. Obviously, the clearer a sermon's structure, the easier it is to memorize.

Interactive preaching. Preaching that actively involves a congregation requires an interactive delivery style. Such interaction may be spontaneous or invited. Jeremiah Wright, in his sermon on Luke 15:1–7, asked his large multiracial congregation to identify with the Pharisees as "church folk."[1] Every time he mentioned "church folk" he expected the congregation to echo "church folk" in a two-way rhythm that created effective interaction. Preachers who collaborate with others in design and delivery of sermons, especially when they employ technology, inevitably have more complex delivery arrangements that necessitate detailed planning.

Impromptu preaching. This method requires no preparation or advance thought about its delivery. It is "on the spur of the moment" preaching. Though such preaching often appears to be extemporaneous, in practice it often draws from a reservoir of previous speaking experiences replete with ideas, structures, and language. Words may indeed be fluent and fresh, but they emerge out of a deposit of themes and ideas. Little conscious memory work is required.

Of course, genuine impromptu preaching does exist. Some great preachers have a gift for extemporaneous preaching, but only after working hard on exegesis and interpretation. C. H. Spurgeon, for example, seems to have needed only a few scratched headings for sermons that held thousands enthralled. In fairness, his apparent photographic memory and remarkable spiritual gifting also helped considerably! For lesser mortals, impromptu preaching runs the risk of repetition.

The Importance of Developing Memory

Of all the choices on this spectrum, preachers should be discouraged from reading sermon manuscripts. Though common and convenient, this option actually flouts basic rules of effective preaching. How preachers preach is crucial within secondary orality. Ideally, twenty-first-century preachers need to develop their memories to the point at which they need no notes at all, though the majority of us recognize that we may fall short of that goal.

Joseph Webb advocates preaching without notes and gives three reasons for its effectiveness. First, it maximizes connectedness by creating the strongest bonds between speaker and audience. "Without notes, human passion is set free, and passion is as close to the cement of human bonding as we ever get."[2] Second, it maximizes participation because the audience senses that words are not preplanned as a sermon unfolds. Third, it gives authentic witness because it comes from a preacher's heart.

He argues convincingly that all preachers have a capacity to develop their "primary memory," that is, their short-term memory. Preachers should develop their short-term memories from the outset of their calling. Of course, other factors help this process, such as physical and mental health, an interest in the material, an ability to concentrate for periods of time, and clear, concise organization of material. By application and persistence, most preachers can extend their short-term memory spans. Webb describes how he works through sermon preparation and designs each sermon to serve short-term memory. He uses four half hour periods during this process when he repeats and memorizes key structural elements.

It is important for twenty-first-century preaching that preachers strengthen their short-term memory. Direct delivery, person to person, is vital for effective preaching. A mid position on the delivery spectrum—memorize the structure—is the most valuable preaching style for today.

Sermon delivery therefore comprises three phases, of which the first entails heavy commitment before the moment of delivery:

Phase 11: Memorize the sermon structure
Phase 12: Deliver with the voice
Phase 13: Deliver with the body

Phase 11: Memorize the Sermon Structure

At this point, many preachers feel an understandable weariness. "Surely," a preacher argues, "now that I have a tested script in my hand I am ready to preach it." Any preacher who has diligently swum down the preaching river this far has invested hours in study, reflection, listening, writing, testing, and designing. At this point, it is tempting to climb out on a near bank, dry off, and relax. Not so fast! Stopping now can cut short the sermon preparation process. Phase 11 is imperative for effective preaching and calls for more commitment so that the earlier hard work is not lost. Preachers have to keep swimming!

Memorizing the structure of a sermon requires preachers to go over their stereo scripts enough times so that they capture key points mentally. This involves memorizing the introduction, the sequence of major sections, and key points and vital expressions that may need accurate repetition. Rather than aim at total recall (recitation), preachers should retain enough of a script's content and flow to do justice to exegesis and interpretation while still being able to engage listeners face to face.

My own practice is to repeat a sermon out loud several times, stopping at those parts at which word choice appears strategic. I visualize how the sermon's main parts belong together and keep their order in mind. Certain sections may already be alive in my thinking and do not require special attention, but the opening sentences, key links, expressions, and quotations require memorization. Though in a preacher's early years this process can seem cumbersome, absorbing too much energy and time, with practice it becomes manageable and indispensable.

Few things disappoint more than listening to preachers who have clearly worked hard on their sermon scripts and yet are so tied to manuscripts that they cannot look up and even stumble over words. Preachers who have memorized the structure and key phrases can know both significant connectedness with hearers and flexibility. Their words can flow as they are open to God's Spirit within the 360-degree dynamic.

Phase 12: Deliver with the Voice

Some books on preaching presume that preachers possess sufficient inherent presentation skills. And some preachers mistakenly assume that delivery is of secondary importance to content. But this is not the case. Miss a preacher's voice, body language, and holistic engagement, and you miss the preaching event itself. A written sermon does not replicate the live experience of preaching. Even an audiotape or videotape can never substitute for personal participation. Ever since Jesus Christ came proclaiming, words have needed to be sounded out and responded to in flesh. Recall the command reverberating through the Gospels: "Let anyone with ears listen" (Matt. 11:15; 13:9, 43; Mark 4:23; 7:16; Luke 8:8; 14:35).

Through preaching, the Holy Spirit connects a preacher's mouth and listeners' ears. "The quality of the preaching is affected most significantly by the level of awareness of the movement of the Spirit shared by those in the pulpit and the pew."[3] The Paraclete collaborator sharpens words during a preacher's preparation, but for these same words to come alive in delivery, they need empowering and anointing, as do hearers' ears. Spiritual connections are necessary between mouth and ears, preacher and listeners.

Within 360-degree preaching, God's anointing is a powerful possibility, never presumed yet always anticipated. Tony Sargent describes an anointed preacher as one who is carried along by a dynamic other than his own. . . . He is being worked on but is aware that he is still working. He is being spoken through but he knows he is still speaking. The words are his but the facility with which they come compels him to realize that the source is beyond himself. . . . He is on fire.[4]

James Massey, in his study of communication and charisma, identifies certain hallmarks of the anointed mouth: a sense of assertiveness by which to act; a sense of being identified with the divine will; a perceived intensity; a sense of self-transcendence. "The anointed preaching carries the hearers beyond the limited benefit of the preacher's personality and rhetorical abilities. . . . It is a contagion between preacher and people."[5] This contagion is the intangible extra of God's working. D. Martyn Lloyd-Jones called this "the congeniality of the Spirit"—the willingness of the Spirit to help the sincere student of Scripture.[6]

However the Holy Spirit may choose to empower preaching, he still needs the dedicated use of a preacher's voice and body. Matters such as breathing, diction, and gestures need close attention. Sadly, nothing wrecks good content more than mumbled or confused delivery. A refusal to work on such things can utterly sabotage otherwise good preaching preparation.

I made a significant discovery in the 1980s when I took singing lessons in a forlorn hope of improving my singing ability. My teacher enforced a strict physical regime. During practice he made me stand erect, practice breathing exercises, and utter a bewildering range of noises in scales. All the while he prodded and poked my diaphragm. He was worryingly accurate about the amount of time I spent practicing daily between lessons. Through these rigorous lessons, I witnessed significant improvements in my breathing and voice control, which undeniably benefited my preaching.

C. H. Spurgeon was renowned for his fine voice; in pre-microphone days he held crowds of over 25,000 rapt. In lecture 8 of his famous *Lectures to My Students*, he advises preachers not to think too much or too little about their voices. Too much and they can forget the importance given to content. "A trumpet need not be made of silver, a ram's horn will suffice; but it must be able to endure rough usage, for trumpets are for war's conflicts."[7] But too little and the outcome can be endangered. "Exceedingly precious truths may be greatly marred by being delivered in monotonous tones."[8] He likened the voice to a drum, which should not be continually struck in the same place or a hole will be worn. Preachers need to develop a mode of speaking that does not come from the throat. He commended frequent preaching. "Twice a week preaching is very dangerous, but I have found five or six times healthy and even twelve or fourteen not excessive."[9] He understood the need to practice so that "your chest, lungs, windpipe, larynx and all your vocal organs may last you till you have nothing more to say."[10]

Much could be written on the use of voice, but we will touch on five basic questions: How are you breathing? What is your mouth doing? Are you standing properly? What is your modulation? What is your variation?

Good voice control depends on controlled breathing. All my preaching classes are put through video exercises with Charles Bartow, who demonstrates three levels of breathing: throat, upper chest, and diaphragm.[11] First, he shows throat breathing that is tight and restricted and can wear out vocal chords. He then invites students to stand and experiment with upper chest breathing; they place their hands under their ribs and feel the pressure of breathing in and out of the upper body. Finally, he encourages them to place their hands around their waists and learn how to fill the diaphragm. This kind of breathing is technically called intercostal diaphragmatic breathing. To attain it, posture has to be upright and relaxed and breath has to fill the lower part of the lungs. Simple exercises can help a person develop breath control such as counting as you breathe in (1, 2, 3, 4, 5) and then out (1, 2, 3, 4, 5). Though this is the natural breathing pattern, especially when sleeping, it must be developed intentionally for public speaking. Surprisingly, little air is actually needed as words are spoken, but the more the diaphragm is used, the less breathy and shallow is the sound.

Obviously, what the mouth does is also important for speech. Lazy diction comes from lazy lips, tongue, and mouth. Clear articulation and sound quality require open mouths and agile tongues. No amount of controlled breathing can compensate for half closed mouths and poor pronunciation.

The question of stance matters too. Good breath control requires a stable stance with legs slightly apart and comfortable uprightness. Leaning forward on a pulpit or being poised awkwardly over a microphone inevitably restricts the voice.

Earlier we noted the significance of modulation for stereo listening, and voice vibration plays a vital part. Out of habit, each of us develops a habitual pitch for our vocal chords, which is sometimes at variance with our optimum pitch, where our voices function best. Experts suggest that a person can find optimum pitch by using a piano and singing to the lowest note he or she can reach comfortably. Five piano keys higher is the pitch he or she should normally use. Of course, we cannot all expect to have velvety deep resonance. But we can improve our habits of voice modulation. G. Robert Jacks is convinced that speech is a habit and advocates many exercises to improve it. "God loves us enough to accept us just as we are. But He loves us too much to leave us that way."[12]

Among all these aspects of voice usage, however, one principle matters the most: variation. Variety is the most significant factor in sustaining interest. Effective speakers demonstrate variety in the following areas: rate, volume, stress, inflection, and the pause.

The rate of delivery is clearly important. Average rates of speaking are roughly 125 to 150 words per minute, though some people speak much faster. President John F. Kennedy once delivered a speech at 327 words per minute![13] An acceptable rate depends much on a speaker's experience, content, and context. Nervousness can speed speakers into babble or slow them down into dirge. With experience, both extremes can be avoided and a varied pace can be found that fits the content. For example, slowing down can emphasize more weighty statements. Mood affects rate too; sadness can slow down rate, but enthusiasm can speed it up. The size of an audience also makes a difference. The larger the group and the room, the slower the speaking rate needed to include everyone. In contrast, a small group in a limited space can be addressed at almost a conversational rate.

Variety in volume is also rewarding for listeners. When preachers first speak publicly, they are often surprised at how loud their voices sound to themselves. They need to find a balance of volume, for extremes of loudness or softness cause irritation for listeners, as well as problems for amplification systems. Yet volume can be appropriately varied throughout a sermon. When a significant point is about to be made, a preacher can use a steady, quieter tone to register authority. Such ups and downs of volume greatly enrich communication.

Variation in stress is also effective—emphasizing certain words so that they stand out from the rest. Nouns and verbs usually carry the most weight and therefore need stressing, especially when qualified by an adjective or adverb. In contrast, other words need to be stressed less. Some inexperienced speakers stress too many words or get into a pattern in which stress acts like a seesaw, which Jacks calls the "teacup effect."[14]

Inflection describes the way in which phrases and sentences rise and fall. Upward inflection indicates a looking forward, a question, or doubt. Downward inflection shows that an action is completed and suggests a sense of closure and confidence. Preachers can vary inflection to great effect.

It is arguable that the most useful speaker's tool for providing variety is the pause. The role of silence is consistently underrated in speaking. A pause at the beginning of a sermon establishes a critical connection with a congregation—it creates serious intent. Throughout a sermon, rather than filling gaps with ums and ers, betraying sloppy preparation and a need for thinking time, a preacher should use intentional pauses that give depth and intensity to the entire preaching event. Well-placed pauses show experience and confidence. They also assault monotony and boredom by helping to vary the rate of delivery, marking changes in volume, and increasing the value of stress.

Phase 13: Deliver with the Body

Attending to the voice is only half of the challenge of delivery. Public speech involves both voice and body. Behavioral science uses the term *kinesics* to describe the interaction between what a voice says and what its owner's body says. Obviously, confident words delivered with confident body language are much preferred to confident words betrayed by awkward body language. According to some statistics, words have a relatively minor role in communication: Seven percent impact comes through the words themselves, 38 percent through the voice, and 55 percent through the facial expressions of the speaker.[15] Whatever the exact proportions, it is undeniable that preaching is much more than words and voices.

The chief way the body communicates is through eye contact. Failure to look at hearers suggests a lack of confidence or that a speaker is unprepared or distant and aloof. John Stott comments, "Look at your people face to face and eyeball to eyeball. Never spray the building with words."[16]

Inexperienced preachers often find it takes prodigious effort to maintain eye contact. It is always easier to examine the far corners of the room, jerking the head from right to left, or to look down at one's notes. Since gazing directly into listeners' faces can be mutually awkward, eye contact is most effective when used more generally. For example, a preacher can look at one section and then another in a large congregation rather than isolating and focusing on one individual.

Facial expressions are extremely important too, as evidenced by the growing use of big screens in larger venues. According to one book, our faces are capable of 250,000 different expressions.[17] Undeniably, facial expressions convey much to listeners, especially the smile. Nothing improves a beginning more than a natural smile. Often, in the pause before I speak, I deliberately establish eye contact and smile. Doing so says volumes about the quality of relationship I anticipate during the preaching event. While speaking, faces need to match words. Solemn issues need solemn faces. Thoughtless facial expressions can undo preachers, especially inappropriate smiles triggered by nerves that contradict a sad moment or scowls that undermine a bright message. C. H. Spurgeon reputedly said, "When you talk about the Savior, let your face light up and shine. When you talk about sin, your normal face will do."

Gestures are movements that accompany speech. Some are unintentional, such as wild hand movements, rocking on the balls of the feet, scratching one's nose, or irritating mannerisms such as rattling keys or coins. Because preachers are inevitably unaware of how distracting these gestures are, they need early encounters with an honest critic or a video camera (or both). As with habits of the voice, unhelpful gestures can be moderated. In contrast, however, intentional gestures can add greatly to a preaching event. Some movements complement words such as stretching arms wide to express inclusivity.

Movement can also help or hinder communication. Some speakers deliberately move around as they speak. Indeed, the design of buildings, platforms, and stages sometimes encourages this, and radio microphones allow high mobility. Other preachers prefer stationary delivery or are tied to it because they use notes. How much a preacher moves depends greatly on personal style, audience expectations, and the amplification system. Both mobile and static deliveries have advantages and disadvantages. Continuous movement can certainly add energy but may tend to wear out listeners. Static delivery can increase dullness but lessen distractions, particularly when accompanied by an appropriate use of eyes, face, and gestures. Preachers must determine the most appropriate, comfortable, and practical style for each context.

All this advice about a preacher's voice and body presumes a fairly traditional approach to preaching. At various points in this book, however, I have encouraged collaborative teamwork and the use of technology. Though I strongly believe in a range of delivery styles and that multimedia resources can add to the preaching event, no amount of electronic wizardry can substitute for inadequate exegesis and interpretation or flat language and dull delivery. Creative presentations cannot conceal an absence of content and spiritual dynamism. Involvement with others and technical know-how can never dismiss the need for preachers to offer the best of voice and body. When they do, preachers, by the grace of God, can witness the positive outcomes of preaching.

12

Stage 5:
Experience the Outcomes

Christian preaching, at its best, is a biblical speaking/listening/seeing/
doing event that God empowers to form Christ-shaped people and
communities.

This final stage crowns the entire purpose of the preaching swim. Preaching is about new things happening, about dead bones coming alive, about God's Word making a difference—returning to him (Isa. 55:11). If nothing happens, it is a waste of breath.

The 360-degree model places as much action *after* the preaching event as before it. Since preaching nourishes renewed life for preacher *and* hearers, everyone should be caught up in the message's impact. I picture this last stage as a joyous mass splashing! Preachers, having immersed themselves in Scripture and preached on a passage's main impact, are joined in the river by listeners plunging in from every side to experience the grace of God. Instead of standing safe (and dry) at a distance, hearers have been drawn by the power of God's Word into fresh experiences together. No longer is a preacher alone in his or her immersion in Scripture; rather, he or she is thronged by others who have heard, seen, tasted, and acted on God's good news. What is more, the dynamic of God's Word is carrying them along together to new places of worship and mission.

Something of this celebrative experience is captured by Frank Thomas. He declares, "The African American sermon was designed to celebrate, to help people experience the assurance of grace that is the gospel."[1]

He defines preaching as "a spiritual gift given by the Holy Spirit to help the church and the world receive and celebrate the good news of Christ."[2] Preaching leads to an exuberance that involves head and heart. "Celebrative design does not intend to move people for the sake of moving people; rather it intends to move people as part of the process of impacting core belief."[3]

How prepared are most listeners to plunge in and participate in this way? Earlier we read George Sweazey's controversial claim that "the skills of the hearers are more important than the skills of the preacher." He went on to argue that hearers "need their own instruction in homiletics. . . . They need to know what the whole idea of preaching is."[4] To say that hearers' skills are more important overstates the case. Yet at the same time, when Jesus called for active listening (as in Mark 4:23; 7:16), he was urging people to respond with minds, hearts, and lives. Hearing words and not putting them into practice is like a foolish person building a house upon sand (Matt. 7:26). Just as believers should love God with all their hearts, souls, minds, and strength (Mark 12:30), so hearers need to respond with all that they are and have.

Of course, preachers have the prime responsibility to ensure that good news is just that. As they exegete, interpret, and design, they need to be conscious of their listeners' context, making connections and applications. But hearers have a critical task too. Too few listeners understand their essential role in 360-degree preaching, and preachers must find ways to alert them. Preachers need to preach about preaching—about how listeners need to respond with heart, soul, mind, and strength.

To do so, preachers must realize that congregations often contain a variety of listening types. Murray Frick generalizes about three groups found in contemporary congregations: those who respond visually and often sit at the back of the church in order to see the big picture; those who respond audibly and sit in the middle so as not to miss anything; and those who sit at the front and respond kinesthetically, preferring to be drawn into the experience by participating physically.[5] Pierre Babin's concept of stereo listening is also helpful when considering listening patterns. Some people respond to conceptual language, while others respond to the symbolic.[6]

Whatever their listening pattern, however, listeners must take some responsibility for their role in the preaching event. In a sermon titled "Good Listeners Make Better Preachers," I gave listeners four challenges. First, prepare for worship expectantly. All worshipers, the preacher included, should make space and time for genuine prayers of preparation (Ps. 24:3–4). "True worshipers will worship the Father in spirit and truth" (John 4:23). Spiritual insensitivity to God before worship promotes spiritual insensitivity during worship. Rather, expectations should be raised that Father, Son, and Holy Spirit are at work. Preachers can share Scripture texts and themes in advance and invite listeners to prepare by reading and reflecting on them. In spite of the clutter of activity before an act of worship, preachers need to model stillness, seriousness, and anticipation (Ps. 46:10). The more preachers practice the presence of God in 360-degree preaching, the more listeners will prepare with them.

Second, listen with all your mind. Active listening involves a willingness to participate mentally with a speaker, to question and interact with a sermon's points and flow. Though the average person speaks at a rate of 125 to 150 words per minute, the average person can listen at a rate of up to 500 words per minute, a difference that allows the mind to wander. Sherwyn Morreale and Courtland Bovee offer several strategies for improving active listening that can be applied to preaching.[7] Improving concentration involves focusing on the speaker, following the words, anticipating the next point, and testing what has been said so far. Focusing on verbal and nonverbal clues involves looking at a speaker's face, posture, and gestures. Withholding judgment means not jumping to conclusions but listening to the whole. Managing personal reactions involves resisting prejudice because of past experiences with certain topics, people, and styles. And taking notes is a practical way to discipline the mind. Many churches, especially those that publish worship bulletins, provide aids for listeners in the form of sermon outlines.

Hearers need to widen their responsiveness by heeding a third challenge: Listen with all your heart and soul. Spiritual engagement always involves more than cognitive and intellectual responses. In Luke 15:1–7, Jesus' parable not only describes the reason for real joy but also expresses God's joy that it may be experienced afresh in repentance. A sermon should stir hearts as the Spirit brings people to full conviction.

And the fourth challenge is: Listen with all your strength, for full conviction should lead to behavioral change. Acting on the words is like building on rock through consistent, daily living that can survive storms (Matt. 7:24–27). Worship should not be concentrated into an hour on Sunday; rather, it should flow through daily living Monday through Sunday. What counts is practical obedience, with all one's strength, to what God calls one to be and to do this week. Preacher and hearers must experience the sermon's main impact so that it makes a difference in their Christian living.

Sometimes, banal comments can follow a sermon, such as, "Nice sermon, pastor!" What tragedy if that is the sum total of reaction. In some traditions, specific responses are expected. In Southern Baptist churches, for example, preaching is associated with "walking the aisle." Salvation Army citadels have their "repentance benches." In a growing number of charismatically influenced churches, invitations are given to "receive ministry." Sometimes an outcome is specific to a particular sermon, as with Tony Campolo's concluding challenge for young people to offer themselves to mission service (described in chap. 3).

More often, however, outcomes are less visible and much more complex. Effective preaching is about long-term formation of Christ-shaped individuals and communities within the mystery of God's triune grace. When I preached my sermon on Luke 15:1–7, I gave an invitation for hearers to receive ministry at the front (the custom of my church). I was aware of at least one direct faith response from an individual. Various conversations during the following week revealed that some listeners had told their own rescue story to others, and one or two were actively concerned about the way in which their busyness in church activities was causing them to miss God's joy. On first appearance it was just an ordinary sermon on an ordinary Sunday. Yet it was also a part of what God is doing week after week in people's lives. And over time that is a very big deal!

The Preacher's Responsibility

Stage 5 also involves preachers in a vital personal exercise of reflection and monitoring. Preachers often undertake this process on their own, though it requires considerable self-discipline and self-awareness. At best, reflection should include other hearers.

Understandably, relief and exhaustion may tempt preachers to excuse themselves from additional effort once a sermon has been delivered. Many preachers also seem to wrestle with personal insecurities when tackling sermon examination. Yet only by asking honest questions and by daring to ask what God said and did in the preaching event can a preacher mature.

Four Rs can summarize a preacher's personal discipline: reflect, review, record, receive.[8] Of these, the last requires the most attention.

Reflect

Through 360-degree preaching, God empowers spoken words to change lives, including the preacher's. Reflection involves asking what difference the sermon's main impact should make on the preacher's own life. Just as prayer was vital before and during the preaching event, so it continues to be important after. A preacher friend of mine was ill for several months and commented that enforced rest made him realize how little he had ever applied his own sermons to himself. Preachers need to be as open and responsive as they hope their congregations will be. Before moving on to the next sermon, preachers should let the one just delivered influence them.

Review

Improvements come by asking honest questions about each sermon event, and preachers have a significant vantage point from which to identify its strengths and weaknesses. Even while they preach, preachers know when something is connecting well or hearers are becoming fidgety. Perhaps one section was too long, too complex, or too rushed. Some preachers take this step to another level and review audio or video recordings. Probably few preachers actually enjoy this process, but as Richard Bewes says, "Faithful are the wounds of the tape machine."[9] He outlines some of the things that preachers should look for and seek to change: excessive length, clichés, unnecessary jargon, inept illustrations, distracting mannerisms, and stale presence.[10]

Record

The third task involves filing and recording the sermon. Computer files can simplify this process. On my computer I have created book and chapter divisions, one for the Old Testament and one for the New. Alongside each text I preach on, I record the title and the date of the sermon. When I wish to find a particular sermon, I first look up its Scripture reference, discover its date, and then locate it in the relevant file, where it is stored chronologically. Whenever a sermon has accompanying clippings or other materials, I put them together in an envelope and write the text, title, and date on the outside. These too are stored chronologically.

Obviously, some preachers have better organizational skills than others, but misplacement of materials can have serious implications when a particular sermon or idea is later needed and cannot be found. I need ways of retrieving helpful materials for future use.

Receive

Honest evaluation by others is essential for a preacher to grow. It is arguable whether praise or criticism does the most damage to a preacher. Praise can too quickly flatter and so deflect preaching's purpose to bring God's message to his people for his glory. But unkind criticism can also inflict damage, especially when a preacher feels vulnerable. Preachers should learn to benefit from comments when discerning people take the trouble to identify positive aspects as well as weaknesses. Such comments are far more valuable than those of naive well wishers, whose bland words may offer no insights and fail to stimulate better preparation.

Several encounters have benefited my preaching. On one occasion a visiting Old Testament scholar wrote me a long letter. After a word of encouragement (so often such letters begin like that), he gave a detailed analysis of my previous six sermons. I read his critique of my exegesis, interpretation, and application. Some of his comments were devastating. My first reaction was defensive: Didn't he know how hard I had to work in the rest of my ministry? But after a short while I recognized the immense value of what he had done. I genuinely thanked him, for nobody had taken the trouble to do this since I had left seminary fifteen years earlier.

This book has encouraged collaboration. Some in ministry are fortunate to have another team leader, perhaps a worship leader, who can help assess the worship event, including the preaching. For several years I benefited from team reflections every Monday morning. Undeniably, individuals need to be secure in their faith and to have good personal relationships with the team members for such a process to work well. Sensitivity is also required for giving and receiving preaching assessments. Levels of review will vary, from basic responses concerning what helped or hindered hearers to a much more demanding exercise that focuses on each stage of the preaching swim.

Each of my preaching classes creates its own set of criteria by which to assess the effectiveness of one another's sermons. Emphases vary from group to group, but always there are questions about faithfulness to Scripture, interpretation for today's listeners, main impact, design, quality of delivery, and what God said and did through the saying and doing of the preaching event. (Appendix C provides a sample evaluation form that preachers and their listeners can use.)

In these changing times, preachers need all the help they can get as they find themselves somewhere along the preaching spectrum. Nothing matters more than that they proclaim truth and continue to find even better ways to do so. Issues such as sermon focus and function are not niceties for the classroom but essentials for a church's good. God's Word must be spoken and not return empty.

Christ-Shaped Communities

This book has made grand claims about how biblical preaching can form Christ-shaped individuals and communities. Sadly, in practice, too much preaching recycles themes for the saints and leaves the world beyond the doors untouched. But effective preaching is and must be possible.

It is not uncommon for preachers to remember certain sermon series and themes that appeared to quicken church life. A discernible intensity and momentum seemed to coincide with significant events in a church's life. For me and many others in my ministry at St. Andrew's Street Baptist Church in Cambridge, one particular period seems to have been genuinely influential in the story of individuals and the community.[11] It dates from the beginning of 1990. After ten years of working, praying, and preaching, the congregation had already developed a mission center alongside the church sanctuary. It was open seven days a week, and through it the members fleshed out the gospel claims that were preached each Sunday. We called it "the laboratory next door" where we could work out our Christian faith and commitment in practical ways.

It was my practice to invite members of the ministry team and deacons to work on preaching themes for a three-month period. Themes were then presented to the church for endorsement. Sometimes, weekly house groups were encouraged to coordinate their Bible studies as follow-up to these Sunday sermons. One series was called "The Upside Down Kingdom."

From the outset of this series, there was a freshness and openness that surprised us. It seemed almost as though Jesus himself were seated in the middle of the church, confronting and inspiring us. There was a gusting veracity of Word that drew us into deeper places together.

The first sermon, based on the Magnificat, was called "Down Is Up" (Luke 1:46–53).

> Most of us are conventional, happily fixed in our own culture, where we've been brought up to do certain things in certain ways. So we try to make Jesus conventional and predictable too. We play it safe and over-spiritualize, concentrating on the comforting words of Jesus. If we come across revolutionary words, we try to avoid their practical implications, which might affect us socially, morally, politically, economically.[12]

How many times had we heard something like that before? But what made this time different was a sense that we were traveling toward new experiences as a community. We were moving toward a fresh edge of living in God's kingdom. The sermon titles sounded hackneyed, and the choice of texts was predictable. Yet we found ourselves pushed into discoveries together. "Blessed Are the Poor" (Luke 6:20) was followed by "Losers Finders" (Matt. 16:21–28). Other titles were "Loveable Enemies" (Luke 6:27–35), "Easy Yokes" (Matt. 11:25–12:8), "Last Is First" (Mark 9:33–37; 10:13–16), "Low Is High" (John 13:1–17), "Peace with a Sword" (Matt. 10:32–42), and "Unseen Is Seen" (Matt. 6:1–8; 10:24–31; 2 Cor. 4:16–18).

A refrain was growing Sunday by Sunday:

> When Christ comes among us, he turns everything that people thought about life upside down. Something new is happening among us right now. God says, "My kingdom is here. It's a kingdom of love and service. The least are the greatest, outcasts are welcomed, adults become like children, enemies love one another, leaders are servants of others."

A subversive yet infectious tone was discernible in our church life, in its worship, group meetings, and commitments. Some outcomes were specific and obvious. The entire fellowship committed itself to shelter some of the city's homeless in the main church hall. Fifty volunteers, many from our own church, offered to form teams to sleep on the premises and support them. Testimonies of new believers preparing for baptism spoke of belonging within a wider dimension of kingdom people. Visitors expressed joy at a tangible quality of togetherness in worship. And as the main preacher, I found myself both bruised and sustained by the demands of preaching to myself and my community in new ways, which exposed me to upside-down ways of living. At no time can I recall such disturbing personal wrestling, such vulnerability, and such answering grace in God's truth. I gained glimpses of the greatest possibility ever granted human beings that, when preacher and congregation commit together within 360-degree preaching, God makes things happen as entire communities participate in his mission to the world.

I am convinced that whenever the church's thinkers, leaders, pray-ers, visionaries, and prophets are also its preachers, there is fire in the land. Effective preaching makes for new kingdom reality. When preaching is biblically dynamic and culturally relevant—prophetic, incarnational, and transformational—and lived out by preachers and people, there is no force that can overturn it. Preaching at its best has always cocreated culture and evoked alternative realities by the grace of the Triune God. As generations of preachers have boldly responded to crises before, so God asks for fresh courage and commitment today. I believe that God can still transform through preaching. Let's offer our best to his transforming power.

Appendix A

The Preaching Swim

Stage 1: Immerse in Scripture

Phase 1: Prayerfully Read Scripture Aloud
Phase 2: Listen and Investigate
Phase 3: Check Out Investigations

Stage 2: Interpret for Today

Phase 4: Listen Now
Phase 5: Sharpen the Main Impact
Phase 6: Throw In Possibilities

Stage 3: Design the Sermon

Phase 7: Choose the Sermon Form
Phase 8: Throw Out Possibilities
Phase 9: Write a Stereo Draft
Phase 10: Test for Impact

Stage 4: Deliver the Sermon

Phase 11: Memorize the Sermon Structure
Phase 12: Deliver with the Voice
Phase 13: Deliver with the Body

Stage 5: Experience the Outcomes

Appendix B

Missing the Joy?

A sermon based on Luke 15:1–7 and preached at Wheaton First Baptist Church, August 11, 2002. This is the stereo draft I developed by adhering strictly to the phases of the preaching swim. I memorized its structure and key sentences. As is my custom, I deliberately left its ending open.

The last couple of weeks I couldn't get enough of the nine Pennsylvania miners' story. I guess it's because I have never forgotten going down a deep coal mine in South Wales as part of a high school trip. Its claustrophobic darkness, four-foot-high tunnels. I remember my utter relief to get back into fresh air. And it's not difficult to imagine the horror when they pierced an unknown underground reservoir and a four-foot-high wall of water rushed at them and began filling the tunnels as they backed up, scrambling to a dead end with the water still rising. How they tied themselves together so no one would die alone. They shared a single pen and a few scraps of soggy cardboard to write farewell to families. A lunch box went by—one corned beef sandwich, one bite each. They conserved lights, sitting, trying to sleep, praying. "Is it 8 in the morning or 8 in the evening?" The breakthrough when oxygen got to them—and the heartbreak when the bit broke and the drilling noise of rescue stopped and they thought the rescuers had given up. Many people thought it impossible. And when the rescue shaft opened up just near them. Seventy-seven hours. And the rescue capsule brought them up 240 feet—one by one into the fresh air, taking lungfuls, and blinking in the lights, the cheers and shrieks of the crowds, and the tears of their families. They tasted the sheer unadulterated wonder of being alive, saved. Joy like they'd never known before. Real joy. Joy in rescue. One miner, Blaine Mayhugh, a man of few words, was interviewed on *Letterman*. "I did think I was going to die. When I came up to all those lights, I can't describe what it meant." And he wore a shirt: "God has blessed us—9 out of 9." Not one missing. What a happy ending—I think that's why I have loved this story too.

Sometimes Jesus seemed to draw on stories in the news. The tower of Siloam fell in a local tragedy, and he speaks about that (Luke 13:4). It may just have been that a local shepherd went out on a rescue mission for one of his sheep. But sheep rescue stories don't sound that dramatic. They don't raise blood pressure. After all, a sheep is a sheep. I know our small children like stories about animals and even vegetables. But a sheep story? But when Jesus tells a story, it is always deeper. And you always have to listen to the ending. Sometimes it sounds really happy, but actually it isn't. We need to listen today.

Jesus lived in conflict. I think sometimes we forget that his ministry began with a fight in the desert with sweat on his brow against temptations that would have finished his mission before it started. And at the end there is a fight in the garden to do his Father's will, and sweat is like great drops of blood. And at every point in between there is conflict with religious people who know who God is and what God is like, and the one thing they are certain about is that Jesus has got it wrong about God. And the longer he goes on like this, mixing with the wrong people, blaspheming, the greater danger he is going to be to others and himself. In fact, he could even be executed.

Actually, we would have admired many of these religious people. Scribes and Pharisees have got a bad name, but many of them were fine people. Actually, Jesus went to eat with Pharisees (Luke 14:1). The majority of Pharisees and scribes were good, clean-living, honest, committed worshipers, perhaps saying grace too loudly at TGI Fridays, but scrupulous tithers, standing for the best in society—God's society, Israel. The very best. They believed they should separate themselves and their children from evil influences. They would recite Psalm 1:5: Sinners will not stand in the congregation of the righteous.

But it seems perversely wrong that this Jesus offends decency and eats with these other people too—dishonest, double-dealing, immoral people, some of whom were even against their society, God's society, Israel. Destructive tax collectors who sided against them—like Al Quaida sympathizers—seemed to be destroying the best. No wonder they grumble, and it's a joyless, negative word against Jesus saying, "This man welcomes sinners and eats with them. He's got it wrong about God."

And Jesus tells a story that the world will never forget. Just eighty-five words. A sheep rescue story. If it were anyone other than Jesus, we wouldn't have the patience. But it *is* Jesus, and his story is always deeper. And you always have to listen to the ending.

He makes it personal: Suppose one of *you* has a hundred sheep? He wants you and me to put ourselves inside the mind of an owner of a hundred sheep. Perhaps you're good with animals. Or you've never thought about sheep much before. One hundred seems quite a lot of sheep. I don't know if you count sheep when trying to get to sleep. I've never quite understood that. There's a current TV advertisement for a mattress in which a flock of sheep is all excited until they see a mattress being delivered. Their faces are full of disappointment. You've seen it?

Recent scientific research in Britain has established that sheep are much more intelligent than previously thought. In laboratory tests, they responded to individual names and performed intelligent tasks that showed them capable of memorizing complex issues.

But one is missing. Perhaps it would have failed the laboratory test. An owner knows this kind of thing. One. Are you sure? Count again. It's the one with the mark on its face. It's missing. How long? Who knows? Could be anywhere. Who cares? Leaving ninety-nine in the open country to find, what? Even if you find it, most likely it will be dead—picked off by hungry predators. Others could wander off. It seems such a waste of energy.

But it's what a good shepherd does who believes in the value of one. Perhaps he had begun his career with just ten in the flock—he will never forget each counts. Which of *you*? *You* go. (After all, this is about *you*.) You go after the lost until you find it. And you concentrate with all you've got. Not there. Try somewhere else. Calling out and listening. And then a pathetic "Baaaa" from way over there. And when you have found it, you lay it on your shoulders and let out a peal of laughter. This pathetic sheep with the mark on its face, so far away, so hopeless, failed to memorize complex issues, is now on its way back. And the shepherd makes light work of the return because when he gets back he's going to have a party. You know what's going to happen. He calls together friends and neighbors, all kinds of people—friends, the people you choose; neighbors, the people you don't. Whose dog barks at night. And he says, "Rejoice with me, for I have found my sheep that was lost."

When Jesus tells a story, it is always deeper. Because the sheep aren't just sheep. They are people (Isa. 53:6). Every kind of person. More intelligent than you might think. People who drift away. And the sheep owner is God, and Jesus has slipped you into seeing with God's eyes, just for once to glimpse what gives God joy. And we didn't know we were going to be asked to think and act like God. We didn't realize it was heavy stuff about his joy. And you always have to listen to the ending: "I tell you, there will be more joy in heaven over one sinner who repents than over ninety-nine righteous persons who need no repentance."

With Jesus the story is always deeper. And you always have to listen to the ending. Is it a happy ending? Not for the ninety-nine. They do not need to repent. They will not be rescued. They miss the joy. It's *not* a happy ending for the religious people at all who thought they knew who God is and what God is like and that they don't need this Jesus, like the tax collectors and sinners do.

Jesus means: You've got it wrong. You all need rescuing. And if you don't think you do, you will close out God's joy from your life. You'll have your religious practices, your sense of duty, your best behavior, but you'll have missed God's rescue joy. You'll have joyless regulations of religious behavior.

But you've seen it, haven't you? God finds joy in the rescue, the searching, finding, carrying, belonging. Whoever would have believed that God is like this if Jesus hadn't told us? God's rescue joy.

A *Chicago Tribune* editorial said, "Before we get distracted by the next crisis, we should take with us a lesson beyond the fact that nine Pennsylvania families still have the husbands, fathers and sons who were resurrected by their friends. Real success in this short life isn't measured by flashy careers or fancy houses or the inexorable accumulation of stuff." Isn't it? Most people think that's exactly what life is about. Careers, real estate, stuff. No. And real success isn't a lot of talk about God, and going to church, being religious, being respectable, and obeying rules and regulations either.

It's knowing you've been rescued, rescued properly—alive from lost to found, darkness to light, death to life. It's having life changed by God's rescue joy. There's nothing more important than that.

I don't know about you, but this makes me think very hard about essentials. I think several stories matter to us right now.

My Rescue Story

I think I have forgotten the wonder of my own rescue story. I was thirteen years old. You know the expression "miserable as sin." Well, it's true. Teenage angst of confusion. One minute conquering the world in my dreams, the next minute realizing I was nothing, not even to my brother. Struggling to be me without knowing who me was. And embarrassment about everything. How I looked, sounded. I had a speech impediment and had to go to a speech therapist. Life was horrible. Really I wasn't a bad kid, just typically mixed up and needing to find direction, and I knew there was a drift pulling me away from God. But brought up in a Christian family, I had heard about Jesus all my life. About him doing something for me that needed my response. His love, which had gone to a cross to bear away sin, my inside mess and all the rest of my life's mess, in order to rescue me. And I needed to invite him as Lord and Savior.

I can remember the spiritual struggle. Did I need to do this? My best friends at school didn't. Was it that serious? Actually, when I went down that mine in South Wales, I made a silly mistake. I wore a white shirt. I thought the miners were being friendly as they greeted me and patted me all over and guffawed to one another. At the end my shirt was dirtier than anyone else's. My life was like that—the longer I went on without Jesus, the dirtier and messier everything was getting.

I don't think I've spent enough time remembering the joy of my rescue. My prayer to Jesus: "Help me. I need you." My baptism. I can still see the colored tiles of the baptismal pool, the faces of my friends, the singing of the hymn's last line: "More of Christ and less of me." Taking lungfuls of eternal life. Sensing the celebration in heaven. My mother saying, "Michael, you are so different." It's true—the most important thing about me and you is the joy in the rescue. Sometimes I have forgotten my rescue, and I miss the joy.

Our Church's Rescue Story

I don't want us to end up on the wrong side, with the ninety-nine unable to be joyful about rescue. Some religious groups seem to forget the joy of the most important thing in our lives. Only a group of the rescued can know God's joy. Christian fellowship is one rescued person rejoicing with another and another, a rejoicing of a new kind of people living in a kingdom that has turned everything upside down. Instead of careers, real estate, and stuff, it's serving, and freeing, and rejoicing in rescue. Everything we're about as a church should ask the question, Will that bring God joy? Because there's nothing more important than the joy of rescue.

William Booth, founder of the Salvation Army, had a dream. He often spoke about it. He said he saw a dark and stormy ocean with terrifying sky and waves, with thousands of poor human beings plunging and floating, shouting and screaming. And then he saw a rock rise up with a vast platform at its base, and poor struggling wretches were jumping back into the water to help others. "But as the numbers grew," he said, "what puzzled me most was the fact that though all had been rescued at sometime or another from the oceans, nearly everyone seemed to have forgotten, and they didn't seem to care."

"Look for yourselves," said William Booth. "All who are not on the rock are in the sea. Look from the standpoint of the great white throne. . . . He is calling you to jump into the sea."

We have all been rescued, and we should care about the rescue of others and what brings God joy. Some of us have forgotten our rescue and we miss the joy.

I don't want to be on the wrong side and miss out on the joy.

Your Rescue Story

What's your story? Many of us have them. Don't forget the wonder of your rescue story. It's the most important thing about you. Tell someone again about it today. This week.

Some perhaps don't yet have a rescue story to tell. For some of you perhaps mine seems far-fetched or conditioned by my upbringing. Rather emotional. Unnecessary. The need to say to Jesus, "Lord, help me. I need you." Because you are not sure whether you could really believe in a caring God like this. Perhaps you've tried and it didn't seem to take.

Outside my church in Cambridge we had large posters at the door. Carol was responsible for writing them. One will always stand out in my memory: "Not many people love you just as you are, but Jesus does. Come in and meet him." And a student called Richard passed it every day on his way from college. Not religious. Never been to church. He said that he couldn't believe it. Not many people did love him. A broken home, disappointing childhood. High hopes to achieve academically. And he knew he should try, just once. And he came in, and it happened to be a believers' baptismal service. People spoke about their rescue, and in the challenge, he met Jesus. It didn't depend on anything human but on the spiritual reality of God's love in Christ. Later he told me his rescue story, about looking at that poster. Jesus does rescue today. It's true. The joy's real.

(Brief evangelistic challenge left unworded)

Appendix C

Sermon Evaluation

Name of speaker_____   Text_____

1. How prepared was the speaker?
2. How did the message relate to the Scripture passage? Did the message *come out of* the text? (Did it say and do what the Bible says and does?)
3. In one sentence, the main impact was:
4. In what ways did the structure and design move the sermon forward?
5. Were the introduction, ending, and illustrations effective? (Was the sermon interesting?)
6. How relevant was the message for today? (Did it connect with listeners?)
7. How effective was the delivery? (voice, gestures, mannerisms, etc.)
8. In what ways did you see evidence of integrity and commitment? (the preacher's own voice, etc.)
9. What outcome was experienced? (a call for action, celebration?)
10. One thing the preacher did well was:
11. One thing the preacher should work on is:
12. What did you get out of this sermon?

Your name_____   Date_____

Notes

Introduction

1. Charles W. Koller, *Expository Preaching without Notes* (Grand Rapids: Baker, 1962, 1964, 1997).

2. Quoted in M. Scott Peck, *The Road Less Traveled and Beyond* (New York: Touchstone, 1997), 13.

Chapter 1

1. George A. Buttrick, *Jesus Came Preaching* (New York: Scribner, 1931), 16.

2. Yngve Brilioth, *A Brief History of Preaching* (Philadelphia: Fortress, 1965).

3. Ibid., 10.

4. Ibid., 75.

5. See "prophetic preaching" in William H. Willimon and Richard Lischer, eds., *Concise Encyclopedia of Preaching* (Louisville: Westminster John Knox, 1995).

6. John R. W. Stott, *The Preacher's Portrait* (London: Tyndale, 1961), 9–11.

7. Sidney Greidanus, *The Modern Preacher and the Ancient Text: Interpreting and Preaching Biblical Literature* (Grand Rapids: Eerdmans, 1988), 1–10.

8. Quoted in ibid., 8.

9. Greidanus, *Modern Preacher*, 8.

10. James Forbes, *The Holy Spirit and Preaching* (Nashville: Abingdon, 1989), 37.

11. Colin Morris, *Raising the Dead: The Art of the Preacher as Public Performer* (London: Harper Collins, 1996), 2.

12. Quoted in John W. Doberstein, *The Minister's Prayer Book* (London: Collins, 1964), 424.

13. Peter Adam, *Speaking God's Words: A Practical Theology of Expository Preaching* (Downers Grove, Ill.: InterVarsity, 1996), 71.

14. Leander Keck, *The Bible in the Pulpit: The Renewal of Biblical Preaching* (Nashville: Abingdon, 1978), 67.

15. Karl Barth, *Prayer and Preaching* (London: SCM, 1964), 65.

16. Pierre Babin, *The New Era in Religious Communication* (Minneapolis: Fortress, 1991), 6.

17. See Andrew Walker, *Telling the Story: Gospel, Mission, and Culture* (London: SPCK, 1996).

18. Gerhard Friedrich in *Theological Dictionary of the New Testament*, ed. Gerhard Kittel, vol. 3 (Grand Rapids: Eerdmans, 1965), 703.

19. C. L. Wilibald Grimm in *Greek-English Lexicon of the New Testament*, ed. Joseph H. Thayer (Edinburgh: T & T Clark, 1901), 256.

20. Ibid., 144.

21. Ibid., 69.

22. Ibid., 139.

23. C. H. Dodd, *The Apostolic Preaching and Its Development* (New York: Harper, 1964), 8.

24. Craig Loscalzo, *Evangelistic Preaching That Connects* (Downers Grove, Ill.: Inter-Varsity, 1995), 54.

25. George E. Sweazey, *Preaching the Good News* (Englewood Cliffs, N.J.: Prentice-Hall, 1976), 5.

26. Bernard L. Manning, quoted in Horton Davies, *Varieties of English Preaching 1900–1960* (London: SCM, 1963), 183.

27. Harry E. Fosdick, quoted in John Killinger, *Fundamentals of Preaching* (London: SCM, 1985), 205.

28. Haddon W. Robinson, *Biblical Preaching: The Development and Delivery of Expository Messages* (Grand Rapids: Baker, 2002), 21.

29. Walter Brueggemann, *The Prophetic Imagination* (Philadelphia: Fortress, 1978), 111.

30. See Peter L. Berger, *A Rumour of Angels: Modern Society and the Rediscovery of the Supernatural* (Garden City, N.Y.: Doubleday, 1969).

31. Quoted in Doberstein, *Minister's Prayer Book*, 398.

32. Quoted in Jean-Jacques von Allmen, *Preaching and Congregation* (London: Lutterworth, 1962), 12.

33. Quoted in Doberstein, *Minister's Prayer Book*, 398.

34. Brueggemann, *Prophetic Imagination*, 13.

35. Ibid., 111.

36. William H. Willimon, *Peculiar Speech: Preaching to the Baptized* (Grand Rapids: Eerdmans, 1992), 17.

37. Robinson, *Biblical Preaching*, 20.

38. Ibid., 20.

39. David Buttrick, *The Mystery and the Passion* (Minneapolis: Fortress, 1992), 1.

40. Stanley Hauerwas and William H. Willimon, *Resident Aliens: Life in the Christian Colony* (Nashville: Abingdon, 1989), 166.

41. Keck, *Bible in the Pulpit*, 11.

42. Edwin C. Dargan, *A History of Preaching*, vol. 1 (Grand Rapids: Baker, 1954), 13.

43. Peter T. Forsyth, *Positive Preaching and the Modern Mind* (London: Hodder & Stoughton, 1907), 3.

44. Paul S. Wilson, *God Sense: Reading the Bible in Preaching* (Nashville: Abingdon, 2001).

45. Brilioth, *Brief History of Preaching*, 22.

46. Ibid., 49–54.

47. Ibid., 60.

48. Martin Luther, quoted in ibid., 110.

49. Ibid., 111.

50. Babin, *New Era in Religious Communication*, 25.

51. Ibid., 24.

52. Richard Molard, quoted in ibid., 25.

Chapter 2

1. Thomas G. Bandy, *Coaching Change: Breaking Down Resistance, Building Up Hope* (Nashville: Abingdon, 2000), 70.

2. Thomas C. Reeves, *The Empty Church: Does Organized Religion Matter Anymore?* (New York: Touchstone, 1996), 24.

3. "Christianity Almost Beaten Says Cardinal," *The London Times*, 6 September 2001.

4. Callum G. Brown, *The Death of Christian Britain* (London: Routledge, 2001), 15.

5. George Barna, *The Second Coming of the Church* (Nashville: Word, 1998), 6.

6. Reeves, *Empty Church*, 198.

7. Donald Bloesch, "Whatever Happened to God?" *Christianity Today*, 5 February 2001, 54.

8. William O'Malley, quoted in Walter Burghardt, *Preaching—the Art and the Craft* (New York: Paulist Press, 1987), 45.

9. Reginald E. O. White, *A Guide to Preaching* (London: Pickering & Inglis, 1973), 5.

10. Michael Quicke, "The Wheel Is Turning, but the Hamster Is Dead," *American Baptist Evangelicals Journal* 10, no. 3 (December 2002): 21–26.

11. See David Norrington, *To Preach or Not to Preach?* (Carlisle: Paternoster, 1996).

12. Jeremy Thomson, *Preaching as Dialogue: Is the Sermon a "Sacred Cow"?* Grove Pastoral Series 68 (Cambridge: Grove Books, 1996), 4.

13. Bandy, *Coaching Change*, 25.

14. See Christian A. Schwarz, *Natural Church Growth* (Carol Stream, Ill.: ChurchSmart, 1999).

15. Jim Herrington, M. Bonem, and J. Furr, *Leading Congregational Change* (San Francisco: Jossey-Bass, 2000), xiii.

16. John Killinger, *Fundamentals of Preaching* (London: SCM, 1985), 164.

17. G. Robert Jacks, *Getting the Word Across: Speech Communication for Pastors and Lay Leaders* (Grand Rapids: Eerdmans, 1995), 36.

18. Donald McKim, *The Bible in Theology and Preaching* (Nashville: Abingdon, 1993), 198.

19. Thomas G. Long, foreword, in Mike Graves, *The Sermon as Symphony* (Valley Forge, Pa.: Judson, 1997), xi.

20. Leander Keck, *The Bible in the Pulpit: The Renewal of Biblical Preaching* (Nashville: Abingdon, 1978), 28–29.

21. James Forbes, *The Holy Spirit and Preaching* (Nashville: Abingdon, 1989), 11.

22. Attributed to Leonard Ravenhill.

23. Forbes, *Holy Spirit and Preaching*, 19.

24. Jana Childers, *Performing the Word: Preaching as Theatre* (Nashville: Abingdon, 1998), 18.

25. Edward K. Rowell, "Working 5 to 9," *Leadership* (spring 1998): 86–92.

26. Killinger, *Fundamentals of Preaching*, 8.

27. Richard L. Eslinger, *A New Hearing: Living Options in Homiletic Methods* (Nashville: Abingdon, 1987), 30.

28. D. Martyn Lloyd-Jones, *Preachers and Preaching* (London: Hodder, 1971), 12.

29. John R. W. Stott, *Between Two Worlds: The Art of Preaching in the Twentieth Century* (Grand Rapids: Eerdmans, 1982).

30. Meic Pearse and Chris Matthews, *We Must Stop Meeting Like This* (Eastbourne: Kingsway, 1999), 106.

Chapter 3

1. Thomas G. Long, *The Witness of Preaching* (Louisville: Westminster John Knox, 1989), 23.

2. T. Keir, quoted in John Killinger, *Fundamentals of Preaching* (London: SCM, 1985), 20.

3. John R. W. Stott, *Between Two Worlds: The Art of Preaching in the Twentieth Century* (Grand Rapids: Eerdmans, 1982), 135–42.

4. Ibid., 138.

5. Ibid., 178.

6. Jean-Jacques von Allmen, *Preaching and Congregation* (London: Lutterworth, 1962), 28.

7. See G. Robert Jacks, *Just Say the Word: Writing for the Ear* (Grand Rapids: Eerdmans, 1996), for his particular emphasis on transparency and presence.

8. Tony Campolo, *Great Preachers*, series 2 (Worcester, Pa.: Gateway Films, 1998).

9. Peter T. Forsyth, *Positive Preaching and the Modern Mind* (London: Hodder & Stoughton, 1907), 97.

10. Quoted in Christoph Schwobel, "The Preacher's Art: Preaching Theologically," in *Theology through Preaching*, ed. Colin Gunton (Edinburgh: T & T Clark, 2001), 2.

11. Ibid., 3.

12. James B. Torrance, *Worship, Community, and the Triune God of Grace* (Downers Grove, Ill.: InterVarsity, 1996).

13. Ibid., 20.

14. Ibid., 20.

15. Ibid., 30–31.

16. Ibid., 32.

17. Ibid., 67.

18. Sidney Greidanus, *The Modern Preacher and the Ancient Text: Interpreting and Preaching Biblical Literature* (Grand Rapids: Eerdmans, 1988), 104–5.

19. Robin Gill, *A Vision for Growth* (London: SPCK, 1994), 15.

20. Donald Coggan, *A New Day for Preaching* (London: SPCK, 1997), 89, italics in original.

21. Peter Adam, *Speaking God's Words: A Practical Theology of Expository Preaching* (Downers Grove, Ill.: InterVarsity, 1996), 89.

22. Elizabeth Achtemeier, *Preaching from the Old Testament* (Louisville: Westminster John Knox, 1989), 14.

23. G. Robert Jacks, *Getting the Word Across: Speech Communication for Pastors and Lay Leaders* (Grand Rapids: Eerdmans, 1995).

24. Ibid., 25.

25. Andre Resner, *Preacher and Cross: Person and Message in Theology and Rhetoric* (Grand Rapids: Eerdmans, 1999), 184.

26. Adam, *Speaking God's Words*, 21.

27. Ibid., 21–22.

28. Steve Holmes, *Toward a Baptist Theology of Ordained Ministry*, unpublished paper, 5.

29. Karl Barth, *Church Dogmatics*, vol. 1, part 1 (New York: Charles Scribner's Sons, 1936), 98–140.

30. Paul S. Wilson, *The Practice of Preaching* (Nashville: Abingdon, 1995), 24.

31. Karl Barth, quoted in Trevor Hart, "The Word, the Words, and the Witness: Proclamation as Divine and Human Reality in the Theology of Karl Barth," *Tyndale Bulletin* 46, no. 1 (May 1995): 93, italics in original.

32. Long, *Witness of Preaching*, 23.

33. Coggan, *New Day for Preaching*, 17.

34. Fred B. Craddock, *As One without Authority* (Nashville: Abingdon, 1971), 46.

35. David J. Schlafer, *Surviving the Sermon—A Guide to Preaching for Those Who Have to Listen* (Cambridge: Cowley, 1992), 56.

36. Wilson, *Practice of Preaching*, 25.

37. See, for example, John D. Zizioulas, "On Being a Person: Toward an Ontology of Personhood," in *Persons, Divine and Human*, ed. C. Schwobel and Colin E. Gunton (Edinburgh: T & T Clark, 1999), 39–42.

38. Dietrich Ritschl, *A Theology of Proclamation* (Richmond: John Knox, 1963), 31.

39. Ibid., 31–32.

40. Humphrey Vellacott, *The Pastor in a Pagan Society* (Ilfracombe, Devon: Arthur H. Stockwell, 1996), 67–68.

41. Hart, "The Word, the Words, and the Witness," 83, italics in original.

42. Coggan, *New Day for Preaching*, 15.

43. James Forbes, *The Holy Spirit and Preaching* (Nashville: Abingdon, 1989), 43.

44. Coggan, *New Day for Preaching*, 16–17.

45. C. E. B. Cranfield, *The Cambridge Greek Commentary on St. Mark* (Cambridge: Cambridge, 1959), 149.

46. I. Howard Marshall, *The Gospel of Luke* (Exeter: Paternoster, 1976), 320.

47. George E. Sweazey, *Preaching the Good News* (Englewood Cliffs, N.J.: Prentice-Hall, 1976), 310.

48. Ibid.

49. Winston Fletcher, "Putting Bums on Pews," *London Evening Standard*, 19 October 1994, p. 63.

50. Martin Luther, quoted in David Buttrick, *Homiletic: Moves and Structures* (Philadelphia: Fortress, 1987), 225.

51. Forbes, *Holy Spirit and Preaching*, 19–20.

52. Torrance, *Worship, Community, and the Triune God of Grace*, 39.

53. Clyde Fant, *Preaching for Today* (San Francisco: Harper & Row, 1975 20), 47.

54. Ibid., 84–85.

Chapter 4

1. John R. W. Stott, *The Contemporary Christian* (Leicester: Inter-Varsity, 1992), 28.

2. Sidney Greidanus, *The Modern Preacher and the Ancient Text: Interpreting and Preaching Biblical Literature* (Grand Rapids: Eerdmans, 1988), xi.

3. See, for example, Bryan Chapell, *Christ-Centered Preaching* (Grand Rapids: Baker, 1994), 169–70.

4. Rick Ezell, *Hitting a Moving Target: Preaching to the Changing Needs of Your Church* (Grand Rapids: Kregel, 1999).

5. Mark Greene, *The Three-Eared Preacher: A Listening Tool for Busy Ministers* (London: London Bible College, 1998).

6. Jimmy Long, *Generating Hope: A Strategy for Reaching the Postmodern Generation* (Downers Grove, Ill.: InterVarsity, 1997).

7. Bill Hybels, Haddon Robinson, and Stuart Briscoe, *Mastering Contemporary Preaching* (Portland, Ore: Multnomah, 1989), 36.

8. Mark I. Pinsky, "Saint Flanders," *Christianity Today*, 5 February 2001, 29.

9. Jon Horowitz, quoted in Mark I. Pinsky, *The Gospel according to the Simpsons* (Louisville: Westminster John Knox, 2001), 1.

10. H. Richard Niebuhr, *Christ and Culture* (New York: Harper & Row, 1951), 32.

11. Quentin Schultze, *Communicating for Life: Christian Stewardship in Community and Media* (Grand Rapids: Baker, 2000), 19.

12. Quoted in ibid., 142.

13. Definition in *Microsoft Encarta College Dictionary* (New York: St. Martin's Press, 2002).

14. David J. Bosch, *Transforming Mission: Paradigm Shifts in Theology of Mission* (New York: Orbis, 1992), 184.

15. Robert E. Webber, *Ancient-Future Faith: Rethinking Evangelicalism for a Postmodern World* (Grand Rapids: Baker, 1999), 16.

16. Andrew Walker, *Telling the Story: Gospel, Mission, and Culture* (London: SPCK, 1996), 103–37.

17. See George Hunter III, *How to Reach Secular People* (Nashville: Abingdon, 1992).

18. Webber, *Ancient-Future Faith*, 34.

19. Lesslie Newbigin, *Foolishness to the Greeks: The Gospel and Western Culture* (Grand Rapids: Eerdmans, 1986).

20. Ibid., 20.

21. Stanley Hauerwas and William H. Willimon, *Resident Aliens: Life in the Christian Colony* (Nashville: Abingdon, 1989), 40–41.

22. Walter Truett Anderson, *The Fontana Post-Modernism Reader* (London: Collins, 1995), 2.

23. Leonard Sweet, *Soul Tsunami: Sink or Swim in New Millennium Culture* (Grand Rapids: Zondervan, 1999), 117.

24. See Neil Howe and William Strauss, *Millennials Rising: The Next Great Generation* (New York: Vintage Books, 2000).

25. Graham Cray (The Jerusalem Lecture, Royal Society of Arts, London, 26 February 2001).

26. Quoted in ibid.

27. George Hunter (address at Worship, Evangelism, and Nurture Mission of the Church, Northern Baptist Theological Seminary, Lombard, Ill., 6 November 2001).

28. Stanley J. Grenz (address at Worship, Evangelism, and Nurture Mission of the Church, Northern Baptist Theological Seminary, Lombard, Ill., 6 November 2001).

29. Craig Loscalzo, *Apologetic Preaching: Proclaiming Christ to a Postmodern World* (Downers Grove, Ill.: InterVarsity, 2000), 19.

30. Graham Johnston, *Preaching to a Postmodern World* (Grand Rapids: Baker, 2001), 23–60.

31. Robertson McQuilkin, "Spiritual Formation through Preaching" (lecture given to the Evangelical Homiletical Society, Reformed Theological Seminary, Orlando, Fla., 20 October 2000).

32. Ed Stetzer lists ten commandments for postmodern U.S. churches in *Western Recorder*, 27 February 2001.

33. Quoted in Gene E. Veith, *Postmodern Times: A Christian Guide to Contemporary Thought and Culture* (Wheaton: Crossway, 1994), 211.

34. Johnston, *Preaching to a Postmodern World*, 149–72.

35. Haddon W. Robinson, *Biblical Preaching: The Development and Delivery of Expository Messages* (Grand Rapids: Baker, 2002), 10.

36. McQuilkin, "Spiritual Formation through Preaching."

37. Robert N. Nash Jr., *An 8 Track Church in a CD World: The Modern Church in a Postmodern World* (Macon, Ga.: Smyth & Helwys, 1997), 18.

38. Walter Ong, *Orality and Literacy: The Technologizing of the Word* (London: Methuen, 1982), 85.

39. Walker, *Telling the Story*, 94.

40. Ibid.

41. Ibid., 95.

42. Pierre Babin, *The New Era in Religious Communication* (Minneapolis: Fortress, 1991), 19.

43. Greidanus, *Modern Preacher*, 313.

44. Ibid., 312.

45. Babin, *New Era in Religious Communication*, 6.

46. Ibid., 21.

47. Ibid., 99.

48. Ong, *Orality and Literacy*, 135.

49. Ibid., 136.

50. Ibid.

51. Babin, *New Era in Religious Communication*, 31–32.

52. Ibid., 151.

53. Ibid., 146.

54. Ibid., 150.

55. Ibid., 149.

56. Ibid., 152.

57. Kevin Bradt, *Story as a Way of Knowing* (Kansas City: Sheed & Ward, 1997), viii.

58. Ibid., ix.

59. Jolyon P. Mitchell, *Visually Speaking* (Edinburgh: T & T Clark, 1999), 193.

60. Michael Rogness, *Preaching to a TV Generation: The Sermon in the Electronic Age* (Lima, Ohio: CSS Press, 1994), 22–23.

61. Ibid., 15.

62. Quoted in ibid.

63. Tex Sample, *The Spectacle of Worship in a Wired World: Electronic Culture and the Gathered People of God* (Nashville: Abingdon, 1998).

64. See resources of Exaltabo: Christian communication between the generations www.jerusalemproductions.org.uk.

65. Terry Mattingley writes a syndicated "On Religion" column for Scripps Howard News Service in Washington, D.C.

66. Charles Colson, "Fuzzy Grammar: Truth in the Age of the Image," Commentary 011107, 7 November 2001, www.breakpoint.org.

67. Sample, *Spectacle of Worship*, 25.

68. Babin, *New Era in Religious Communication*, 58.

69. Sample, *Spectacle of Worship*, 37.

70. Ibid., 47.

71. Ibid., 78.

72. Ibid., 104.

73. J. A. Sanders, "Hermeneutics," in *Concise Encyclopedia of Preaching*, ed. William H. Willimon and Richard Lischer (Louisville: Westminster John Knox, 1995).

74. Gordon D. Fee and Douglas Stuart, *How to Read the Bible for All Its Worth: A Guide to Understanding the Bible*, 2d ed. (Grand Rapids: Zondervan, 1993), 13.

75. Ibid., 64.

76. See R. J. Allen, *Contemporary Biblical Interpretation for Preaching* (Valley Forge, Pa.: Judson, 1984), 132–33.

77. Anthony C. Thiselton, *New Horizons in Hermeneutics* (London: Harper Collins, 1992), 5.

78. Thomas G. Long, *Preaching and the Literary Forms of the Bible* (Philadelphia: Fortress, 1989), 29.

79. Michael J. Glodo, "The Bible in Stereo," in *The Challenge of Postmodernism: An Evangelical Engagement*, ed. David S. Dockery (Grand Rapids: Baker, 1995), 148–72.

80. Ibid., 153, 160.

81. Walter Ong, quoted in Thomas Long, "Preaching with Ordered Passion," *Leadership* 12, no. 2 (spring 1991): 139.

Chapter 5

1. Phillips Brooks, *Lectures on Preaching* (Grand Rapids: Baker, 1978), 5.

2. David J. Schlafer, *Your Way with God's Word* (Cambridge: Cowley, 1995), 57–74.

3. Malcolm Goldsmith and Martin Wharton, *Knowing Me, Knowing You* (London: SPCK, 1993), 181.

4. Roy M. Oswald and O. Kroeger, *Personality Type and Religious Leadership* (Washington, D.C.: Alban Institute, 1988), 43–49.

5. Carol M. Noren, *The Woman in the Pulpit* (Nashville: Abingdon, 1992), 31–45.

6. See Henry H. Mitchell, *Black Preaching: The Recovery of a Powerful Art* (Nashville: Abingdon, 1990).

7. Patricia A. Gould-Champ, "Women and Preaching: Telling the Story in Our Own Voice," in *Born to Preach*, ed. Samuel K. Roberts (Valley Forge, Pa.: Judson, 2000), 100–112.

8. This model has been adapted from Bill Allen's work at Spurgeon's College, which itself draws on John Adair's three-circle model from "Action-Centered Leadership," the 1990 Methodist conference report.

9. John Westerhoff, *Spiritual Life: The Foundation for Preaching and Teaching* (Louisville: Westminster John Knox, 1994), 1.

10. Donald English, *An Evangelical Theology of Preaching* (Nashville: Abingdon, 1996), 7.

11. Fred B. Craddock, *Preaching* (Nashville: Abingdon, 1985), 69–75.

12. James Black, *The Mystery of Preaching* (London: Marshall, Morgan & Scott, 1977), 6, 44.

13. John Killinger, *Fundamentals of Preaching* (London: SCM, 1985), 188.

14. David J. Schlafer, *Surviving the Sermon—A Guide to Preaching for Those Who Have to Listen* (Cambridge: Cowley, 1992), 38–39.

15. Thomas H. Troeger, *Imagining a Sermon* (Nashville: Abingdon, 1990), 15.

16. Ibid., 35, 139.

17. Colin Morris, *Raising the Dead: The Art of the Preacher as Public Performer* (London: HarperCollins, 1996), 88.

18. Ibid., 89.

19. David Buttrick, *Homiletic: Moves and Structures* (Philadelphia: Fortress, 1987), 146.

20. Quoted in Morris, *Raising the Dead*, note 11.

21. W. E. Sangster, *The Craft of the Sermon* (London: Epworth, 1954), 15.

22. H. H. Farmer, *The Preaching of the Word* (Digswell Place, U.K.: Nisbet, 1941), 27.

23. Helmut Thielicke, *Encounter with Spurgeon* (London: Clarke, 1964), 13.

24. Ibid., 23.

25. John R. W. Stott, *Between Two Worlds: The Art of Preaching in the Twentieth Century* (Grand Rapids: Eerdmans, 1982), 262–337.

26. Craddock, *Preaching*, 24.

27. Fred B. Craddock, *As One without Authority* (Nashville: Abingdon, 1971), 17.

28. Westerhoff, *Spiritual Life*, 29–39.

29. See Michael Quicke, "Applying God's Word in a Secular Culture," *Preaching* 17, no. 4 (January–February 2002): 7–15.

30. Killinger, *Fundamentals of Preaching*, 8.

31. Quoted in Clyde Fant, *Preaching for Today* (San Francisco: Harper & Row, 1987), 109.

32. Gordon D. Fee, *Listening to the Spirit in the Text* (Grand Rapids: Eerdmans, 2000), 5.

33. Westerhoff, *Spiritual Life*, 76.

34. Quoted in Tony Sargent, *The Sacred Anointing: The Preaching of Dr. Martyn Lloyd-Jones* (London: Hodder & Stoughton, 1994), 127, 129.

35. Fant, *Preaching for Today*, 67.

36. Thomas G. Long, *The Witness of Preaching* (Louisville: Westminster John Knox, 1989), 23–47.

37. Killinger, *Fundamentals of Preaching*, 53.

38. Stephen Olford, with David L. Olford, *Anointed Expository Preaching* (Nashville: Broadman & Holman, 1998), 149.

39. Long, *Witness of Preaching*, 80.

40. Craddock, *As One without Authority*, 51–76.

41. Long, *Witness of Preaching*, 28.

42. Quoted in ibid., 25.

43. Quoted in Richard A. Jensen, *Telling the Story* (Minneapolis: Augsburg, 1980), 65.

44. John Claypool, "Life Is a Gift," in *A Chorus of Witnesses: Models for Today's Preacher*, ed. Thomas G. Long and Cornelius Plantinga Jr. (Grand Rapids: Eerdmans, 1994), 120–30.

45. Ibid., 130.

46. Eugene Lowry, *How to Preach a Parable: Designs for Narrative Sermons* (Nashville: Abingdon, 1989), 27–28.

47. Quoted in Long, *Witness of Preaching*, 36.

48. Eugene Lowry, *The Homiletical Plot* (Atlanta: John Knox, 1975).

49. Ibid., 43.

50. See Eugene Lowry, *The Sermon: Dancing the Edge of Mystery* (Nashville: Abingdon, 1997), 19.

51. Lowry, *How to Preach a Parable*, 38–41.

52. Ibid., 115–41.

53. Ibid., 120.

54. Joel B. Green, *The Gospel of Luke*, New International Commentary on the New Testament (Grand Rapids: Eerdmans, 1997), 36.

55. Long, *Witness of Preaching*, 95.

56. Paul S. Wilson, *The Four Pages of the Sermon: A Guide to Biblical Preaching* (Nashville: Abingdon, 1999), 10.

57. Sidney Greidanus, *The Modern Preacher and the Ancient Text: Interpreting and Preaching Biblical Literature* (Grand Rapids: Eerdmans, 1988), 122–40.

58. Ibid., 122.

59. Leander Keck, quoted in ibid., 124.

60. Francis C. Rossow, "Topical Preaching," in *Handbook of Contemporary Preaching*, ed. Michael Duduit (Nashville: Broadman, 1992), 84–92.

61. Thomas G. Long, *Preaching and the Literary Forms of the Bible* (Philadelphia: Fortress 1989), 12.

62. Gordon D. Fee and Douglas Stuart, *How to Read the Bible for All Its Worth: A Guide to Understanding the Bible*, 2d ed. (Grand Rapids: Zondervan, 1993).

63. Mike Graves, *The Sermon as Symphony* (Valley Forge, Pa.: Judson, 1997), 7.

64. Ibid., 9.

65. Haddon W. Robinson, *Biblical Preaching: The Development and Delivery of Expository Messages* (Grand Rapids: Baker, 2002), 116–31.

66. Craddock, *Preaching*, 57.

67. Fred Craddock, quoted in Long, *Witness of Preaching*, 98.

68. Buttrick, *Homiletic,* xii, italics in original.

69. Ibid., 26.

70. See Mitchell, *Black Preaching.*

71. Henry H. Mitchell, *Celebration and Experience in Preaching* (Nashville: Abingdon, 1990), 49.

72. Ibid., 55.

73. Ibid., 66.

Chapter 6

1. "The Heavenly Host Is Fined for Low Flying," *The London Times,* 13 March 1998, p. 3.

2. Lyle E. Schaller, *The Change Agent* (Nashville: Abingdon, 1972), 11–12.

3. See Lucy Atkinson Rose, *Sharing the Word: Preaching in a Round Table Church* (Louisville: Westminster, 1997).

4. John Broadus, *On the Preparation and Delivery of Sermons,* 4th ed. (San Francisco: Harper & Row, 1986).

5. H. Grady David, *Design for Preaching* (Philadelphia: Fortress, 1958).

6. Rose, *Sharing the Word,* 59.

7. Fred B. Craddock, *As One without Authority* (Nashville: Abingdon, 1971).

8. Paul S. Wilson, *The Practice of Preaching* (Nashville: Abingdon, 1995), 12.

9. See Al Fasol, "Textual Preaching," in *Handbook of Contemporary Preaching,* ed. Michael Duduit (Nashville: Broadman, 1992), 77–83.

10. Eugene Lowry, *The Sermon: Dancing the Edge of Mystery* (Nashville: Abingdon, 1997), 20–28.

11. Quoted in Samuel K. Roberts, *Biblical Criticism and the Art of Preaching* (Valley Forge, Pa.: Judson, 2000), 13.

12. Harold T. Bryson, *Expository Preaching* (Nashville: Broadman, 1995), 39.

13. Ibid., 7–8, italics in original.

14. Rose, *Sharing the Word,* 33.

15. Ronald J. Allen and Gilbert L. Bartholomew, *Preaching Verse by Verse* (Louisville: Westminster John Knox, 2000), 11.

16. Richard A. Jensen, *Thinking in Story* (Lima, Ohio: CSS Publishing, 1993), 57.

17. Robert E. Webber, *Ancient-Future Faith: Rethinking Evangelicalism for a Postmodern World* (Grand Rapids: Baker, 1999), 13.

18. Michael Rogness, *Preaching to a TV Generation: The Sermon in the Electronic Age* (Lima, Ohio: CSS Publishing, 1994), 36.

19. John Westerhoff, *Spiritual Life: The Foundation for Preaching and Teaching* (Louisville: Westminster John Knox, 1994), 24.

20. Andrew Walker, *Telling the Story: Gospel, Mission, and Culture* (London: SPCK, 1996), 17.

21. Kevin Bradt, *Story as a Way of Knowing* (Kansas City: Sheed & Ward, 1997), 14.

22. G. Robert Jacks, *Getting the Word Across: Speech Communication for Pastors and Lay Leaders* (Grand Rapids: Eerdmans, 1995), 34.

23. See Mike Graves, *The Sermon as Symphony* (Valley Forge, Pa.: Judson, 1997).

24. Thomas Swears, *Preaching to Head and Heart* (Nashville: Abingdon, 2000), 50.

25. Quoted in Horton Davies, *Varieties of English Preaching 1900–1960* (London: SCM, 1963), 86.

26. Rogness, *Preaching to a TV Generation,* 40.

27. Paul S. Wilson, *The Four Pages of the Sermon: A Guide to Biblical Preaching* (Nashville: Abingdon, 1999), 11.

28. Jolyon Mitchell, *Visually Speaking* (Edinburgh: T & T Clark, 1999), 6.

29. Ibid., 39.

30. Pierre Babin, *The New Era in Religious Communication* (Minneapolis: Fortress, 1991), 58–59.

31. Tex Sample, *The Spectacle of Worship in a Wired World: Electronic Culture and the Gathered People of God* (Nashville: Abingdon, 1998), 49.

32. Lori Carrell, *The Great American Sermon Survey* (Wheaton: Mainstay Church Resources, 2000), 23.

33. Allen and Bartholomew, *Preaching Verse by Verse*, viii.

34. H. Beecher Hicks, "Applying God's Word in a Secular Culture" (paper presented at preaching conference, Philadelphia, 8 May 2001).

35. Thomas G. Bandy, *Coaching Change: Breaking Down Resistance, Building Up Hope* (Nashville: Abingdon, 2000), 25.

36. Ibid., 51.

37. Ibid.

38. John McClure, *The Round Table Pulpit* (Nashville: Abingdon, 1995), 7.

39. Ibid., 8.

40. Donald Coggan, *The Sacrament of the Word* (London: Fount, 1987).

41. Ibid., 99.

42. See Carrel, *Great American Sermon Survey*, 13.

43. David Schlafer, *Kindling Points for Sacred Fire*, unpublished manuscript.

44. Association of Christian Theological Schools, D.Min. program.

45. Sample, *Spectacle of Worship*, 15.

46. Jimmy Long, *Generating Hope: A Strategy for Reaching the Postmodern Generation* (Downers Grove, Ill.: InterVarsity, 1997), 35.

47. Michael Slaughter, *Out on the Edge: A Wake-up Call for Church Leaders* (Nashville: Abingdon, 1998), esp. chaps. 4 and 7.

48. Len Wilson, *The Wired Church* (Nashville: Abingdon, 1999), 40–41.

Chapter 7

1. Eugene Lowry, *The Sermon: Dancing the Edge of Mystery* (Nashville: Abingdon, 1997), 15.

2. Michael Quicke (E. Y. Mullins Lectures, Southern Baptist Seminary, Louisville, 3 March 1995).

3. Charles W. Koller, *How to Preach without Notes* (Grand Rapids: Baker, 1997), 14.

4. YMCA of USA, *Teaching Swimming Fundamentals* (Champaign, Ill.: Human Kinetics Publishers, 1999), 10–11.

5. Quoted in John W. Doberstein, *The Minister's Prayer Book* (London: Collins, 1964), 428.

6. Tony Sargent, *The Sacred Anointing: The Preaching of Dr. Martyn Lloyd-Jones* (London: Hodder & Stoughton, 1994), 2.

7. Thomas G. Long, *The Witness of Preaching* (Louisville: Westminster John Knox, 1989), 20.

8. William H. Willimon, *Peculiar Speech: Preaching to the Baptized* (Grand Rapids: Eerdmans, 1992).

9. See David J. Schlafer, *Your Way with God's Word* (Cambridge: Cowley, 1995), 28.

10. Ronald J. Allen and Gilbert L. Bartholomew, *Preaching Verse by Verse* (Louisville: Westminster John Knox, 2000), viii.

11. Eugene Lowry, *Living with the Lectionary* (Nashville: Abingdon, 1992), 35.

12. James Black, *The Mystery of Preaching* (London: Marshall, Morgan & Scott, 1977), 20.

13. W. E. Sangster, *The Craft of the Sermon* (London: Epworth, 1954), 44.

14. See John McClure, *Roundtable Preaching: Where Leadership and Preaching Meet* (Nashville: Abingdon, 1995).

15. David J. Schlafer, unpublished manuscript.

16. See Donald Coggan, *A New Day of Preaching* (London: SPCK, 1996).

17. Michael Slaughter, *Out on the Edge: A Wake-up Call for Church Leaders* (Nashville: Abingdon, 1998), 65–87.

18. Richard Bewes, *Speaking in Public—Effectively* (Fearn, U.K.: Christian Focus, 1998), 55–56.

19. Paul Wilson, *The Four Pages of the Sermon: A Guide to Biblical Preaching* (Nashville: Abingdon, 1999), 27.

20. Joseph M. Webb, *Preaching without Notes* (Nashville: Abingdon, 2001), 36.

Chapter 8

1. John H. Hayes and Carl R. Holladay, quoted in Thomas G. Long, *The Witness of Preaching* (Louisville: Westminster John Knox, 1989), 60.

2. David J. Schlafer, *Surviving the Sermon—A Guide to Preaching for Those Who Have to Listen* (Cambridge: Cowley, 1992), 22.

3. O. H. Steck, *Old Testament Exegesis: A Guide to the Methodology* (Atlanta: Scholars Press, 1998), 7.

4. Eugene H. Peterson, *Working the Angles: The Shape of Pastoral Integrity* (Grand Rapids: Eerdmans, 1987), 101.

5. Ibid., 125.

6. Gordon D. Fee, *Listening to the Spirit in the Text* (Grand Rapids: Eerdmans, 2000), 11.

7. David A. Currie and Susan P. Currie, "Preaching as *Lectio Divina:* An Evangelical and Expository Approach" (lecture given to the Evangelical Homiletical Society, Reformed Theological Seminary, Orlando, Fla., 20 October 2000).

8. David Day, *A Preaching Workbook* (London: Lynx, 1998), 17.

9. Barbara Brown Taylor, *A Preacher's Life* (Cambridge: Cowley, 1993), 147.

10. K. M. Yates, *Preaching from Great Bible Chapters* (Waco: Word, 1957), 102.

11. Walter Brueggemann, *The Prophetic Imagination* (Philadelphia: Fortress, 1978), 111.

12. Mike Graves, *The Sermon as Symphony* (Valley Forge, Pa.: Judson, 1997), xii.

13. Ibid., 15–25.

14. G. Robert Jacks, *Getting the Word Across: Speech Communication for Pastors and Lay Leaders* (Grand Rapids: Eerdmans, 1995), 61.

15. Ibid., 63.

16. Long, *Witness of Preaching*, 68–70.

17. Ibid., 86.

18. I. H. Marshall, *The Gospel of Luke* (Exeter: Paternoster, 1976), 597.

19. Joel B. Green, *The Gospel of Luke*, New International Commentary on the New Testament (Grand Rapids: Eerdmans, 1997), 576.

20. Norval Geldenhuys, *Commentary on the Gospel of Luke* (Grand Rapids: Eerdmans, 1952), 401–3.

21. Robert C. Tannehill, *Luke*, Abingdon New Testament Commentaries (Nashville: Abingdon, 1996), 238.

22. Fred B. Craddock, *Luke*, Interpreters' Commentary (Louisville: John Knox, 1990), 185.

Chapter 9

1. Haddon W. Robinson, *Making a Difference in Preaching* (Grand Rapids: Baker, 1999), 85.
2. Bryan Chapell, *Christ-Centered Preaching* (Grand Rapids: Baker, 1994), 216.
3. David Mains, Mainstay Ministries, Carol Stream, Ill.
4. Tex Sample, *The Spectacle of Worship in a Wired World: Electronic Culture and the Gathered People of God* (Nashville: Abingdon, 1998), 25.
5. David J. Schlafer, *Your Way with God's Word* (Cambridge: Cowley, 1995), 3–4.
6. Michael J. Glodo, "The Bible in Stereo," in *The Challenge of Postmodernism: An Evangelical Engagement*, ed. David S. Dockery (Grand Rapids: Baker, 1995), 167–68.
7. Haddon W. Robinson, *Biblical Preaching: The Development and Delivery of Expository Messages* (Grand Rapids: Baker, 2002), 35.
8. Fred B. Craddock, *Preaching* (Nashville: Abingdon, 1985), 122.
9. David Day, *A Preaching Workbook* (London: Lynx, 1998), 27.
10. David J. Schlafer, *Surviving the Sermon—A Guide to Preaching for Those Who Have to Listen* (Cambridge: Cowley, 1992), 55–56.
11. See Schlafer, *Your Way with God's Word*, 10.
12. Thomas H. Troeger, *Imagining a Sermon* (Nashville: Abingdon, 1990), 15–16.
13. Ibid., 15.
14. Ibid., 26.
15. Day, *Preaching Workbook*, 48.
16. Craddock, *Preaching*, 86–90.
17. See Mark Greene, *Supporting Christians at Work* (Sheffield, U.K.: Administry, 2001).
18. Schlafer, *Surviving the Sermon*, 50.
19. Rick Ezell, *Hitting a Moving Target: Preaching to the Changing Needs of Your Church* (Grand Rapids: Kregel, 1999).
20. See Mark Greene, *The Three-Eared Preacher: A Listening Tool for Busy Ministers* (London: London Bible College, 1998).
21. Bill Hybels, Haddon Robinson, and Stuart Briscoe, *Mastering Contemporary Preaching* (Portland, Ore: Multnomah, 1989), 36.
22. David Peacock, "Preparing for Sunday Worship," *Ministry Today* 4 (June 1995): 27.
23. Lectionary, Season after Pentecost, proper 3 from Sunday closest to May 21.
24. Quoted in Robinson, *Biblical Preaching*, 37.
25. Richard Bewes, *Speaking in Public—Effectively* (Fearn, U.K.: Christian Focus, 1998), 57.
26. James Forbes, *The Holy Spirit and Preaching* (Nashville: Abingdon, 1989), 81–82.
27. Helmut Thielicke, *Encounter with Spurgeon* (London: Clarke, 1964), 40.
28. Ibid., 41.
29. Thomas G. Long, *The Witness of Preaching* (Louisville: Westminster John Knox, 1989), 86.
30. Mark Galli and Craig Brian Larson, *Preaching That Connects* (Grand Rapids: Zondervan, 1994), 24.
31. Ibid., 22–33.

Chapter 10

1. David Day, *A Preaching Workbook* (London: Lynx, 1998), 35.
2. Andrew W. Blackwood, *The Preparation of Sermons* (London: Church Book Room, 1951), 19.

3. Walter C. Kaiser Jr., *Toward an Exegetical Theology* (Grand Rapids: Baker, 1981), 193.

4. Jerry Vines and Jim Shaddix, *Power in the Pulpit: How to Prepare and Deliver Expository Sermons* (Chicago: Moody, 1999), 28.

5. Fred B. Craddock, *Preaching* (Nashville: Abingdon, 1985), 84.

6. Thomas G. Long, *The Witness of Preaching* (Louisville: Westminster John Knox, 1989), 93.

7. Ibid., 96.

8. Ibid., 104.

9. Murray Frick, *Reach the Back Row: Creative Approaches for High-Impact Preaching* (Loveland, Colo.: Vital Publishing, 1999).

10. Bryan Wilkerson, *A Wonderful Night* (Carol Stream, Ill.: Preaching Today, 2001), tape 220.

11. Tim Stratford, *Interactive Preaching: Opening the Word Then Listening* (Cambridge: Grove Books, 1998), 22.

12. Long, *Witness of Preaching*, 126–30.

13. Paul S. Wilson, *The Practice of Preaching* (Nashville: Abingdon, 1995), 179–81.

14. Haddon W. Robinson, *Biblical Preaching: The Development and Delivery of Expository Messages* (Grand Rapids: Baker, 2002), chaps. 6, 7, and 115–64.

15. Haddon W. Robinson, ed., *Biblical Sermons: How Twelve Preachers Apply the Principles of Biblical Preaching* (Grand Rapids: Baker, 1989), 153–71.

16. Ibid., 165.

17. Jeremiah Wright, "The Good Shepherd" (message recorded at Fourth Presbyterian Church, Chicago, 2 May 2002, Festival of Homiletics—Preaching 2002, tape TH 6) (High Point, N.C.: Goodkind of Sound, 2002).

18. Barbara Brown Taylor, *A Preacher's Life* (Cambridge: Cowley, 1993), 147–53.

19. Ibid., 150.

20. Ibid., 151.

21. Ibid., 152.

22. Ibid., 153.

23. Day, *Preaching Workbook*, 91.

24. Jolyon P. Mitchell, *Visually Speaking* (Edinburgh: T & T Clark, 1999), 193.

25. See Clyde Fant, *Preaching for Today* (San Francisco: Harper & Row, 1987), 252–74.

26. G. Robert Jacks, *Just Say the Word: Writing for the Ear* (Grand Rapids: Eerdmans, 1996), 92–95.

27. Long, *Witness of Preaching*, 138–47.

28. Richard Bewes, *Speaking in Public—Effectively* (Fearn, U.K.: Christian Focus, 1998), 64–65.

29. Wilson, *Practice of Preaching*, 184–86.

Chapter 11

1. Jeremiah Wright, "The Good Shepherd" (message recorded at Fourth Presbyterian Church, Chicago, 2 May 2002, Festival of Homiletics—Preaching 2002, tape TH 6) (High Point, N.C.: Goodkind of Sound, 2002).

2. Joseph M. Webb, *Preaching without Notes* (Nashville: Abingdon, 2001), 26.

3. James Forbes, *The Holy Spirit and Preaching* (Nashville: Abingdon, 1989), 20.

4. Tony Sargent, *The Sacred Anointing: The Preaching of Dr. Martyn Lloyd-Jones* (London: Hodder & Stoughton, 1994), 14.

5. Quoted in Forbes, *Holy Spirit*, 53–54.

6. Sargent, *Sacred Anointing*, 245.

7. Charles H. Spurgeon, *Lectures to My Students* (London: Marshall, Morgan, & Scott), 117.

8. Ibid.

9. Ibid., 129.

10. Ibid., 135.

11. Charles Bartow, *The Preaching Moment: A Hands-on Speech Course for Scripture Reading and Preaching*, video series (Princeton, N.J.: Princeton Theological Seminary Media, 1998).

12. G. Robert Jacks, *Just Say the Word: Writing for the Ear* (Grand Rapids: Eerdmans, 1996), 150.

13. Sherwyn P. Morreale and Courtland L. Bovee, *Excellence in Public Speaking* (New York: Harcourt Brace College Publishers, 1998), 296.

14. G. Robert Jacks, *Getting the Word Across: Speech Communication for Pastors and Lay Leaders* (Grand Rapids: Eerdmans, 1995), 33–34.

15. Jerry Vines and Jim Shaddix, *Power in the Pulpit: How to Prepare and Deliver Expository Sermons* (Chicago: Moody, 1999), 324.

16. Quoted in ibid.

17. Morreale and Bovee, *Excellence in Public Speaking*, 302.

Chapter 12

1. Frank A. Thomas, *They Like to Never Quit Praisin' God* (Cleveland: United Church Press, 1997), 3.

2. Ibid., 27.

3. Ibid., 11.

4. George E. Sweazey, *Preaching the Good News* (Englewood Cliffs, N.J.: Prentice-Hall, 1976), 310.

5. Murray Frick, *Reach the Back Row: Creative Approaches for High-Impact Preaching* (Loveland, Colo.: Vital Publishing, 1999).

6. For a fuller analysis, see my "Let Anyone with Ears to Hear, Listen" (lecture given to the Evangelical Homiletical Society, Trinity Evangelical Divinity School, Deerfield, Ill., 18 October 2002), at www.evangelicalhomiletics.com.

7. Sherwyn P. Morreale and Courtland L. Bovee, *Excellence in Public Speaking* (New York: Harcourt Brace College Publishers, 1998), 76–82.

8. Richard Bewes, *Speaking in Public—Effectively* (Fearn, U.K.: Christian Focus, 1998), 151–58 suggests three of these, to which I have added the first.

9. Ibid., 153.

10. Ibid., chap. 7, 173–83.

11. This story was shared in Paul Fiddes, ed., *Doing Theology in a Baptist Way* (Oxford: Whitley Publications, 2000), 59–62.

12. Sermon preached on 21 January 1990, St. Andrew's Street Baptist Church, Cambridge.

Index